HISTORICAL ATLAS OF MISSOURI

Historical Atlas of Missouri

By Milton D. Rafferty

University of Oklahoma Press: Norman

BY MILTON D. RAFFERTY

Atlas of Missouri (with Russel Gerlach and Dennis Hrebec)
  (Springfield, Missouri, 1970)
Economic and Social Atlas of Missouri (with David Castillon and
  William Cheek) (Springfield, Missouri, 1975)
The Ozarks: Land and Life (Norman, 1980)
Historical Atlas of Missouri (Norman, 1981)

Library of Congress Cataloging in Publication Data

Rafferty, Milton D., 1932–
   Historical atlas of Missouri.

   Includes bibliography and index.
   1. Missouri—Geography, Historical—Maps. 2. Missouri—
Description and travel. 3. Missouri—Economic conditions—
Maps. 4. Missouri—History. 5. Missouri—Social conditions—
Maps. I. Title.
G1436.S1R3   1981   911'.778   81-675048
                        AACR2

PREFACE

In one respect the history of Missouri reflects our European origins and the subsequent development of a national culture in the American colonies. In another respect Missouri's development has been distinctive and exceptional if not unique. These two aspects of Missouri's history are represented in this atlas.

The atlas does not purport to be a "history"; rather, it is an aid to historians and geographers and to teachers and students of history and geography. It is intended to be used as a reference book by those who wish to look up particular points. Each map is a synopsis, as it were, of the raw materials for historical and geographical research. The text gives enough information to enable the reader to understand fully what the maps portray. The selected references for each map not only provide the reader with the primary sources that were used in compiling the maps, but also are the basis for further inquiry into the subject.

The *Historical Atlas of Missouri* addresses most topics from a historical point of view, but it is designed to serve the needs of educators, students, state officials, businessmen, and interested citizens. Missouri's physical diversity, historical development, population characteristics, transportation facilities, agricultural production, political patterns, and other features are presented in map form, with interpretation of geographical features and areal differences. Maps derived from census data provide information on contemporary regionalism and differences from place to place.

Specific aspects of the history and geography of Missouri are presented in a series of maps. The first maps show the location of Missouri within the nation, give information about the size of the state, and locate the places with populations of more than five hundred. These are followed by a series of maps which show the major physical features. The next series of maps depicts the chronology of exploration and the historical development of land claims. Then follows a series of maps showing various aspects of settlement, population change, and the economic, political, and social characteristics of Missouri.

The maps in the atlas are numbered consecutively. All numbers in the index are map numbers. There are no page numbers in the maps section of the book. References for the maps and accompanying text are listed at the end of the book.

I wish to extend thanks to several agencies and individuals who have helped me in several ways. State agencies that provided maps, data, and other assistance include the Missouri Department of Natural Resources, the Missouri Department of Commerce and Industrial Development, the Missouri Department of Conservation, and the Missouri Tourism Commission. James C. Kirkpatrick, Missouri Secretary of State, furnished political data. Several of the maps were adapted from an earlier *Atlas of Missouri,* and special acknowledgment is extended to Russel Gerlach and Dennis Hrebec, my coauthors on that project. Special thanks are also extended to the following: Duane Meyer, President, Southwest Missouri State University, who first suggested that I undertake the project; Elias Johnson, Professor of Geography, Southwest Missouri State University, who made numerous valuable suggestions for map design and assisted by advising student cartographers in the Department of Geography and Geology at Southwest Missouri State University; and Nancy Schanda, my coworker in the department, who assisted with typing. In large part the atlas is a product of faculty and students in the Department of Geography and Geology at Southwest Missouri State University. Components of research for many of the maps have been carried out by students in my classes, and encouragement and ideas for maps have stemmed from my colleagues. Students who are extended special acknowledgment include Helen Welborn, who assisted with archival research and map compilation, and Susan Baldwin, Danny Clevinger, Christopher Eveler, Terry Faber, Michael Fink, Ron Hough, Cynthia Rutledge, John Williams, and Joe Wilson, who compiled, designed, and drafted maps.

It has been my desire to produce an atlas that will not only aid the professional scholar, but will also help secondary-school and college students gain a better understanding of the historical-geographical relationships by which the state of Missouri has developed. It is my sincere hope that readers will find it both enjoyable and profitable to peruse the atlas, to note recurrent geographic patterns and significant historical themes, and to speculate on the relationships therein.

MILTON D. RAFFERTY

Springfield, Missouri

CONTENTS

HISTORICAL ATLAS OF MISSOURI

MISSOURI

1. LOCATION WITHIN THE UNITED STATES

Missouri, in the central part of the United States, is situated between 89°05′ and 95°45′ west longitude and between 36°00′ and 40°30′ north latitude. Because of its location it is often called the "Center State." The geographical center of the contiguous forty-eight states is only 250 miles west of Missouri, near Lebanon, Kansas, and the population center of the United States is just a few miles southwest of St. Louis. From St. Louis, on the east side of Missouri, someone traveling straight east to the Atlantic Ocean would pass through five states: Illinois, Indiana, Kentucky, West Virginia, and Virginia; from Kansas City, on the west side, a traveler to the Pacific Ocean would also pass through five states: Kansas, Colorado, Utah, Nevada, and California. From the northern boundary of Missouri a traveler heading due north to Canada would pass through two states: Iowa and Minnesota. Two states also are between Missouri's southern boundary and the Gulf of Mexico: Arkansas and Louisiana. Missouri is also a border state, both historically and today. It borders on four great geographic regions of the United States: the Middle West, the South, the Southwest, and the Great Plains.

What does this central location mean to Missouri? First, because Missouri is nearer to all parts of the country than any other state, it means lower cost and shorter time in hauling goods. In no more than two days Missourians can secure oranges from Florida, fresh lettuce from California, lumber from Oregon, or manufactured goods from Massachusetts. It also means that goods from any section of the country to another section on the opposite side are likely to pass through Missouri, giving employment to many persons in the transportation industry.

Both St. Louis and Kansas City are well-known convention centers because of their central location in the United States.

Missouri shares common boundaries with eight other states. Only Tennessee has as many neighbors. Bordering Missouri are Iowa on the north, Nebraska on the northwest, Kansas and Oklahoma on the west, Arkansas on the south, Tennessee and Kentucky on the southeast, and Illinois on the east.

Missouri is the seventeenth-largest state in area, containing a total of 69,686 square miles. It is larger than any state east of it and smaller than any state west of it except Washington and Hawaii. Missouri is approximately one-eighth the size of Alaska, but it is fifty-seven times the size of Rhode Island. In fact, Missouri has a greater area than that of all six New England states combined.

From the Arkansas boundary on the south to the Iowa boundary on the north, the distance is 285 miles, while the east–west distance from the Kansas border at Kansas City to the Illinois boundary at St. Louis is about 250 miles. The distance from the extreme northwest part of the state to the extreme southeast part of the Bootheel is slightly more than 450 miles. The latitudinal location of Missouri, as well as its great size, has had a definite influence on the cultural activities of its inhabitants. Missouri is in the transition zone between the humid eastern and the drier western parts of the nation, between the forests of the East and the grasslands of the West, between the Cotton Belt in the South with its long growing season and the Corn Belt in the North with its rich glacial and loessal soils, and includes the low elevations of the Coastal Plain and the higher elevations of the Ozark Upland.

BOUNDARY OF 1836

MISSOURI AT STATEHOOD

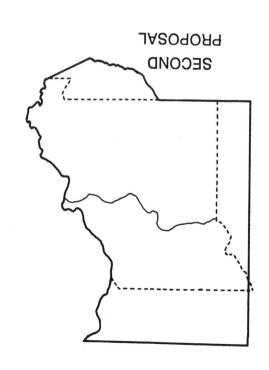

SECOND PROPOSAL

FIRST PROPOSAL

2. THE HISTORIC BOUNDARIES OF MISSOURI

The precise meaning of the name Missouri is uncertain, but it is probably a Sioux word. It first appeared on maps of French explorers in the 1600s. It was the name of a group of Indians living near the mouth of a river, and the name was naturally given to that river. From the river it was transferred to the state through which the river ran. Even Missourians cannot agree how to pronounce the name. A recent survey by the Automobile Club of Missouri showed that slightly more than half of the people pronounced the name "Missour-uh," while a little fewer than half pronounced it "Missour-ee." More people in eastern Missouri pronounce the name "Missour-ee," while western Missourians prefer "Missour-uh."

The first boundary proposal was to encompass the territory between 36°30′ and 40° north latitude, with the Mississippi River as the eastern boundary and the Osage boundary on the west. The southern boundary was to be an extension of the Virginia–North Carolina and Tennessee-Kentucky boundaries. Specific mention was made that the Missouri River should be a unifying factor and should not serve as a boundary.

In 1818 the territorial legislature requested Congress to enlarge the boundaries of Missouri. Had this request been honored, the state of Missouri would have included territory now in the adjoining states of Arkansas, Kansas, and Iowa.

The boundaries at statehood included the Bootheel and excluded territory in the northwestern part of the state. J. Hardeman Walker, founder of Caruthersville and large-scale property owner, was instrumental in the acquisition of the Missouri Bootheel. He used his considerable influence to have the territory in Pemiscot, Dunklin, and New Madrid counties added to the state.

In 1837 the state was further enlarged by the addition of the so-called Platte Purchase. The Sauk, Fox, and Pottawatomie Indians who occupied the area agreed to exchange their land for land farther west.

Since the addition of the Platte Purchase, the boundaries of Missouri have remained fixed except for minor adjustments due to the shifting of the channels of the rivers that form boundaries. Two of the more important disputes involved Wolf Island and Arsenal Island, both in the Mississippi River. Missouri lost in both cases to Kentucky and Illinois, respectively. For a brief time the state of Kansas had designs on Kansas City, Missouri, but nothing came of them. For a time there was litigation with Iowa over the northern boundary. This dispute was settled in favor of Iowa.

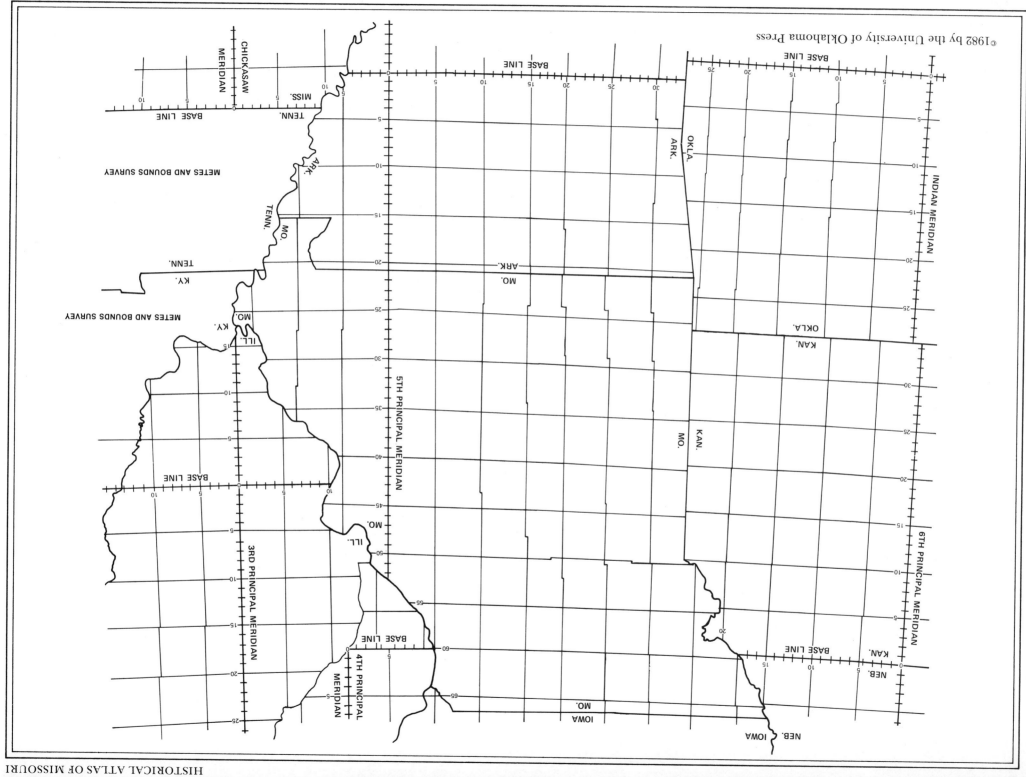

3. THE UNITED STATES LAND OFFICE SURVEY

Topographic maps of the central and western United States show the civil division of land according to the United States Land Office Survey. The system, sometimes called the rectangular land survey, was first authorized for the survey of land lying north and west of the Ohio River. To avoid the irregular and unsystematic type of land survey (metes and bounds) that had been used in seaboard states during colonial times, Congress specified that the new lands be subdivided into six-mile squares, now called congressional townships. The original survey specified that the grid of townships should be based on a carefully surveyed east-west base line, designated the "geographer's line." Meridians and parallels laid off at six-mile intervals from the base line formed the boundaries of the townships. This plan, believed to have been proposed by Thomas Jefferson, was used earlier for subdivision of small tracts of land in New England and may have stemmed from the types of surveys used in the reclaimed polder land in the Low Countries of Europe. The general plan was subsequently used to subdivide the remainder of the central and western states.

Principal meridians run north and south from selected points whose latitude and longitude were calculated astronomically. Thirty-two meridians have been surveyed. Westward from Pennsylvania these are numbered from one through six, after which they are designated by names. Through the initial starting point for the principal meridian was run an east-west line corresponding to a parallel of latitude for that point. North and south of the base line, horizontal six-mile tiers of townships were laid off and numbered accordingly (T1S, T2S, T1N, T2N,

and so on). Correspondingly, vertical rows of ranges were laid off to the right and left of the principal meridian and numbered accordingly (R1E, R2E, R1W, R2W, and so on).

The area covered by one principal meridian and its base line is confined to a particular section of the country. Where two systems meet, they do not correspond, because they were laid out and surveyed independently of one another. While a relatively small amount of land in Missouri near the Missouri and Mississippi rivers was surveyed under the Spanish and French land survey system, the remainder of the state's land survey is based on the Fifth Principal Meridian. The land surveyed under the Fifth Principal Meridian covers the largest area of all the systems. Its most northerly tier of townships is numbered 163; the most westerly range is numbered 104. Thus, the total north-south extent of the survey is 1,122 miles, and the east-west spread is 726 miles.

The origin of the Fifth Principal Meridian is the midpoint of the Arkansas River where it flows into the Mississippi River. The portion of this meridian from its origin to the south bank of the Missouri River, a distance of 317 miles, was surveyed by Prospect K. Robbins in 1815. Joseph C. Brown surveyed the Arkansas Base Line west from the mouth of the St. Francis River in the same year.

Because of the curvature of the earth's surface, the range lines progressively narrow as they are extended northward. To avoid reduction in township widths in the more northerly tiers, new base lines, known as standard parallels, are surveyed every four tiers of townships.

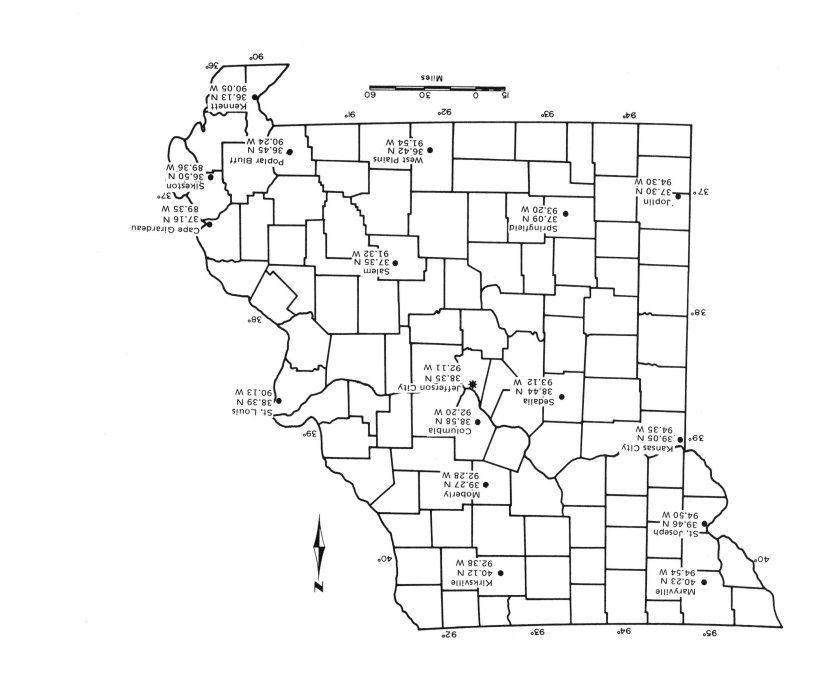

Kennett
36.13 N
90.05 W

Poplar Bluff
36.45 N
90.24 W

West Plains
36.42 N
91.54 W

Sikeston
36.50 N
89.36 W

Cape Girardeau
37.16 N
89.35 W

Joplin
37.30 N
94.30 W

Springfield
37.09 N
93.20 W

Salem
37.35 N
91.32 W

St. Louis
38.39 N
90.13 W

Jefferson City
38.35 N
92.11 W

Sedalia
38.44 N
93.12 W

Columbia
38.58 N
92.20 W

Kansas City
39.05 N
94.35 W

Moberly
39.27 N
92.28 W

St. Joseph
39.46 N
94.50 W

Maryville
40.23 N
94.54 W

Kirksville
40.12 N
92.38 W

Miles

15   0   30   60

N

4. LONGITUDE AND LATITUDE OF MISSOURI

Missouri's latitude extends from 36° north, which is the latitude of the southern boundary of the Bootheel, to 40°35' north, the latitude of the Iowa-Missouri boundary. The southern boundary, from the St. Francis River westward, follows the parallel of 36°30' north.

The easternmost part of Missouri, where the Mississippi River makes an eastward bend in Mississippi County, is at longitude 89°06' west. The westernmost point in Missouri is at the extreme northwestern tip where the Missouri River enters the state. The longitude at that point is 95°46' west. The western boundary, extending southward from the mouth of the Kansas River in Kansas City, follows the meridian of 94°37' west longitude.

Jefferson City, at latitude 38°15' north, longitude 92°07' west, is near the center of the state.

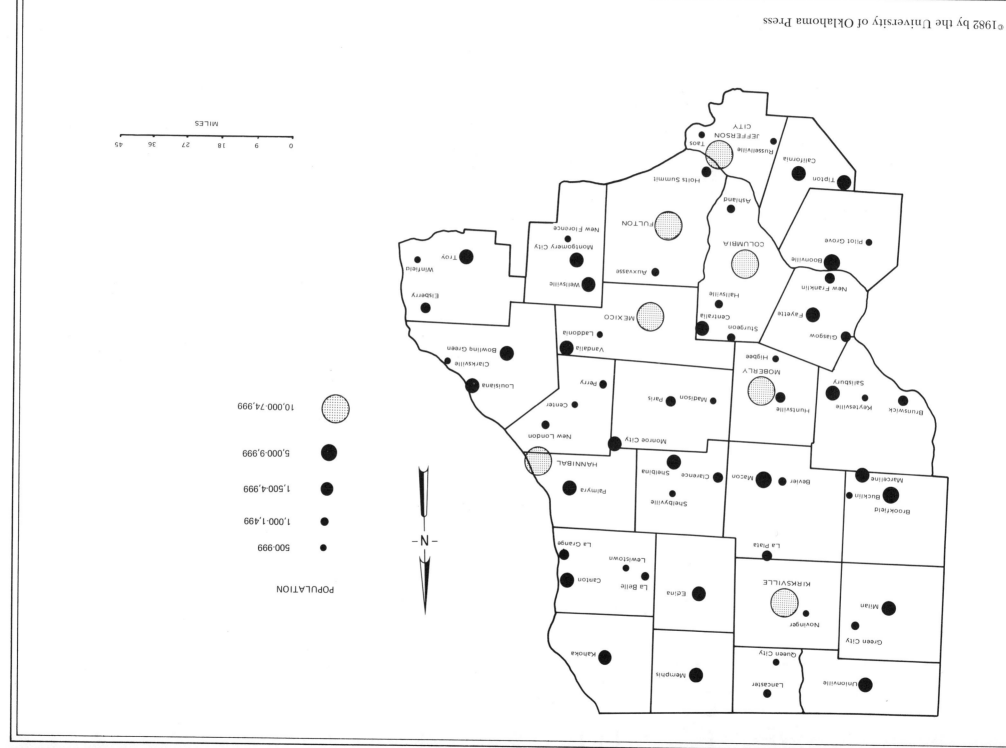

MILES

0   9   18   27   36   45

—N—

POPULATION

500-999

1,000-1,499

1,500-4,999

5,000-9,999

10,000-74,999

JEFFERSON CITY
Taos
Russellville
Holts Summit
California
Tipton
Ashland
Pilot Grove
FULTON
COLUMBIA
New Florence
Boonville
Montgomery City
New Franklin
Troy
Auxvasse
Fayette
Winfield
Wellsville
Hallsville
Glasgow
Elsberry
Centralia
MEXICO
Sturgeon
Laddonia
Higbee
Bowling Green
Vandalia
MOBERLY
Clarksville
Salisbury
Louisiana
Perry
Huntsville
Keytesville
Center
Madison
Paris
Brunswick
New London
Monroe City
Marceline
Clarence
Macon
HANNIBAL
Shelbina
Bevier
Palmyra
Buckklin
Shelbyville
Brookfield
La Plata
La Grange
Lewistown
La Belle
Canton
Edina
KIRKSVILLE
Novinger
Milan
Kahoka
Green City
Queen City
Memphis
Lancaster
Unionville

5. NORTHEASTERN MISSOURI

Northeastern Missouri includes the hilly belts underlain by glacial till and loess that border the Chariton, Wyaconda, and Missouri rivers, the limestone hills that border the Mississippi River, and the level uplands in Audrain, Randolph, and Monroe counties. St. Louis and its suburbs lie just outside the region's southern border.

Included in the region is the Columbia Standard Metropolitan Statistical Area (SMSA) which includes the city of Columbia and Boone County. Columbia, county seat of Boone County, the site of the main campus of the University of Missouri, and a major medical and trade center, has a population of 58,804.

Six other towns share leadership with Columbia. The largest of these, Jefferson City, has a population of 31,921. It owes its growth and importance to the fortune of being designated the state capital. Government and finance play a large role in the economy of the city. Because, over the years, government has assumed a larger and larger role in the affairs of business, social services, and commerce, there has been a steady growth in the number of state and national governmental agencies and civil employees.

Most of the remainder of the outlying towns are agricultural service centers. Towns with populations over five thousand include (1) Moberly, seat of Randolph County, rail junction and manufacturing center; (2) Fulton, seat of Callaway County and the site of the state mental hospital; (3) Macon, seat of Macon County, a trading center and livestock market; (4) Hannibal, seat of Marion County; (5) Kirksville, seat of Adair County and site of Northeast Missouri State University; and (6) Mexico, a town long supported by the manufacture of firebrick.

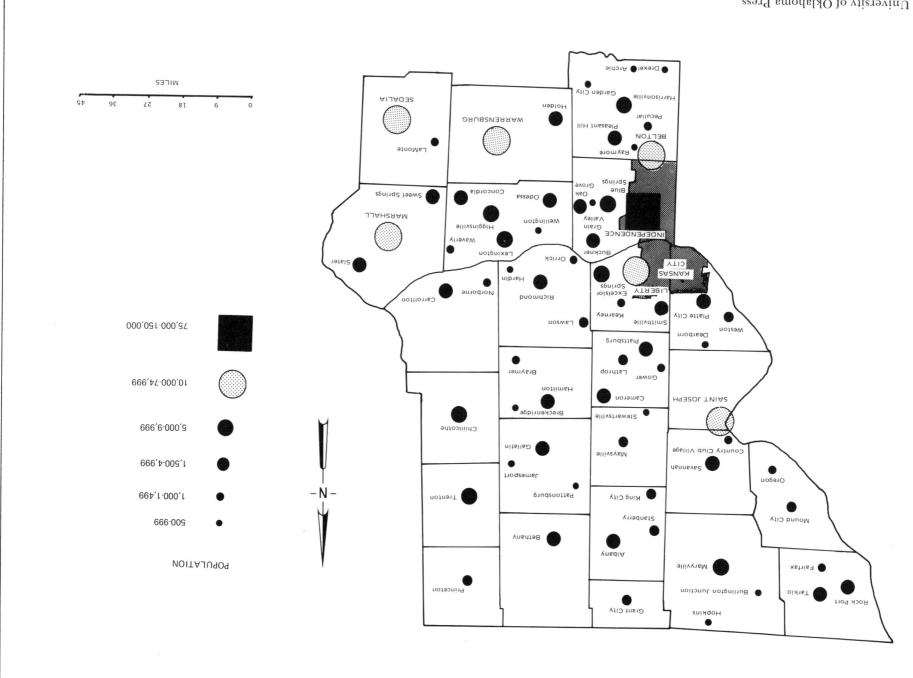

POPULATION

500-999

1,000-1,499

1,500-4,999

5,000-9,999

10,000-74,999

75,000-150,000

-N-

MILES
0   9   18   27   36   45

6. NORTHWESTERN MISSOURI

Northwestern Missouri includes: the loessal hills bordering the Missouri River, western and west central Missouri, and the loess-covered uplands and valley hills drained by the Grand River and its tributaries. Outside the Kansas City and St. Joseph metropolitan areas the land is the chief resource, and the economy is predominantly agricultural.

Within this region is the Kansas City Standard Metropolitan Statistical Area (SMSA) with its population of 1,256,649 (including the Kansas portion) in 1970. Kansas City, Missouri, alone accounted for 507,087. In the Missouri portion of the Kansas City SMSA there were more than twenty cities with populations over 1,000 in 1970. The largest of these places include Independence (110,790), Raytown (32,965), Gladstone (23,100), Grandview (17,480), Lee's Summit (16,188), and Liberty (13,604). The St. Joseph SMSA includes the city of St. Joseph and Buchanan County. St. Joseph's population in 1970 was 72,691.

The largest of the outlying towns is Sedalia (22,244), the site of the Missouri State Fair and an important transportation, commercial, and manufacturing center. Sedalia was founded in 1857 when General George R. Smith purchased land and laid out the town along the proposed route of the Pacific Railroad. During the Civil War, Sedalia benefited by the protection and trade generated by the military post established there. Later the Missouri Pacific Railroad and the Missouri-Kansas-Texas Railroad established shops in Sedalia.

Most of the remaining outlying towns in northwestern Missouri are small agricultural service centers. Those over five thousand population include: (1) Warrensburg (13,242), a central service center and trade center of importance and the location of Central Missouri State University; (2) Maryville, seat of Nodaway County, service and trade center and the site of Northwest Missouri State University; (3) Chillicothe, seat of Livingston County, service and trade center, and site of Chillicothe Business College and the Missouri State Industrial School for Girls; (4) Trenton, seat of Grundy County and a service and trade center; and (5) Brookfield, a former railroad division point and an agricultural service, trade, and manufacturing center.

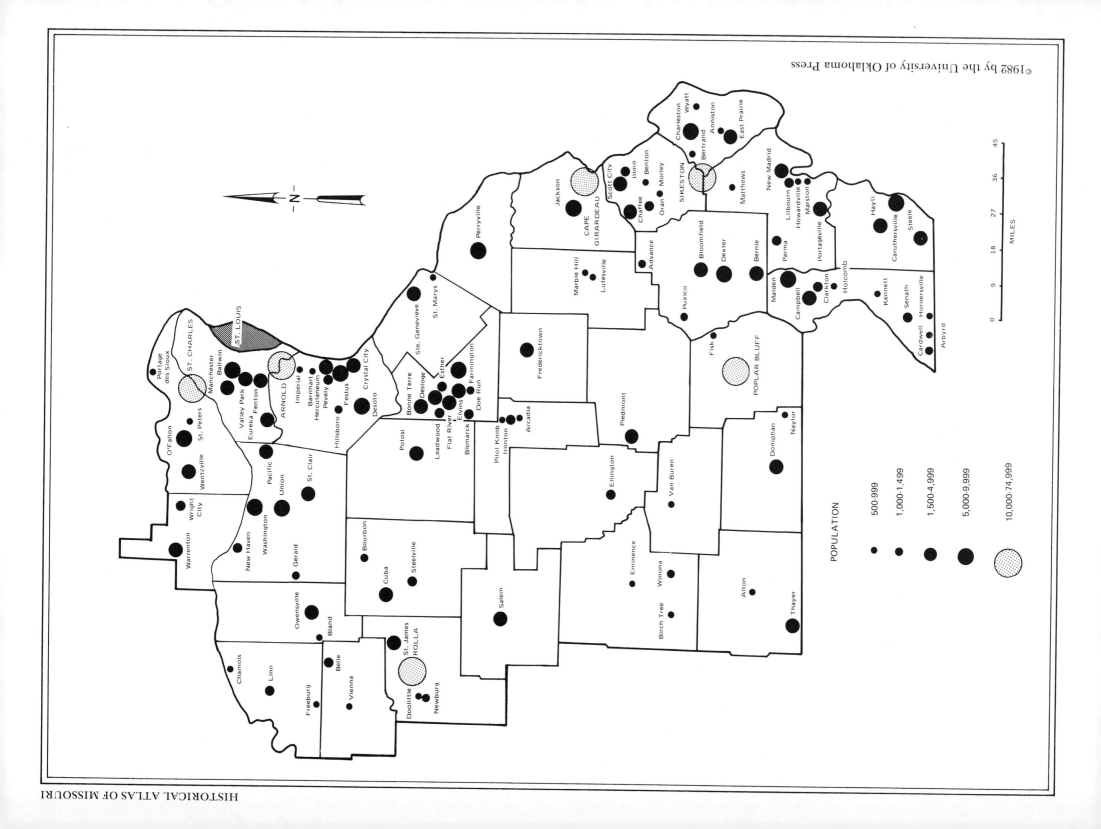

N

Portage des Sioux
ST. CHARLES
ST. LOUIS
Manchester
Ballwin
O'Fallon
St. Peters
Valley Park
Eureka
Fenton
Wentzville
Wright City
Warrenton
Pacific
Union
St. Clair
New Haven
Washington
Gerald
Chamois
Linn
Owensville
Bland
Belle
Freeburg
Vienna
Doolittle
Newburg
St. James
ROLLA
Bourbon
Cuba
Steelville
Salem
Birch Tree
Winona
Eminence
Alton
Thayer
ARNOLD
Imperial
Barnhart
Herculaneum
Pevely
Festus
Crystal City
Hillsboro
Desoto
Bonne Terre
Desloge
Potosi
Leadwood
Flat River
Esther
Farmington
Elvins
Doe Run
Bismarck
Pilot Knob
Ironton
Arcadia
Piedmont
Ellington
Van Buren
Doniphan
Naylor
Ste. Genevieve
St. Marys
Perryville
Fredericktown
Marble Hill
Lutesville
Advance
Puxico
Fisk
POPLAR BLUFF
Jackson
CAPE GIRARDEAU
Scott City
Ilmo
Benton
Chaffee
Oran
Morley
SIKESTON
Bloomfield
Dexter
Bernie
Charleston
Wyatt
Anniston
East Prairie
Bertrand
Matthews
New Madrid
Lilbourn
Howardville
Marston
Parma
Malden
Campbell
Portageville
Clarkton
Holcomb
Kennett
Senath
Hornersville
Cardwell
Arbyrd
Hayti
Caruthersville
Steele

POPULATION

500-999
1,000-1,499
1,500-4,999
5,000-9,999
10,000-74,999

MILES
0   9   18   27   36   45

7. SOUTHEASTERN MISSOURI

Southeastern Missouri encompasses the rugged limestone plateaus of the eastern Ozarks, including the knobs and valleys in the St. Francis Mountains, and the fertile lowlands extending to the tip of the Bootheel. In terrain, economy, and population density it is Missouri's most diverse region.

The primary city of southeastern Missouri, and of the entire state, is St. Louis. Founded in 1764 as a fur trading post, St. Louis, because of its superior geographic situation for commerce, quickly became the leading city in Missouri.

St. Louis City, because of its independent status (since 1875), its fixed boundaries, and the movement of people to suburban subdivisions, has experienced a decline of more than a quarter of a million people over the past two decades. Nevertheless, the St. Louis Standard Metropolitan Statistical Area (SMSA), which includes St. Louis City, St. Louis County, Jefferson County, Franklin County, and St. Charles County in Missouri and Madison and St. Clair counties in Illinois, experienced substantial growth during this period. The total population of the SMSA in 1970 was 2,340,000, or 11.2 per cent more than in 1960. In the Missouri portion of the St. Louis SMSA there are fourteen cities over 20,000 population and sixty-eight places over 1,000 population. The total population in the Missouri portion is 1,826,907.

Outlying towns over five thousand population in the vicinity of St. Louis include (1) Washington, the seat of Franklin County and a manufacturing and trade center; (2) Sullivan, a prosperous trade town on Interstate 44; (3) the closely packed Mineral Area towns in St. Francois County (Bonne Terre, Flat River, Elvins); (4) Farmington, the county seat of St. Francois County; and (5) DeSoto and Festus, two towns in Jefferson County that are growing industrial and bedroom suburbs of St. Louis.

Other major growth centers in southeastern Missouri include Cape Girardeau, Sikeston, Poplar Bluff, and Kennett. Cape Girardeau has profited from river trade, Bootheel agriculture, education, and industry. There are more than seventy-five manufacturing plants in the city. Poplar Bluff has a geographic site similar to that of Cape Girardeau. It is perched on the Ozark escarpment where the Black River exits from the Ozarks into the southeastern alluvial plain. Founded in 1850 as the seat of Butler County, Poplar Bluff has always been supported by the lumber industry, the mining of small iron deposits, employment in the Missouri Pacific and Frisco switching yards and shops, and trade with farms and smaller towns. Sikeston, at the junction of Interstate 55 and U.S. 60, is well located to capitalize on modern truck transportation. It has a long history as a milling center, a market for farm products, a railroad junction, and a shipping point. Kennett has been the business and governmental center for Dunklin County since the county was organized. It was until recently a "cotton town." Its economy continues to rest upon an agricultural base, but now there is less emphasis on cotton and more emphasis on other crops such as soybeans, wheat, and corn.

Most of the remaining outlying towns of southeastern Missouri are agricultural service centers. The larger places have the advantage of being a county seat or a location on one of the better federal highways.

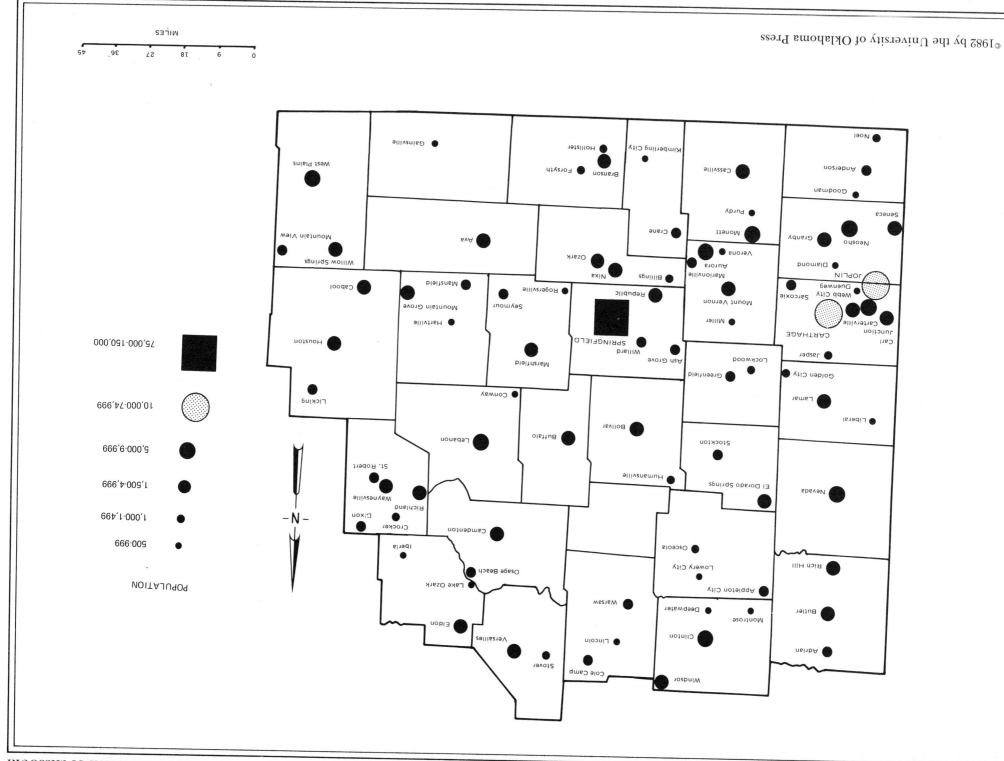

MILES

45   36'   27   18   9   0

POPULATION

75,000–150,000

10,000–74,999

5,000–9,999

1,500–4,999

1,000–1,499

500–999

– N –

West Plains

Gainsville

Hollister

Kimberling City

Branson   Forsyth

Cassville

Noel

Anderson

Goodman

Purdy

Mountain View

Willow Springs

Ava

Crane

Monett

Seneca

Verona

Granby   Neosho

Cabool

Mansfield

Rogersville

Nixa   Ozark

Billings

Aurora

Marionville

Diamond

JOPLIN

Mountain Grove

Seymour

Republic

Mount Vernon

Sarcoxie

Webb City   Duenweg

Carterville

Hartville

Houston

Willard   Ash Grove

SPRINGFIELD

Miller

CARTHAGE

Carl Junction

Marshfield

Lockwood

Jasper

Licking

Conway

Greenfield

Golden City

Bolivar

Lamar

Buffalo

Liberal

Lebanon

Stockton

St. Robert

Humansville

El Dorado Springs

Nevada

Waynesville

Richland

Dixon

Crocker

Camdenton

Osceola

Rich Hill

Iberia

Lowry City

Osage Beach

Appleton City

Lake Ozark

Warsaw

Butler

Eidon

Deepwater

Montrose

Versailles

Lincoln

Clinton

Adrian

Stover

Cole Camp

Windsor

8. SOUTHWESTERN MISSOURI

Southwestern Missouri includes the western Ozarks and the western unglaciated plains. Terrain varies from nearly level tracts in the shale beds of the western plains to rugged hill districts carved from the thick Ozark limestones.

The largest city in southwestern Missouri is Springfield. With a metropolitan population of more than 150,000, the city serves a large trade area. The Springfield Standard Metropolitan Statistical Area includes Green and Christian counties. Founded in 1830, the city has experienced steady growth except for a brief period during the Civil War. Non-agricultural employment accounts for 60,000 of the 65,000 work force. Major manufacturers include the Zenith Corporation, Springday, Inc., and the Paul Mueller Company. Other major employers include the Frisco Railroad, the Assemblies of God Church, hospitals, and local, state, and federal government offices. Southwest Missouri State University, Drury College, Evangel College, Baptist Bible College, and Central Bible College have a combined enrollment of nearly twenty thousand.

Joplin, in Newton and Jasper counties, with 39,000 population, is the second major city in southwestern Missouri. Within a fifty-mile radius of the city is a population of more than 350,000. Joplin has long been the marketing, commercial, and transportation hub of this area, which covers parts of Missouri, Kansas, Oklahoma, and Arkansas. As the chief town in the Tri-State Mining District, Joplin has accumulated a number of industries, and in recent years several trucking firms have located there. Missouri Southern College, a four-year state-supported college, is located in Joplin.

The larger outlying towns in southwestern Missouri are mainly county seats that have become good shopping and service centers. Carthage, platted in 1842, prospers as the seat of Jasper County and as a trade and manufacturing center; Neosho, platted in 1839 as the seat of Newton County, experienced boom periods brought on by mining and the establishment of Camp Crowder, an army induction and training center. Now that the boom periods have ended, Neosho prospers as a trade and service center. Webb City, one of the larger mining towns, declined in population when the mines were closed but has now recovered as a trade and manufacturing town. Monett, the largest town between Springfield and Neosho, is important for the processing of agricultural products. Lebanon, the seat of Laclede County, is the chief town on Interstate 44 between Rolla and Springfield. It is a good shopping town that has accumulated several new industries. Rolla is an educational center and the seat of Phelps County. Major employers include the University of Missouri, the U.S. Geological Survey (USGS), and the Missouri Department of Natural Resources. West Plains, seat of Howell County, is the largest town in south central Missouri. It has a long tradition as a livestock market as well as serving as a retail trade and service center for Howell and Oregon counties and parts of Texas, Shannon, and Carter counties. A branch of Southwest Missouri State University is located at West Plains.

Smaller towns in southwestern Missouri function as centers for retail trade and services. Most towns of fifteen hundred or more have one or two small manufacturing plants.

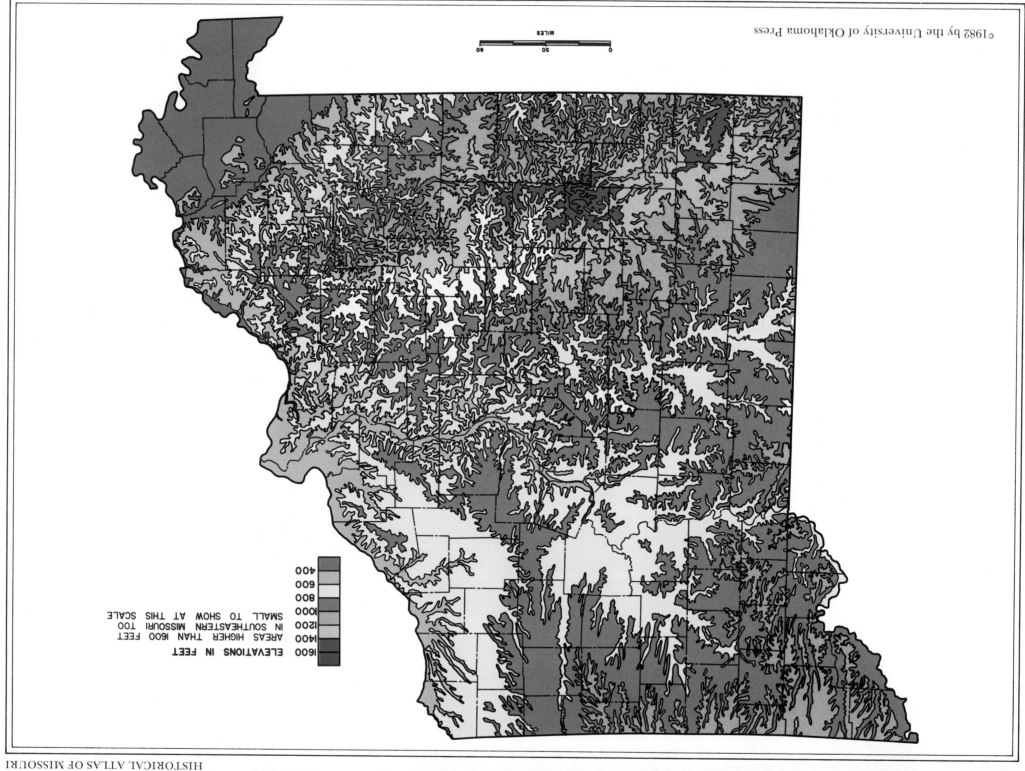

MILES

0 30 60

ELEVATIONS IN FEET

400
600
800
1000
1200
1400
1600

AREAS HIGHER THAN 1600 FEET
IN SOUTHEASTERN MISSOURI TOO
SMALL TO SHOW AT THIS SCALE

9. RELIEF OF MISSOURI

Elevations in Missouri extend from 245 feet, where the St. Francis River exits from the southwestern tip of the Bootheel, to 1,772 feet on Taum Sauk Mountain in Iron County some seventy miles southwest of St. Louis. The highest elevations are in the St. Francis Mountains in southeastern Missouri, where numerous mountain summits exceed 1,700 feet. The lowest elevations, mainly under 350 feet, are in the Southeast Lowlands. Extremes in local relief are found in the same two locales—from as much as 600 to 700 feet in the St. Francis Mountains to as little as 5 feet in extensive areas in the Southeast Lowlands.

The elevation of the country around the foot of the Ozark region varies from 600 to 800 feet above sea level, while the crest of the eroded dome varies from 1,400 to 1,700 feet. Extensive upland areas in the central Ozarks in south central Missouri are between 1,000 and 1,200 feet. Local relief of 200 to 400 feet near major streams that drain the plateau is typical. Near Cedar Gap in Wright County, an eastern prong of the Springfield Plain forms a cuesta 1,728 feet above sea level. This summit is the second highest point in the state.

The prairie region is lowest along the borderline between it and the Ozark region and rises gradually westward, or slightly northwestward. Along the Ozark border the elevation varies from six hundred to eight hundred feet. In the northwestern part of the region upland elevations are one thousand to eleven hundred feet. The rise occurs in a series of steps which are successively higher westward.

The Missouri River forms a lowland across the midsection of the state. Floodplain elevations vary from about 400 feet, where the Missouri debouches into the Mississippi north of St. Louis, to 900 feet at the extreme northwest corner of the state. Floodplain elevations along the Mississippi River vary from 250 feet where the Mississippi exits the state in the south to 480 feet at the mouth of the Des Moines River in the northeastern corner of Missouri. Local relief along the Missouri and Mississippi rivers is between 150 and 300 feet.

The most striking relief feature of the Southeast Lowland region is Crowley's Ridge. This remarkable landform feature, including the Commerce Hills in Scott and Cape Girardeau counties—three to twenty miles wide and stretching nearly one hundred miles in a general north-south alignment—varies between 350 feet and 500 feet in elevation. The adjacent lowland is between 250 and 350 feet above sea level.

ELEVATIONS OF SELECTED MISSOURI CITIES

City	Elevation (ft.)	City	Elevation (ft.)
Cape Girardeau	340	Moberly	872
Columbia	730	Poplar Bluff	340
Jefferson City	557	St. Joseph	850
Joplin	990	St. Louis	455
Kansas City	750	Salem	1,173
Kennett	262	Sikeston	315
Kirksville	969	Springfield	1,300
Maryville	1,036	West Plains	949

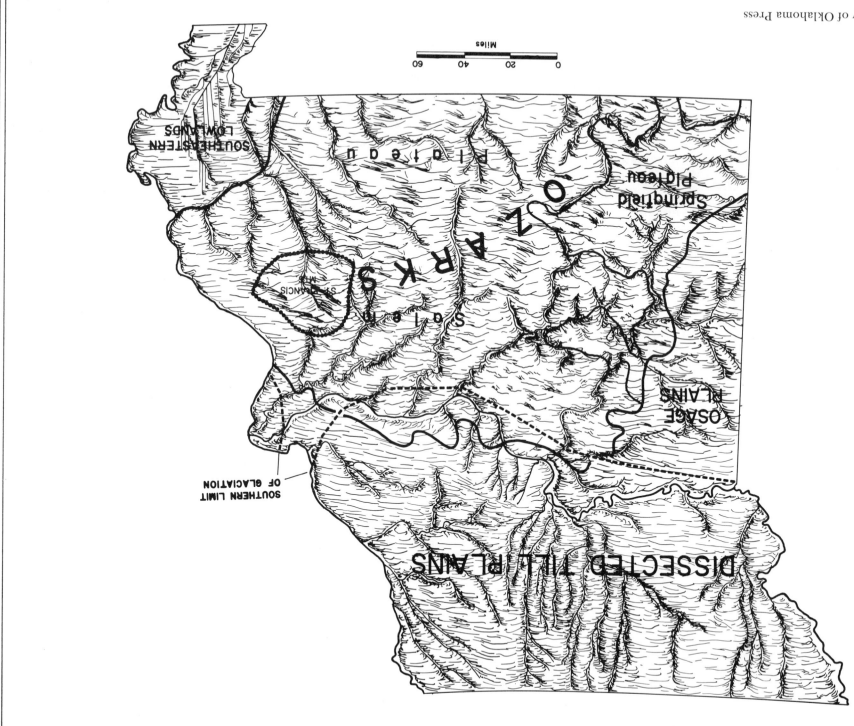

0   20   40   60

Miles

SOUTHEASTERN
LOWLANDS

Plateau

OZARKS

Springfield
Plateau

ST. FRANCIS MT.

Salem

OSAGE
PLAINS

SOUTHERN LIMIT
OF GLACIATION

DISSECTED TILL PLAINS

10. PHYSIOGRAPHIC REGIONS OF MISSOURI

Much of the landscape of today is the result of three major geologic factors: the uneven arching or uplifting of the bedrock, the weathering and erosion of the various rocks, and, in the northern part of the state, the result of glaciers spreading a thick mantle of clay, sand, and gravel over the bedrock.

For a short discussion of the landforms of the state, it is convenient to divide the state into four major geomorphic regions: (1) the Ozarks, (2) the Osage Plains to the west of the Ozarks, (3) the Dissected Till Plains of the northern half of the state, and (4) the Southeast Lowlands.

The Ozarks. The name Ozarks is a corruption of the abbreviated liaison of the French words *aux-Arcs,* meaning "to Arkansas." There is no general agreement concerning the boundaries of the Ozarks, especially the western margin. Traditionally the Springfield Plain has been included as a part of the Ozarks, although it resembles the western plains both culturally and geologically in many ways.

The topography of the Ozarks is one of hills, plateaus, and deep valleys. Limestones and dolomites are quite common, and many of the Ozark rocks contain much chert. Igneous rocks (granite and porphyry) crop out only in the Ozarks.

Ozark streams are typically deeply entrenched and follow meandering courses. Springs, caves, and sinkholes are common, constituting one of the major karst regions in the United States.

The maximum elevations in Missouri are in the Ozarks. The highest point is Taum Sauk Mountain (1,772 feet), but large areas are more than 1,400 feet above sea level.

The Osage Plains. The western plains are underlain by Pennsylvanian sedimentary strata which dip gently westward. Because of differential erosion of resistant sandstones and limestones and weaker shales, the topography is cuestaform, but with more subdued relief than that of the Ozarks.

The Dissected Till Plains. The southern limit of glaciation in Missouri is near the Missouri River. To the west of Jefferson City, glaciation extended south of the river into northern Pettis County.

Beneath the glacial material much of the bedrock in the Dissected Till Plains is identical to that of the Osage Plains. As the glaciers melted, the rock debris or "drift" contained in the ice was deposited, often accumulating to great depths in stream valleys. As the glaciers retreated, the landscape was mantled with a thick, yellow, wind-deposited silt called loess. Along the Missouri and Mississippi rivers the bluffs are formed of loess deposits as much as a hundred feet in thickness.

The Southeast Lowlands. The lowlands result from intermittent sinking of the area, the relatively late invasion of seas, and the shiftings of the Mississippi River. The main resulting landform is a poorly drained alluvial plain with hills scattered across the northern part. The Mississippi at one time flowed west of Crowley's Ridge. The lowlands are still in a state of geologic unrest, as shown by the New Madrid earthquakes of 1811–12 and lesser earthquakes of more recent times.

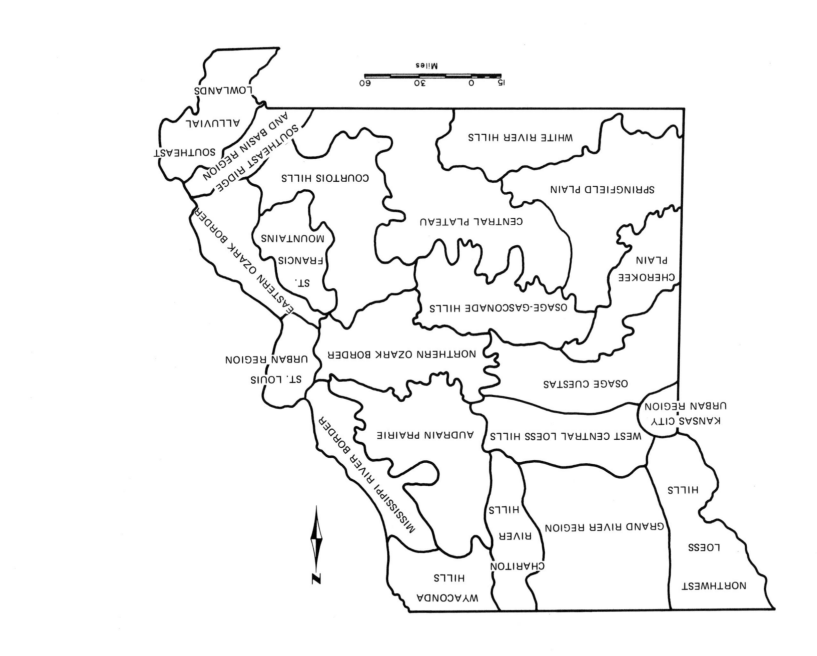

Miles
60   30   0   15   60

LOWLANDS

ALLUVIAL

SOUTHEAST

SOUTHEAST RIDGE AND BASIN REGION

COURTOIS HILLS

WHITE RIVER HILLS

SPRINGFIELD PLAIN

CENTRAL PLATEAU

ST. FRANCIS MOUNTAINS

EASTERN OZARK BORDER

CHEROKEE PLAIN

OSAGE-GASCONADE HILLS

ST. LOUIS URBAN REGION

NORTHERN OZARK BORDER

OSAGE CUESTAS

KANSAS CITY URBAN REGION

MISSISSIPPI RIVER BORDER

AUDRAIN PRAIRIE

WEST CENTRAL LOESS HILLS

CHARITON RIVER HILLS

GRAND RIVER REGION

HILLS

LOESS

NORTHWEST

WYACONDA HILLS

N

11. GEOGRAPHIC REGIONS OF MISSOURI

The most comprehensive attempt to regionalize Missouri's diverse geography was by James E. Collier in 1955. Earlier efforts based on more selected criteria include those of Marbut and Sauer. The geographic regions delineated on the map are based mainly on physical features, especially relief and slope, but soil fertility, land use, and population density are also considered.

REGIONAL DATA

Region	Area (sq. mi.)	1970 Pop.	Pop. Increase or Decrease (Since 1960)	Pop. per Sq. Mile	Value of Crops per Acre	Total Cropland (acres)	Landforms
Northwest Loess Hills	3,600	232,223	32,649	82	$73.08	996,403	Rolling upland, roughland near major streams, deep loessal soils
Grand River Loess Flats and Drift Hills	5,856	106,546	− 9,769	18	61.38	1,742,900	Gently rolling uplands, more rugged near larger streams, moderately deep loessal soils
West Central Loess Hills	3,486	290,955	40,024	83	61.99	707,747	Rolling loessal hills extending 25 miles either side of the Missouri River. Broad flood plains.
Chariton River Hills	2,723	83,935	6,327	31	53.62	464,286	Steep-sided and closely spaced hills. Thin loess cover.
White River Hills	3,486	61,742	4,280	18	32.56	120,793	Rugged, heavily forested hills with elongate ridges, balds and knobs, cedar glades.
Central Plateau	7,286	161,620	9,084	22	42.71	332,130	Terrain varies from rolling upland prairies or flats to sharply hilly forested areas. Cherty soils.
Osage-Gasconade Hills	3,597	118,275	17,698	33	46.65	226,609	Sharply hilly with streams entrenched deeply into limestone bedrock. Heavily forested with clearings in bottoms and on ridges. Cherty soils.
Courtois Hills	4,676	71,470	4,626	15	42.57	132,821	Rugged hills with relief as much as 200 to 400 feet. Mainly forested with clearings on bottoms and on ridges. Cherty soils.
St. Francis Mountains	1,711	54,205	− 95	32	41.08	68,607	Granite and felsite knobs with small basins underlain by limestones. Heavily forested and thin soils except in the lowlands.
Southeast Alluvial Lowlands	2,684	127,656	− 39,201	48	57.61	1,111,893	Broad alluvial lowland with low, sandy ridges. Relief seldom more than 10 feet.
St. Louis Urban Region	1,114	1,644,175	136,240	1,475	60.67	191,500	Rolling hills, heavily urbanized.
Kansas City Urban Region	682	500,287	29,328	733	73.85	90,212	Rolling hills, heavily urbanized.
Andrain Prairie	3,309	107,334	12,050	32	57.84	664,568	Wide, flat tablelands, fertile loessal and fluvial soils.
Mississippi River Border	2,738	107,152	16,679	39	62.35	506,844	Gently rolling to steep. Relief as much as 200 to 300 feet, karst landforms. Steep slopes forestal.
Wyaconda Hills	2,023	37,322	− 1,595	19	58.38	449,180	Level uplands with prairie soils, wide alluvial valleys, hilly near larger streams. Steep slopes forested.
Osage Cuestas	4,390	184,072	− 18,677	42	58.01	770,295	Cuesta landforms developed on limestones, sandstone, and shales.
Cherokee Plain	2,552	56,369	− 3,544	22	53.00	577,929	Loco hills developed on weak shales. Scattered limestone and sandstone buttes.
Springfield Plain	4,855	309,288	29,519	67	44.39	515,395	Rolling tableland cut by deeply entrenched streams. Steep slopes forested. Cherty soils locally.
Northern Ozark Border	4,014	182,772	27,557	45	53.12	356,045	Steeply rolling hills covered by loess. Uplands and lowlands cultivated. Steep slopes forested.
Eastern Ozark Border	2,345	131,372	24,192	56	55.23	253,180	Hilly with relief as much as 200 to 300 feet. Loessal soils. Steep slopes forested.

AVERAGE PRECIPITATION FOR
THE THREE-MONTH PERIOD
SEPTEMBER, OCTOBER, AND
NOVEMBER

INCHES

12
11
10
9
8

AUTUMN PRECIPITATION

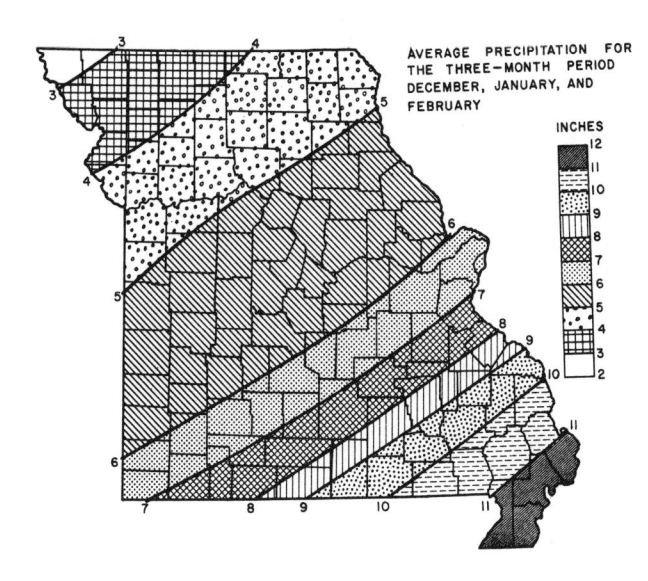

AVERAGE PRECIPITATION FOR
THE THREE-MONTH PERIOD
DECEMBER, JANUARY, AND
FEBRUARY

INCHES

11
10
9
8
7
6
5
4
3
2

WINTER PRECIPITATION

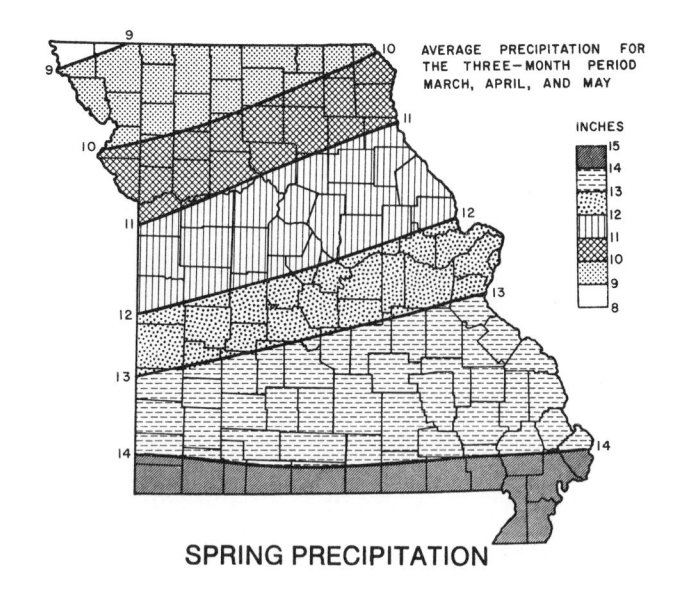

AVERAGE PRECIPITATION FOR
THE THREE-MONTH PERIOD
MARCH, APRIL, AND MAY

INCHES

15
14
13
12
11
10
9
8

SPRING PRECIPITATION

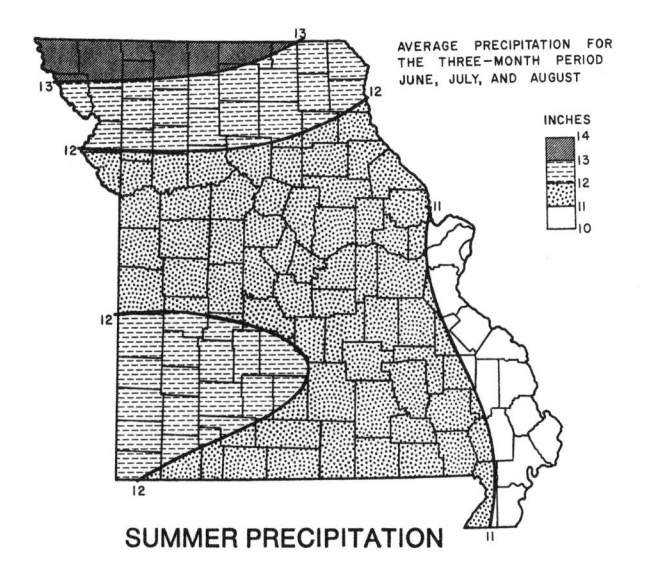

AVERAGE PRECIPITATION FOR
THE THREE-MONTH PERIOD
JUNE, JULY, AND AUGUST

INCHES

14
13
12
11
10

SUMMER PRECIPITATION

12. PRECIPITATION BY SEASON

The average annual precipitation in Missouri ranges from thirty-four inches in the northwest to fifty inches in the extreme southeast. The hourly climatic records of Kansas City, in the heart of the midwestern agricultural belt, may be considered as representative of the greater part of the area. The distribution in the Kansas City area is of the type favorable to plant growth. Considering the year as a whole, 64 per cent of measurable precipitation falls between sunset and sunrise, and 77 per cent falls between 11:00 P.M. and 11:00 A.M. During the dormant season for plants there is only slight variation in precipitation through the average twenty-four-hour day. However, during the vegetal period, 88 per cent of the hours with measurable precipitation are between 11:00 P.M. and 11:00 A.M., with maximum frequency at sunrise.

Autumn and Winter Precipitation. Autumn in Missouri is a season of variable precipitation. When high pressure dominates the state, some of the most pleasantly cool and clear weather may occur, but at other times fronts may produce extended periods of rain. Autumn precipitation ranges from nine inches in the northwest to eleven inches in the southeastern half of the state. The most pronounced precipitation gradient occurs during the winter season. Because the northwestern part of the state is more often under the influence of cold, dry Arctic air, it receives only three inches of precipitation, with much of that as snow. Southeastward, the influence of air from the Gulf of Mexico becomes progressively greater so that more of the precipitation falls as rain or drizzle and the total winter accumulation amounts to eleven inches or more.

In northern Missouri the average amount of snowfall ranges from 5 to 18 inches a year. Average snowfall at Springfield is about 3.5 per cent of total precipitation, or 15.9 inches, less than half the snowfall of Chicago or New York.

Spring and Summer Precipitation. The greatest amount of precipitation falls in the spring and summer. The spring rainfall ranges from nine inches in the northwest to fourteen inches along the southern border. Most of the spring precipitation is frontal, resulting from the meeting of moist Gulf air and the cooler and drier air from the north.

Summer rains occur as heavy convectional thundershowers usually of short duration. The distribution and occurrence of rainfall are often erratic in summer months. The amount of summer rainfall increases from southeast to northwest, but the distribution over the state is more even. When dry air masses stagnate over the state, prolonged periods of time may pass without significant precipitation.

Heavy downpours are associated with squall lines, fronts, and isolated thunderstorms. On June 22, 1947, the most remarkable of all intense small-area rainfalls occurred at Holt, Missouri, approximately thirty miles northeast of Kansas City. The point rainfall total of twelve inches in forty-two minutes is a world record. Although flash floods and the even larger floods that inundate the bottomlands of major river valleys cause heavy property damage, droughts have done more damage than periods of heavy rains. The droughts cover a larger area and are more prolonged, they affect both uplands and river bottomland, they do permanent injury to field crops, and they affect farm and village alike by depleting water supplies as reservoirs are lowered and springs stop flowing.

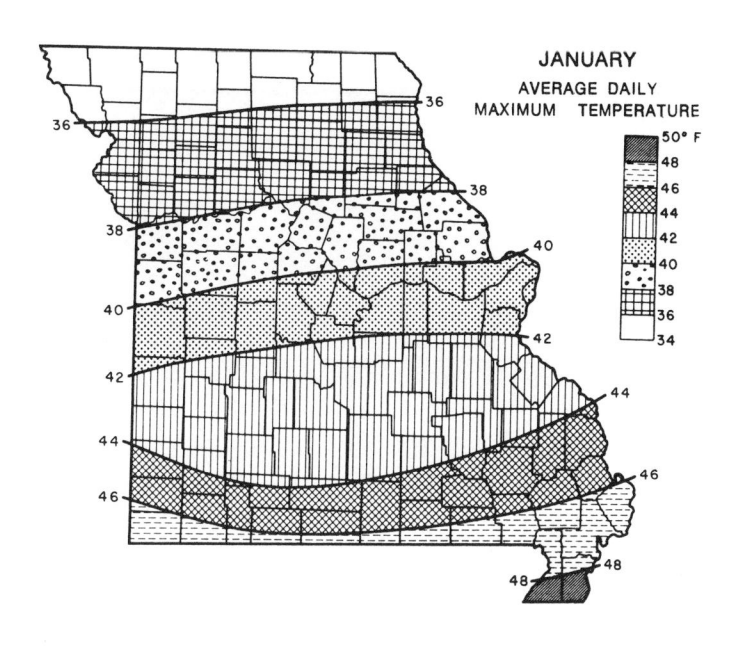

JANUARY
AVERAGE DAILY
MAXIMUM TEMPERATURE

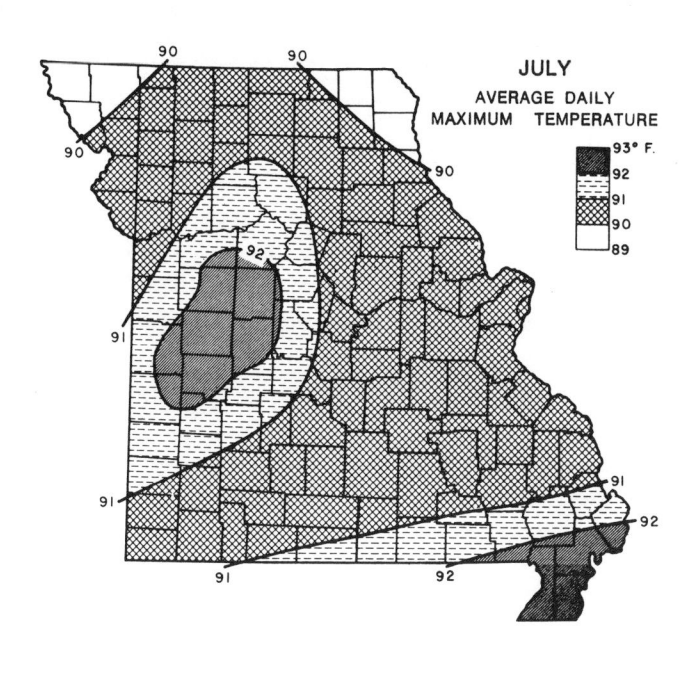

JULY
AVERAGE DAILY
MAXIMUM TEMPERATURE

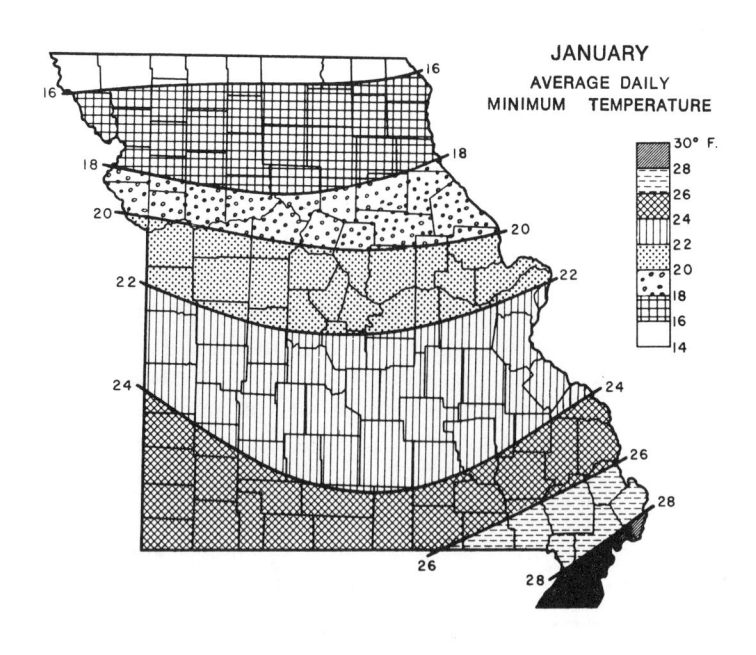

JANUARY
AVERAGE DAILY
MINIMUM TEMPERATURE

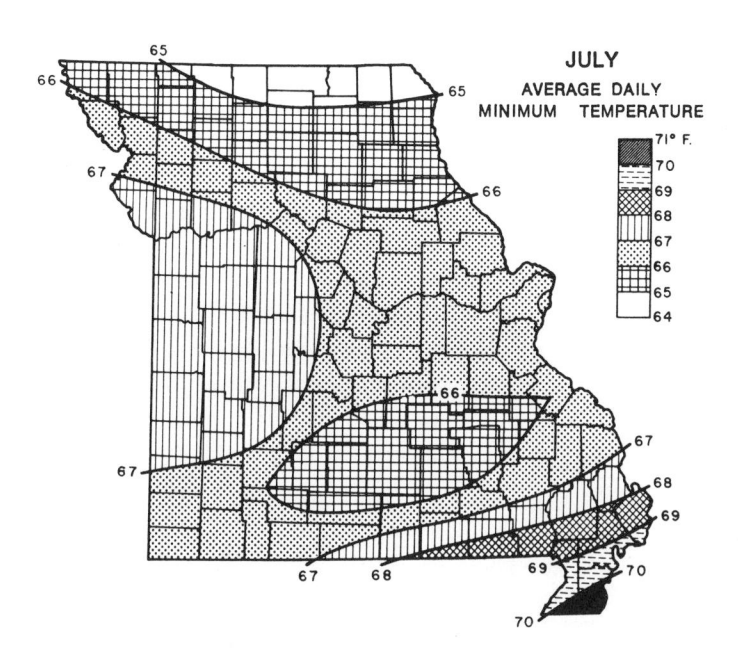

JULY
AVERAGE DAILY
MINIMUM TEMPERATURE

©1982 by the University of Oklahoma Press

13. SEASONAL AND DIURNAL TEMPERATURES

Missouri's climate is continental. There are frequent changes in weather, both from day to day and from season to season. The state's midcontinental location places it in the path of cold air moving down out of Canada; warm, moist air coming up from the Gulf; and dry air from the west.

January Temperatures. Winter in Missouri usually sets in about the second half of December and continues through January and February, with occasional cold periods in early March. Each of the winter months has twenty-two to twenty-seven days when the temperature during the warmest part of the day is at 32° F or above and only one to three days when the temperature goes below zero. In northern Missouri the cold periods last a bit longer, and in the southeast, particularly in the Bootheel, the cold weather is less severe and of shorter duration. The low temperature of January nights averages 28° F in the Bootheel, while the low in the north averages 16° F. In both locations many nights are much colder or much warmer. The daily maximum temperature in January varies from 48° F in the southeast to 36° F in the north. About three cold waves a season sweep over the state, and the average length of each wave is about three days. The mean daily range in temperature throughout the year is 18.2 degrees; in winter it is 16.8 degrees, in spring 19 degrees, in summer 18.3 degrees, and in autumn 18.8 degrees. Northern Missouri winters usually experience several days in a row when the temperatures never rise above freezing. Missouri's record low of −40° F was registered at Warsaw on February 13, 1905.

July Temperatures. Extreme temperatures of 100° F or above may be expected during a Missouri summer. For the state as a whole, extremely high temperatures are likely to occur on one or two days in late June, three to five days during each of the months of July and August, and perhaps a day or two in early September. Average minimum temperatures in July are in the upper sixties, except in the extreme southeast, where they reach 70° F. The average minimum of 65° F is lowest in the northern part of the state, but even there many summer nights are uncomfortably warm. Residents of northern Missouri refer to the hot, humid nights of July and August as "corn growing weather." Average daily maximums in July exceed 90° F over most of the state. There is little variation over the state. Missouri's record high of 118° F was recorded at Lamar and at Warsaw.

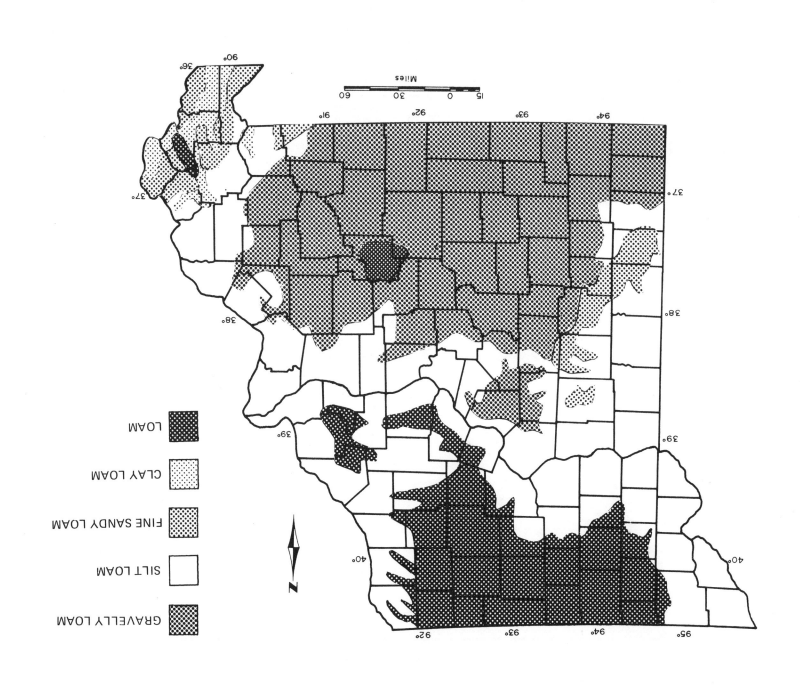

LOAM

CLAY LOAM

FINE SANDY LOAM

SILT LOAM

GRAVELLY LOAM

Miles
15 0   30   60

N

14. SOIL TEXTURES

For the pioneers who settled Missouri, the single most important factor for economic development of the region was the quality of soil resources. Today, after more than a century of agricultural settlement, the well-being and prosperity of the people are dependent on the continued use of the soil.

Soil is a complex material. It is composed of weathered rock material, decayed and partially decayed organic matter, air, and water in various conditions. The chief parent materials of Missouri soils are loess, glacial till, limestone and dolomitic limestone, shales, and alluvial deposits. Sandstone and granite are of minor importance.

The texture of soils greatly affects their fertility, tilth (tillability), and capability to retain water. Sands have very low available water storage capacity. Special soil horizons such as fragipan horizons, rocky or gravelly layers, and bedrock also are factors affecting fertility and plant growth.

The textures of Missouri's soils are mainly loam or silt loam. Such soils of medium textures have the greatest moisture-holding capacity, best tilth, and widest crop adaptations. Bottomland soils range widely in soil texture, from sticky, plastic clay to loose sand. Most of the soils of the Ozark region are silty, but are usually cherty or stony. Sandy soils occur in the southeastern plains and locally in the Ozarks.

Most of the upland soils have clayey subsoils. This is especially true of the glaciated section, but even the Ozarks subsoils often have stony clay textures. Claypan soils are common on level uplands in northern Missouri, while fragipans of accumulated clay and iron compounds are found on Ozark uplands. Such pan developments are detrimental to root penetration and place limits on natural vegetation and crop growth.

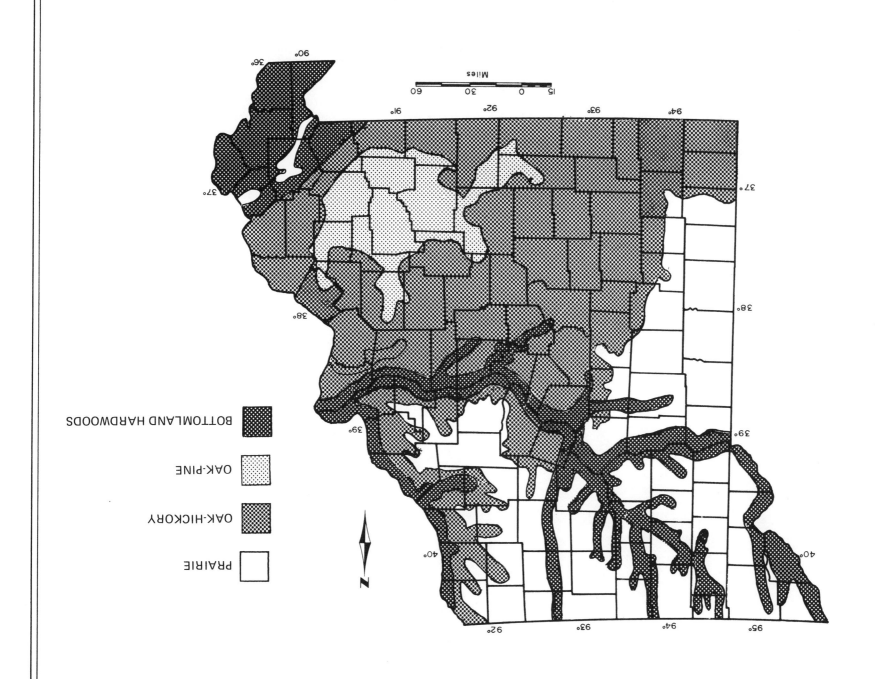

BOTTOMLAND HARDWOODS

OAK-PINE

OAK-HICKORY

PRAIRIE

Miles

60   30   0   15

15. VEGETATION

Maps of natural vegetation are mainly historical maps, because man has cut over most of the forests and plowed most of the humid grasslands of the world. Forests covered two-thirds of the state in its primeval condition. The remainder of the state was covered by a tall-grass prairie with big and little bluestem grasses especially prominent. Virtually all of the prairie land has been plowed and converted to agricultural uses, and the forested land likewise has been reduced in area. Today forest covers about one-third of the state. Not only has the area in forests been reduced, but the quality of the forests also has been depleted by logging of the commercially valuable timber.

Two-thirds of the existing forested land is in the Ozarks, where it occurs in large blocks of forested land and as wood-lots in more level areas. Outside the Ozarks the timberland is confined to the dissected land along streams and as small farm woodlots. Most of the forested land is privately owned, and the average size of landholding is small. Mark Twain national forest contains approximately 8 per cent of the forested area.

Reports of pioneers and the field notes of surveyors who carried out the first land surveys indicate that the trees on uplands were often stunted. Hard, cemented fragipan layers in the soil under level upland tracts may have retarded penetration of tree roots and caused slower tree growth. There were small prairies in the eastern Ozarks, such as the "Barrens" in Perry County, but the western Ozarks were about 50 per cent parklike grasslands. Extensive forests of short-leaf pine were found in early years in Reynolds, Carter, Shannon, and Oregon counties. The virgin pine and oak timber of the Ozarks and the Southeast Alluvial Lowlands was cut over by large lumber companies between 1880 and 1920.

The prairies, even more than the forests, have been modified by man. Most of the prairies, consisting of bluestems and other tall grasses, were plowed when agriculture became more intensive. The prairie lands of northern and western Missouri today produce abundant yields of corn, soybeans, wheat, and grain sorghums.

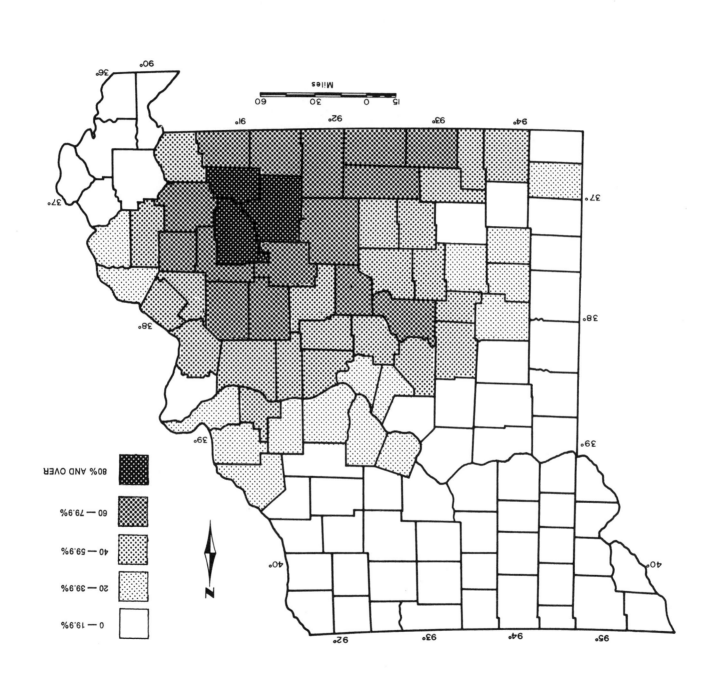

80% AND OVER

60 — 79.9%

40 — 59.9%

20 — 39.9%

0 — 19.9%

Miles

15   0   30   60

16. PERCENTAGE OF LAND IN FORESTS

Missouri lies in the border belt between land that was naturally forested and land that was in grass. When white men first entered the state, more than two-thirds of the state was virgin forest wilderness. An estimated 30 million acres were covered with trees. The forest cover was dominated by oak and pine in portions of the Ozark region and by oak and hickory forests through the remainder of the state.

Today the state is approximately 34.5 per cent forested. The percentage of land in forests corresponds rather closely to the landform divisions of the state. Northern and western Missouri counties are all less than 20 per cent forested. These areas are well suited to crop production, so that a large share of the land is under cultivation. The counties of the Southeast Lowlands are similarly lacking in forest cover.

The Ozark region is heavily forested, and especially so in the interior portions. Most of the interior Ozark counties are over 60 per cent forested, while Reynolds, Shannon, and Carter counties are more than 80 per cent forested.

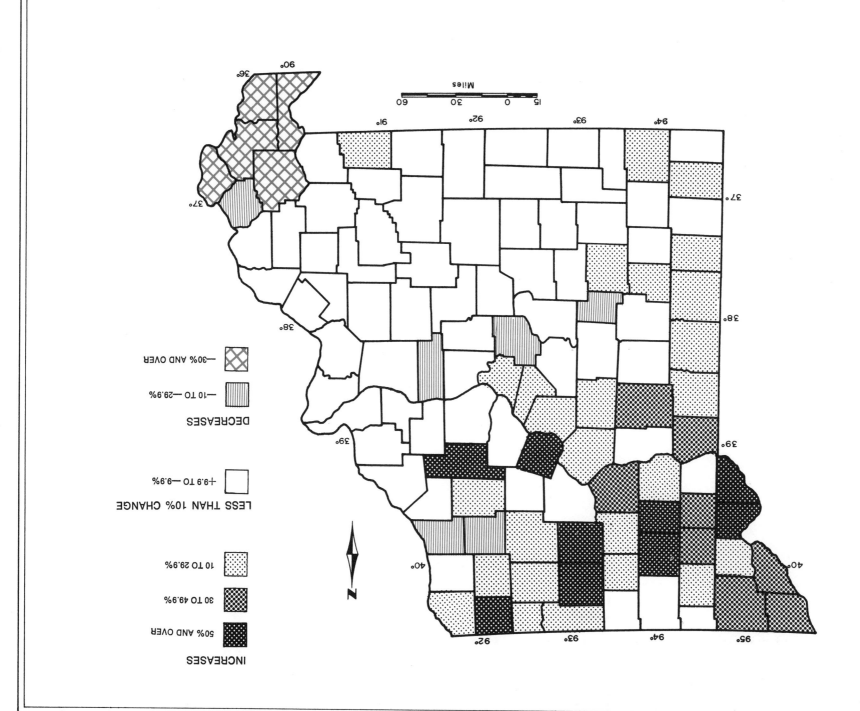

17. PERCENTAGE OF CHANGE IN FORESTED LAND, 1947–72

The map of percentage of change in forest land between 1947 and 1972 shows three general areas of change. Counties in the agricultural north and west have shown moderate to large percentages of gain, probably due to the advance of timber on former cropland. This trend has been stimulated by the federal program of acreage restriction and conservation reserve which allows farmers to divert land unsuited to crops to other uses. It should also be noted that the large percentages of increase do not reflect very large actual acreage gains, since the forest base is small in these counties.

Throughout the Ozarks the percentage of land in forest has remained rather stable, although the general condition of the forest has deteriorated in many areas. It should be recognized that many of the heavily forested Ozark counties such as Wash- ington, Iron, Reynolds, Madison, Wayne, Shannon, and Carter have only a small amount of dollar production for the large amount of forest land. Significant decreases in forested area occurred in the Southeast Lowlands, reflecting the continuing expansion of drainage and crop agriculture in that section.

Sawtimber volume out of total growing stock volume (6 billion cubic feet) is an important factor, because sawtimber potential represents potential lumber products. The sawtimber portion of growing stock increased between 1959 and 1972 by 13 per cent from 13.3 billion board feet to 15.1 billion board feet. Because softwoods grow at a faster rate than hardwoods, the softwood volume increased 58 per cent and hardwood volume increased 10 per cent.

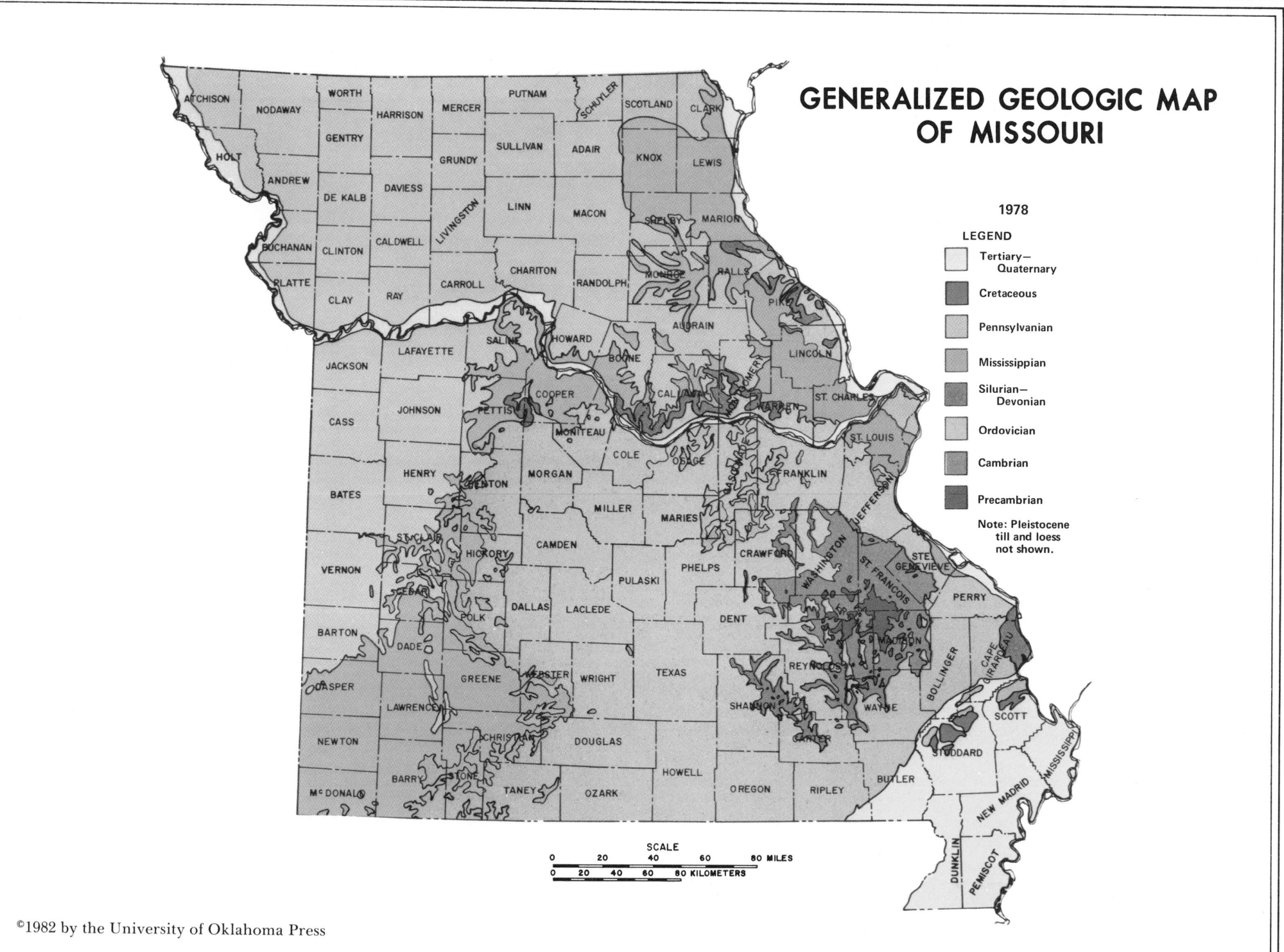

GENERALIZED GEOLOGIC MAP OF MISSOURI

1978

LEGEND

- Tertiary—Quaternary
- Cretaceous
- Pennsylvanian
- Mississippian
- Silurian—Devonian
- Ordovician
- Cambrian
- Precambrian

Note: Pleistocene till and loess not shown.

SCALE

0   20   40   60   80 MILES

0   20   40   60   80 KILOMETERS

18. GEOLOGY

Missouri rocks are mainly sedimentary, formed by settling into beds of masses of sediment, and igneous, formed by the solidification of hot mixtures of minerals. The oldest rocks are the igneous rocks that appear at the surface in the St. Francis Mountains in southeastern Missouri. The igneous rocks are of two kinds, granites and porphyries.

The sedimentary rocks are of two main groups. One is composed of limestone formed while Missouri was not only covered by water but also far from any land area. The other group of rocks was formed when Missouri was either part of a continent or covered by a shallow sea near land. Sandstones, shales, and certain limestones fall into this group.

The rocks of the earth's surface may also be classified according to age. Three of the four major time spans (eras), Cenozoic, Mesozoic, Paleozoic, and Precambrian (Proterozoic and Azoic), are represented in Missouri along with eight or nine of the subdivisions of the ages (periods). If all these subdivisions were superimposed at any one place, they would make a column thirty-five hundred feet high from the top of the granites and felsites. The thickness of the igneous rocks is unknown.

For purposes of mapping, the rocks are divided into groups, each group usually including more than one kind of rock or more than one formation. The Precambrian granites and rhyolites are found in the St. Francis Mountains and in Shannon County where the Current River has cut deeply into the overlying sedimentary rock layers. A long period later, an ocean invaded the valleys and rose high on the rounded igneous rock hills. Weathered gravel and boulders were cemented to form the sandstones and conglomerates of the Cambrian Lamotte formation.

The second period of the Paleozoic era, the Ordovician, began with the advances of seas over all of Missouri. Deposits of dolomite up to five hundred feet thick were laid down. Then the seas retreated from most of the state, and many narrow valleys were eroded in the emerging surface. During this period sand was deposited over large areas forming the St. Peter sandstone.

During Silurian and Devonian times the seas covered only the extremities of Missouri, in the southeast, northeast, and northwest. Limestones and shales accumulated to thicknesses of less than one hundred feet. After erosion in the late Devonian, seas of the Mississippian period advanced and covered the state. Thick deposits of limestone—notably the St. Louis, Keokuk, and Burlington formations—were laid down. The end of Mississippian time was the final chapter of Missouri's marine history. It was under the sea at times thereafter, but for short periods only.

The later stratified rocks of Missouri are made up of land material. The first formation, the Cherokee shales, probably was deposited around an Ozark island. The coal beds of Missouri contain an estimated 83 billion tons. Limestones and shales were subsequently deposited on top of the coal-bearing formations.

Most of the bedrock of northern Missouri is buried under rock rubble laid down by two great glaciers that spread southward as far as the Missouri River and in places a few miles beyond. Later these glacial till deposits were covered with a wind-blown silt called loess. The loess, which reaches depths as much as a hundred feet in bluffs along the Missouri River, probably was derived from material deposited by glacial meltwater and later blown across the landscape by winds.

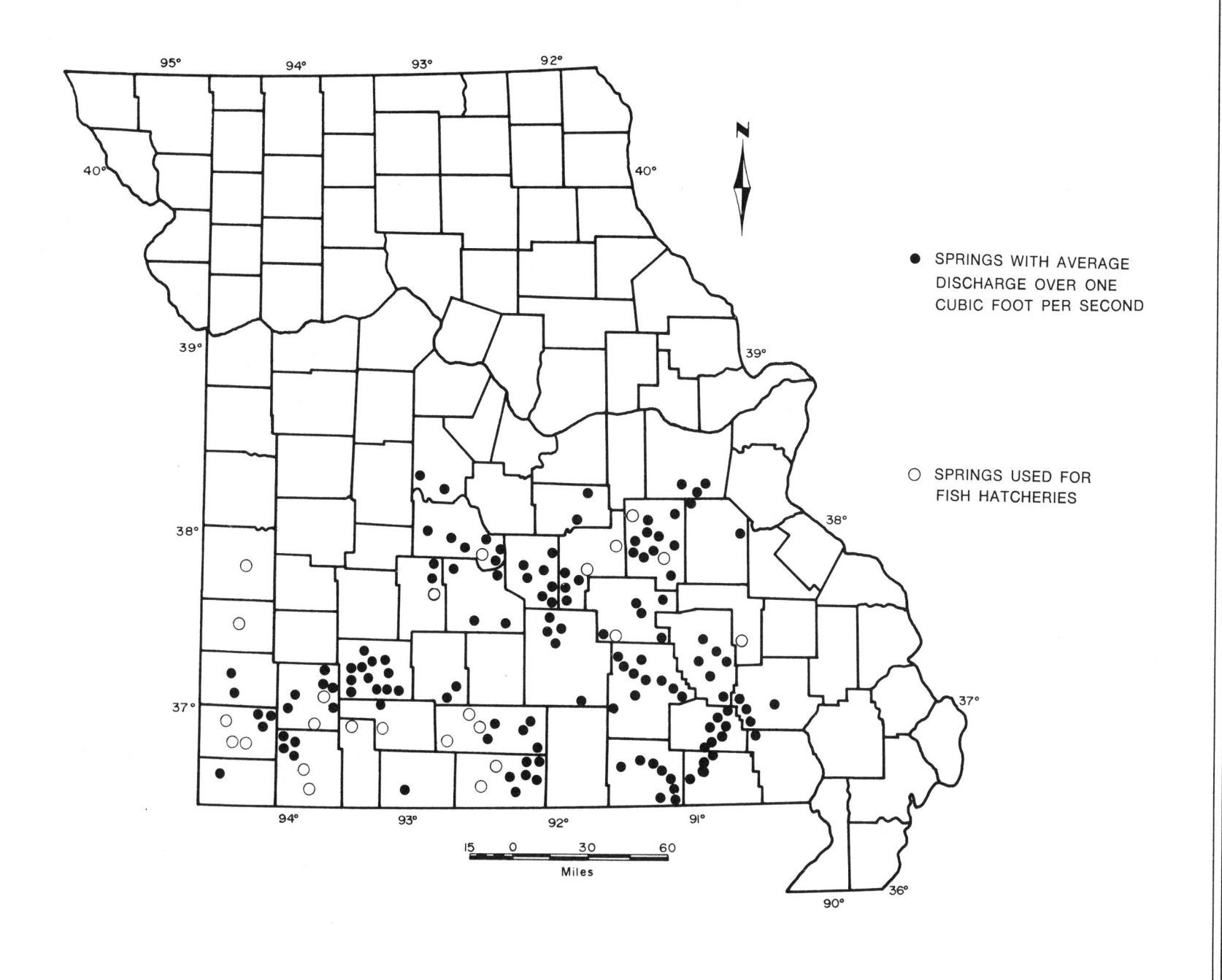

● SPRINGS WITH AVERAGE
 DISCHARGE OVER ONE
 CUBIC FOOT PER SECOND

○ SPRINGS USED FOR
 FISH HATCHERIES

19. SPRINGS

Springs are an important part of the water resources of Missouri, particularly in the Ozarks, where some of the world's largest springs are located. Only a minor part of the discharge of Missouri springs is used directly for municipal and domestic water supplies, medicinal purposes, and commercial fisheries, but the springs contribute indirectly to the economy by sustaining the flow of streams and by serving as focal points for scenic and recreational developments.

The springs of the Ozarks are in a very scenic part of the state. Attempts to preserve the aesthetic qualities of the springs, their surroundings, and the rivers into which they flow have led to the establishment of the Ozark National Scenic Railways. The Current River and its principal tributary, Jacks Fork, are included in this new national preserve.

The Ozark region contains the largest and greatest number of springs in Missouri. Springs with year-round flow occur at altitudes as high as fifteen hundred feet above sea level. Most Ozark springs are outlets for subterranean streams intersected by surface streams as the latter deepen their valleys. The interconnected solution channels that form spring supply systems, filled or partly filled with water, are caves in various stages of formation. Similar openings, now above the water table, create the large cave system for which the state is noted. The combination of considerable relief, the repeated uplifting of a sequence of more than one thousand feet of carbonate rocks, and the fracturing resulting from the uplifting and other stresses have created the conditions necessary for the development of an extensive spring and cave system.

The springs are located at many points along the streams and add much to the beauty of the streams. Among these streams are the Current River and Jacks Fork, Eleven Point River, North Fork River and its tributary Bryant Creek, the White and James rivers, Shoal Creek, Spring River, the lower Osage, the Gasconade, Big Piney and Meramec rivers, and the Black and St. Francis rivers, all well known to float trippers, fishermen, and those who enjoy spectacular scenery. In areas bordering the Salem Plateau, springs generally are small by comparison, but many are large by standards of other states.

The most favorable environment for the development of large spring systems is the sequence of Cambrian and Ordovician dolomites of the Ozarks. The major cavernous formations are the Gasconade, Eminence, and Potosi dolomites. Groundwater moves freely through these formations, and where they are deeply buried, they are good aquifers.

There are fifteen springs in the Missouri Ozarks which have an average daily flow (ADF) in excess of 24 million gallons. The four largest springs have average daily flows of 100 million gallons or more. The largest is Big Spring (276 million gallons ADF), followed by Greer Spring (214 million gallons ADF), Double Spring (100 million gallons ADF), and Bennett Spring (100 million gallons ADF).

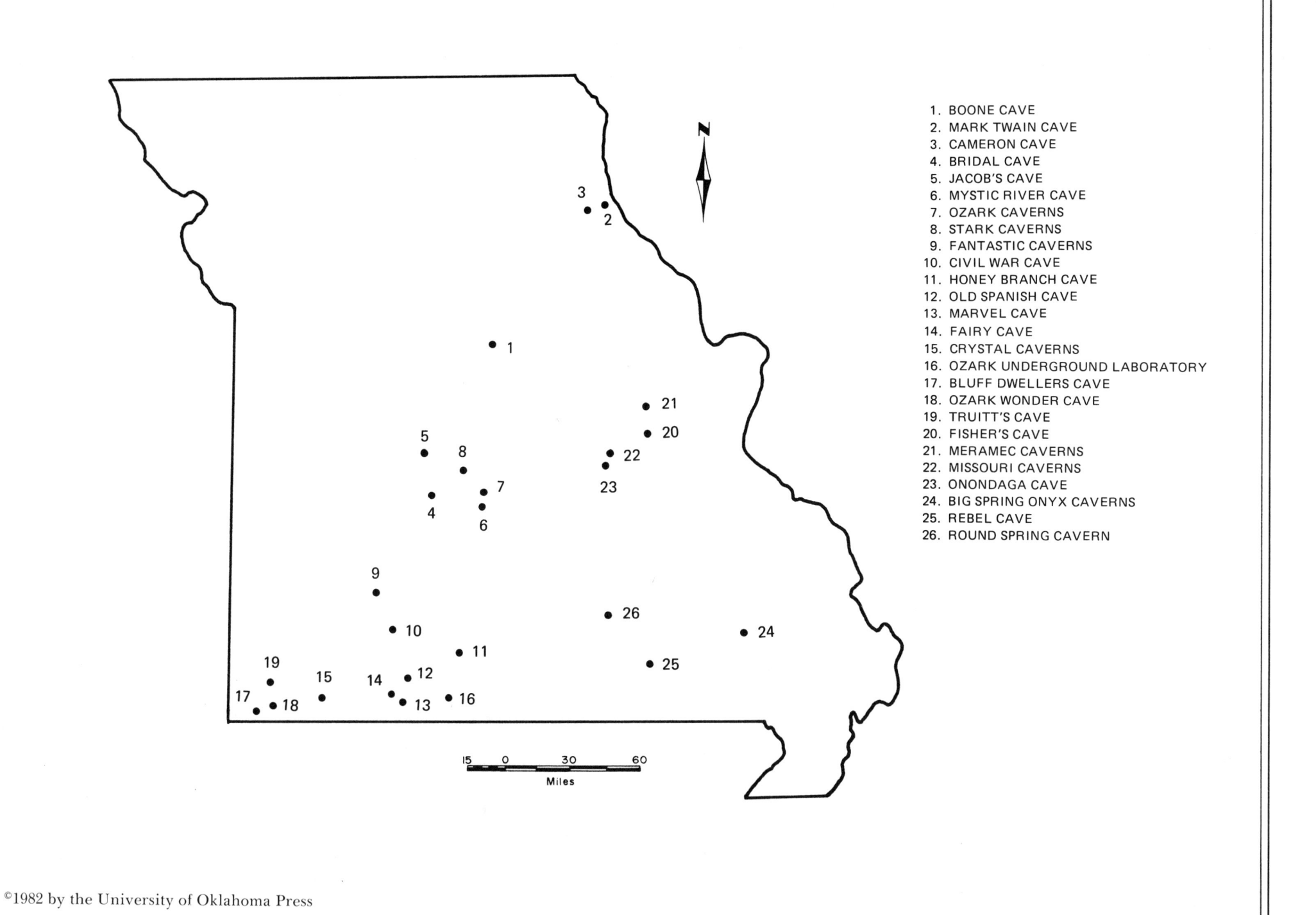

1. BOONE CAVE
2. MARK TWAIN CAVE
3. CAMERON CAVE
4. BRIDAL CAVE
5. JACOB'S CAVE
6. MYSTIC RIVER CAVE
7. OZARK CAVERNS
8. STARK CAVERNS
9. FANTASTIC CAVERNS
10. CIVIL WAR CAVE
11. HONEY BRANCH CAVE
12. OLD SPANISH CAVE
13. MARVEL CAVE
14. FAIRY CAVE
15. CRYSTAL CAVERNS
16. OZARK UNDERGROUND LABORATORY
17. BLUFF DWELLERS CAVE
18. OZARK WONDER CAVE
19. TRUITT'S CAVE
20. FISHER'S CAVE
21. MERAMEC CAVERNS
22. MISSOURI CAVERNS
23. ONONDAGA CAVE
24. BIG SPRING ONYX CAVERNS
25. REBEL CAVE
26. ROUND SPRING CAVERN

Miles

Missouri has more commercial caves than any other state. Most kinds of limestone cave formations may be seen in them.

Boone Cave (1), near Rocheport in Boone County, contains bones of the musk ox, woolly mammoth, and extinct bison. Mark Twain Cave (2), near Hannibal, was described by Mark Twain in *The Adventures of Tom Sawyer*. Nearby Cameron Cave (3) is in the same rock formation.

Five caves are operated near Lake of the Ozarks. Bridal Cave (4), near Camdenton, was supposedly named from the marriage there of an Osage Indian princess. It has been the scene of hundreds of weddings. Jacob's Cave (5), near Camdenton, is noted for its travertine formations. Near Osage Beach is Ozark Caverns (7), which features tours that include a speedboat ride and a wagon ride. Stark Caverns (8), near Eldon, has many indications of occupancy by prehistoric man.

Fantastic Caverns (9), just north of the city limits of Springfield, features a one-mile jeep tour and stage shows on Saturday evenings during the peak tourist season. Near Ozark is Civil War Cave (10), known locally as Smallin's Cave. The huge entrance to the cave was described by Henry Rowe Schoolcraft in 1818. The cave was commercialized in 1962. Honey Branch Cave (11), near Ava, was discovered in 1835 and commercialized in 1956. Old Spanish Cave (12), near Reeds Springs, is linked by legend to an old Spanish map, silver mining, and buried bodies. A few miles south, on the property of Silver Dollar City, is Marvel Cave (13), which features an entrance-way into a spectacular room twenty stories high, a waterfall five hundred feet beneath the surface, and a cable train that carries visitors to the surface. Fairy Cave (14), near Reed's Spring, was first explored by Truman S. Powell in 1896, and the Powell family still runs the cave. Crystal Caverns (15), in Cassville, is linked by legend to an Indian maiden. Ozark Underground Laboratory (16), near Protem, is operated as an experimental cave for research on speleology and groundwater hazards. Bluff Dwellers Cave (17), near Noel, takes its name from the stone tools and human bones found in the detritus accumulated at the entrance. Also near Noel is Ozark Wonder Cave (18), reportedly used as an ammunition dump during the Civil War. Truitt's Cave (19), near Lanagan, has an underground fireplace with a natural flue which opens to the surface by way of a rock fissure. The cave was commercialized in 1935.

The caves along Interstate 44 are among the most visited in Missouri. Fisher's Cave (20), one of twenty caves in Meramec State Park, is the only one in the park in which guided tours are conducted. Meramec Caverns (21), near Stanton, has twenty-six miles of explored passages. Near Leasburg, Missouri Caverns (22) is opened on request for educational tours. Onondaga Cave (23) was visited by Daniel Boone in 1798. The cave was first opened to the public to attract visitors from the St. Louis World's Fair in 1904.

Near Van Buren is Big Spring Onyx Caverns (24). About four miles north of Greenville, near the hamlet known as Silva, is Rebel Cave (25), reportedly named for seven Southern sympathizers who were executed on May 28, 1865, nearly six weeks after General Lee's surrender. Round Spring Cavern (26), north of Eminence along State Highway 19, adjoins Round Spring State Park and the Ozark National Scenic Riverways.

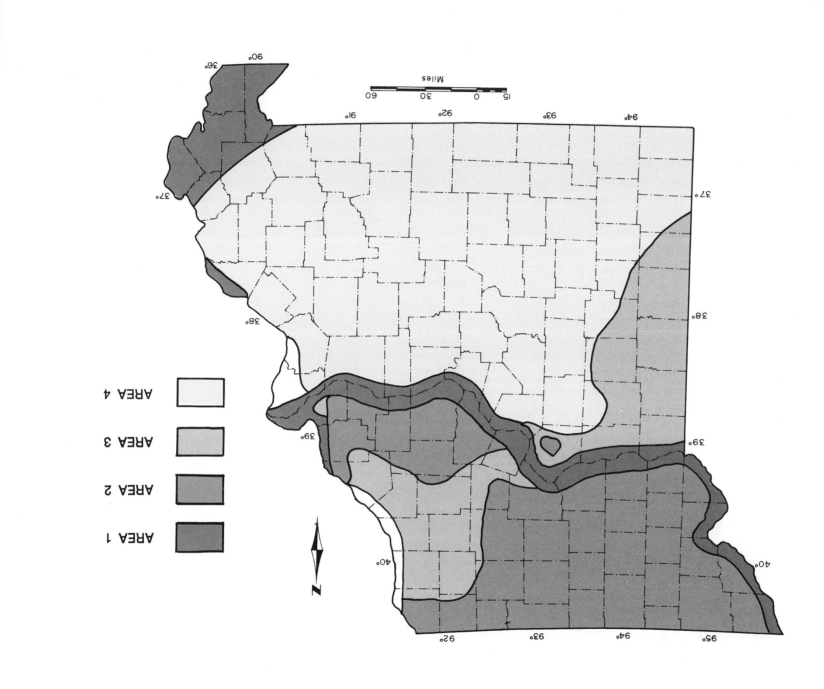

AREA 4

AREA 3

AREA 2

AREA 1

Miles
15   0   30   60

21. GROUNDWATER RESOURCES

Water constitutes one of the important natural resources of Missouri. Groundwater is of special importance because its qualities of uniform temperature and relative freedom from pollutants make it well suited for municipal and industrial uses.

The importance of groundwater in the development of the state is indicated by the number of communities obtaining water supplies from this source. About 60 per cent of the public water systems of Missouri depend on groundwater as the primary supply. In addition, many institutions, industries, and most farms depend upon groundwater supplies. It is generally more economical for the small community to use wells instead of surface supplies if a good source of groundwater is present, since well water normally does not need a filtration plant.

Groundwater sources, aside from springs and mines, are either shallow wells or deep wells. The term *deep wells* generally refers to wells one hundred feet or more deep.

Groundwater occurs throughout most of the geologic formations, filling voids below the water table in the zone of saturation. The availability of the water depends upon the depth below the surface to highly porous saturated formations known as aquifers.

The groundwaters of Missouri are divided into four provinces. Province 1 covers the area in the northwest part of the state overlain by the heaviest glacial deposits. Wells drilled into these glacial sands and gravels yield sufficient water for farms and communities. Deeper wells that penetrate bedrock formations yield mineralized water. Province 2 occupies a belt extending from the northeastern part of Missouri to south of Kansas City. Wells have limited yields of fresh water up to depths of five hundred feet but salty or sulfurous water at greater depths depending on location. Province 3 covers the Southeast Lowlands and the alluvial valleys of the Missouri and Mississippi rivers. Wells produce unlimited yields from the alluvial valleys and 600 to 1,000 gallons a minute from the Ripley sands in southeastern Missouri. Province 4 occupies most of the Ozark region and includes over half the state. Wells drilled into several formations in this province have fairly large capacity, commonly yielding from 150 to 600 gallons a minute. Among the more important deep aquifers in this section are the St. Peter, Roubidoux, Gunter, and Lamotte formations.

All of the waters that drain from Missouri eventually find their way to the Mississippi River. Most of the area of the state is drained by rivers flowing to the Missouri and Arkansas rivers. Only a relatively small part of extreme eastern Missouri drains directly to the Mississippi River.

The rivers of northern Missouri flow to either the Missouri or the Mississippi. Those flowing into the Missouri River have a southerly course, usually almost due south, while those flowing to the Mississippi flow southeastward. The larger streams, such as the Nodaway, One Hundred and Two, Platte, Grand, Chariton, Des Moines, Wyaconda, Fabius, Salt, and Cuivre, have valleys as much as five miles wide, with flat, meadowlike floors over which the stream channels meander in winding courses. Meander scars, oxbow lakes, backwater swamps and marshes, and sandbars are typical floodplain landforms.

The Ozark dome forms the major drainage divide in Missouri midway between the Missouri River and the southern boundary of the state. The two major streams flowing north to the Missouri River are the Osage and the Gasconade. Major streams flowing south to the White River include the James, North Fork, Eleven Point, Current, and Black rivers. The largest streams flowing to the Mississippi are the Meramec, which enters the larger stream just south of St. Louis, and the St. Francis, which flows southward out of Missouri to join the Mississippi near Helena, Arkansas. The streams of the Ozarks are distinctive in that even though they are deeply entrenched into the plateau surface, they follow meandering courses. Such streams have numerous localities where dams are easily constructed at bedrock narrows.

All of Missouri's large lakes are man-made. The first, Lake Taneycomo, was formed when the Powersite Dam was constructed on the White River by the Ozark Power and Water Company in 1912. Power transmission lines were extended from the dam to Springfield and to the cities and mines in the Tri-State Mining District. The second major impoundment, Lake of the Ozarks, was formed when Bagnell Dam was completed in 1931. The dam and power plant built by Union Electric and Power Company supplied electrical power to St. Louis and the towns and mines in the Lead Belt in St. Francois County.

Beginning in 1948 with the construction of Clearwater Lake on Black River, the Corps of Engineers assumed the role of dam builder in Missouri. The 1950s and 1960s saw several large reservoirs completed: Bull Shoals, Table Rock, Pomme de Terre, and Stockton. The largest and most expensive impoundment, Truman Reservoir, began filling in early 1978 when the dam on the Osage River was closed.

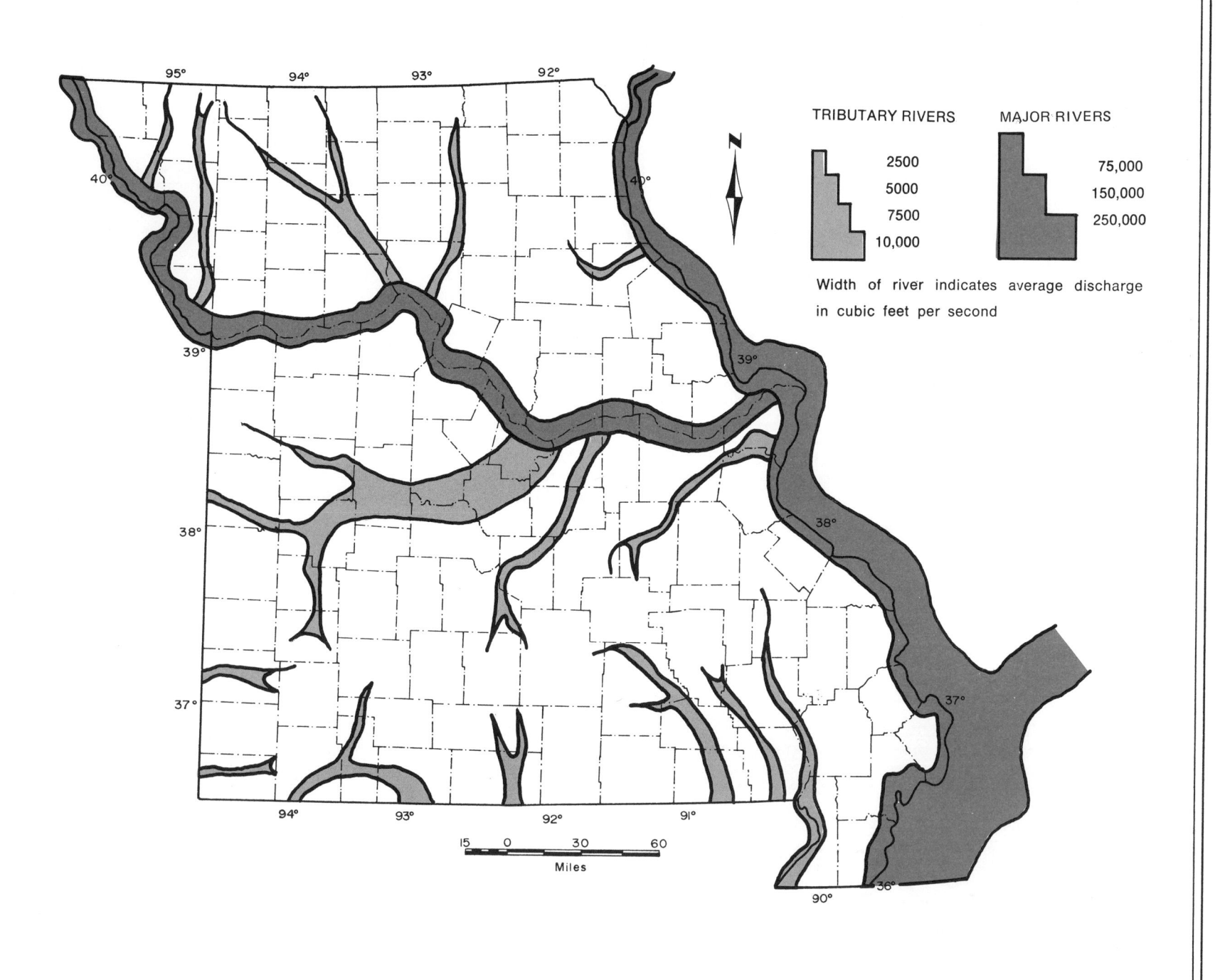

TRIBUTARY RIVERS

2500
5000
7500
10,000

MAJOR RIVERS

75,000
150,000
250,000

Width of river indicates average discharge
in cubic feet per second

As the population has increased and as the use of water has become greater, interest has grown in the state's water resources. The kind of water supply developed for purposes other than hydroelectric power in Missouri is determined by the sources of water available. If surface water and groundwater sources are both available, the comparative cost of obtaining and treating the water is taken into account. Along the major rivers where big cities and their industries require large quantities of water, the source is principally the river. North of the Missouri River where development of groundwater supplies is difficult and minimum flows of streams are inadequate without storage, reservoirs store the drainage for small areas. During extended dry spells some of these supplies are inadequate, and water must be hauled to supply emergency domestic needs of small towns and farms.

The average annual runoff from streams in the state varies from four inches in the northwest to twenty-two inches in the southeast. Runoff for selected locations is as follows: Maryville, five inches; Kansas City and Kirksville, six inches; Sedalia, Jefferson City, and St. Louis, ten inches; Springfield, twelve inches; Poplar Bluff, eighteen inches; and Kennett, twenty-two inches.

All of Missouri is drained either directly or indirectly by the Mississippi and Missouri rivers. Distinctive low-flow regimens (the volume of water after a prolonged dry period) exist in each of Missouri's physiographic regions. In the plains, the low-flow potential of the streams is small because of the low storage capacity of the shales and clays of the area. In the Ozarks, where the base flow is almost entirely from springs, the base flows of streams are the highest in the state. In the Southeast Lowlands, large amounts of surface water are available without storage,

and the region ranks second to the Ozarks in terms of available surface water. The yield of streams during long periods of low precipitation is larger south of the Missouri River in the Ozark region than in the glaciated areas of northern Missouri. The rock formations underlying the Ozarks contribute more water to sustain the low flow of streams than do those underlying the glaciated region.

STREAM FLOW DATA FOR MISSOURI RIVERS

River	Location	Drainage Area (sq. mi.)	Average Discharge (cu. ft./sec.)	Maximum Discharge (cu. ft./sec.)	Minimum Discharge (cu. ft./sec.)
Mississippi	Keokuk, Iowa	119,000	60,670	314,000	5,000
Mississippi	St. Louis	701,000	173,800	1,019,000	18,000
Wyaconda	Canton	447	315	16,000	0
Salt	New London	2,480	1,498	64,700	0
Missouri	Rulo, Nebr.	418,905	36,180	358,000	4,420
Missouri	Kansas City	489,200	54,710	573,000	1,500
Missouri	Hermann	528,000	78,570	676,000	4,200
Tarkio	Fairfax	508	187	16,300	0
Platte	Agency	1,760	820	50,000	0
Grand	Sumner	6,880	3,700	180,000	10
Chariton	Prairie Hill	1,870	1,068	25,600	4
Osage	Bagnell	14,000	9,516	220,000	220
Gasconade	Rich Fountain	3,180	2,939	96,400	271
Meramec	Eureka	3,788	3,025	120,000	196
St. Francis	Wappapello	1,311	1,308	22,300	0
White	Forsyth	4,544	4,959	209,000	0
James	Springfield	246	176	24,800	0
Black	Poplar Bluff	1,245	1,258	52,600	70
Current	Doniphan	2,038	2,712	94,000	852
Eleven Point	Bardley	793	744	40,000	152
Spring	Waco	1,164	828	103,000	4
Shoal Creek	Joplin	439	386	54,000	1

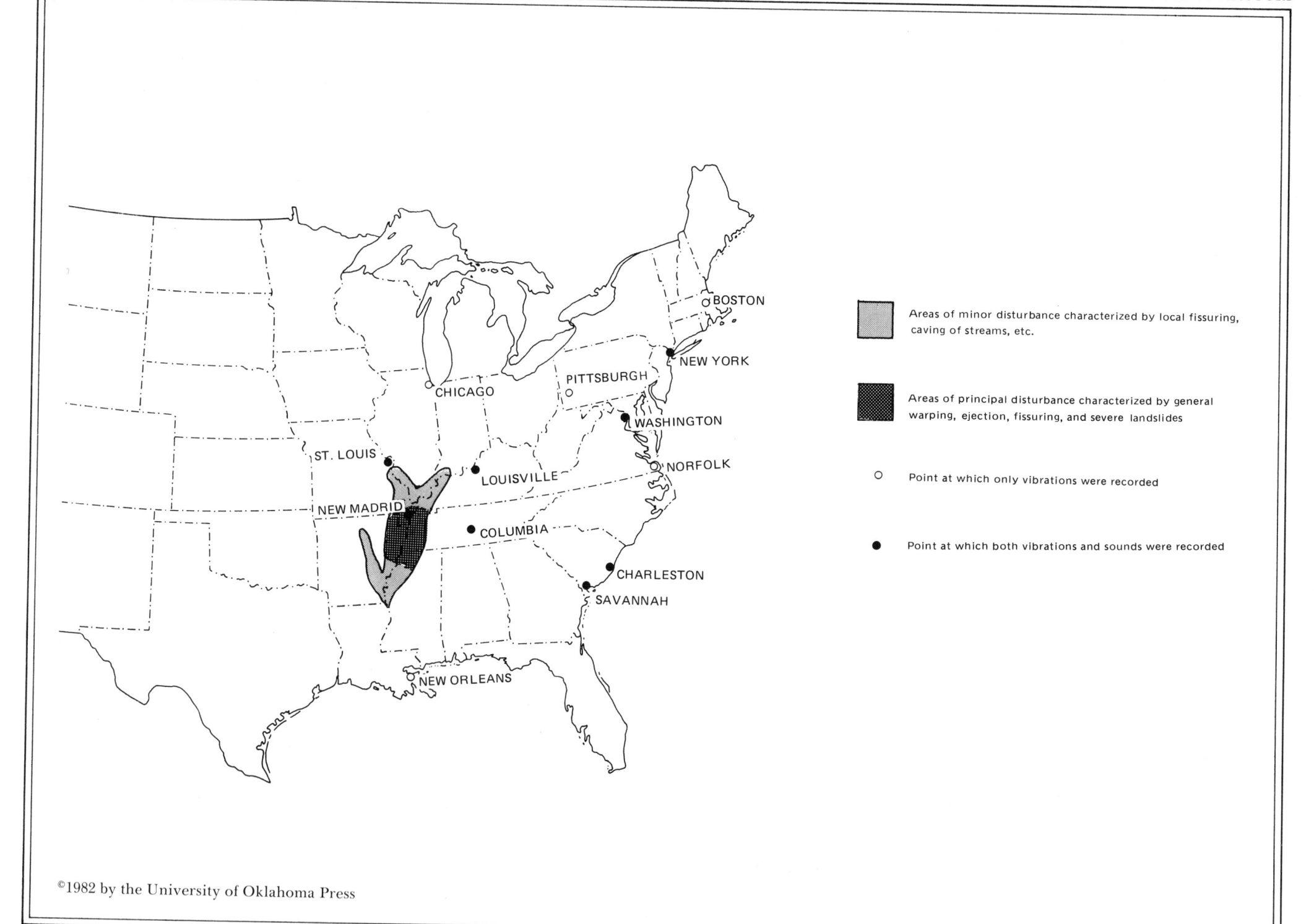

Areas of minor disturbance characterized by local fissuring, caving of streams, etc.

Areas of principal disturbance characterized by general warping, ejection, fissuring, and severe landslides

○ Point at which only vibrations were recorded

● Point at which both vibrations and sounds were recorded

BOSTON

NEW YORK

PITTSBURGH

CHICAGO

WASHINGTON

ST. LOUIS

NORFOLK

LOUISVILLE

NEW MADRID

COLUMBIA

CHARLESTON

SAVANNAH

NEW ORLEANS

24. THE NEW MADRID EARTHQUAKE, 1811–12

The succession of shocks designated collectively the New Madrid Earthquake occurred in an area of the central Mississippi Valley including southeastern Missouri, northeastern Arkansas, and western Kentucky and Tennessee. Beginning December 16, 1811, and lasting more than a year, these shocks have not been surpassed or even equaled for number, continuance of disturbance, area affected, and severity by the more recent and better-known shocks at Charleston and San Francisco. Because the region was almost unsettled at that time, relatively little attention was paid to the phenomenon, the published accounts being few in number and incomplete in details. Therefore, the New Madrid Earthquake is little known by the public, although scientific literature has given it a place among the great earthquakes of the world.

The exact cause of the New Madrid Earthquake is uncertain, but it is believed to be the result of fracturing and readjustment of the earth's crust deep beneath he surface. Because of the unconsolidated nature of the surface materials in the Mississippi alluvial plain, the effects of the shock waves were magnified.

Contemporary accounts are doubtless exaggerated, for calm observation and recording of an earthquake is impossible if the shocks are severe and dangerous. Fortunately, a number of scientists or men of education were in or near the region during the period of disturbance.

The first shock came a little after two o'clock on the morning of December 16. Inhabitants of the region were awakened by groaning, creaking, and cracking of the timbers of their houses and by the rattle of furniture and the crash of falling chimneys.

Inhabitants remained outside their cabins shivering in winter weather while repeated shocks kept them from returning to their houses during the night. In the early morning there was a second severe shock which caused the ground to rise and fall, tilted trees, and opened the soil in deep cracks as the surface bent. Landslides swept down the steeper bluffs, areas were uplifted, and even larger areas sank and became covered with water emerging from below through fissures or accumulating from the interruption of surface flow. Great waves swept up the Mississippi, overwhelming numerous boats and washing others high up on the shore. High banks caved in, sandbars and points of islands gave way, and whole islands disappeared.

During January 16 and 17 the shocks continued at short intervals, but with diminished intensity. They continued at longer intervals until January 23, 1812, when there was another shock similar in intensity and destructiveness to the first. For two weeks there was relative quiet, but on February 7 there were several alarming and destructive shocks, the last equaling or surpassing any previous disturbance, and for several days the earth was in nearly constant tremor.

The shock known as the New Madrid Earthquake was not the first felt in the region nor the last, but it was by all odds the most severe. There are certain accounts of earthquakes in the same region in 1776, 1791 or 1792, 1795, 1796, and 1804. Since seismographs have been installed at several locations, numerous small tremors originating in the Mississippi Valley are recorded each year. The most notable shocks in recent years occurred in 1967 and 1976.

PRINCIPAL INDIAN TRIBES OF MISSOURI

INDIAN TRAILS IN MISSOURI

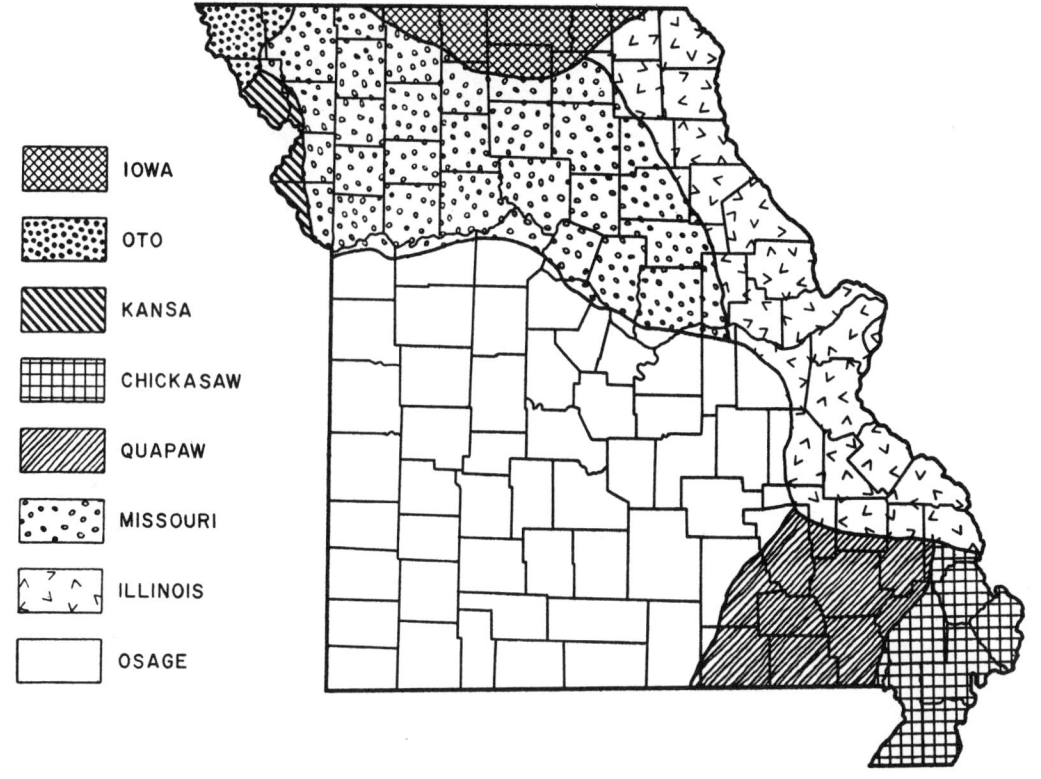

IOWA

OTO

KANSA

CHICKASAW

QUAPAW

MISSOURI

ILLINOIS

OSAGE

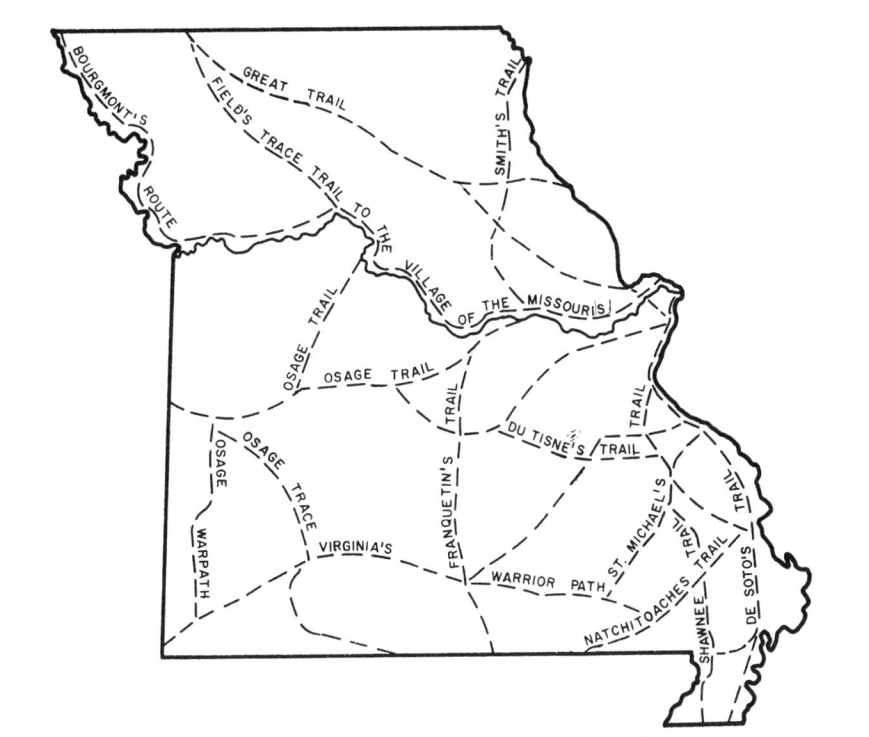

Information about the early inhabitants of Missouri, especially the geographic distribution of the various Indian peoples, is incomplete. This notable gap in our understanding of the early anthropogeography of Missouri stems from several causes. Among these causes are the long period of Indian occupance, from more than ten thousand years ago to the middle of the nineteenth century; the wandering and transient nature of many of the Indians, especially as eastern tribes were displaced westward in recent times; and the fragmentary nature of the archaeological research in both time and place.

Time periods extending back into prehistory have been described for Missouri. The periods, their approximate durations, and their names are as follows:

Historic Period	A.D. 1700–A.D. 1835	European Contact
Mississippian Period	A.D. 900–A.D. 1700	Village Farmer
Woodland Period	1000 B.C.–A.D. 900	Prairie-Forest Potter
Archaic Period	7000 B.C.–1000 B.C.	Forager
Dalton Period	8000 B.C.–7000 B.C.	Hunter-Forager
Paleo-Indian Period	12,000 B.C.–8000 B.C.	Early Hunter

The final period of Indian occupation of Missouri was marked by the appearance of groups which were present during the time of European contact. The larger native tribes include the Osages, Missouris, Otos, Iowas, Kansas, Illinois, Caddos, and Quapaws. The Missouris occupied most of nothern Missouri, while the Osages occupied most of the western and interior Ozarks. The Illinois, Caddos, Quapaws, Otos, and Iowas lived along the present borders of Missouri and foraged into the state on extended hunts. While it probably would be impossible to verify the exact location and chronology of each boundary, the map is of use to show the main Indian groups that occupied the state and the locations of their main areas of occupance.

The map of Indian trails is adapted from a map in Houck's *History of Missouri,* Vol. I. Since space does not permit a complete discussion of the various trails, readers are referred to the analysis in that source.

Certainly it would be a mistake to assume that the aborigines dwelling in Missouri did not have established and well-known traces or trails leading from their villages to hunting grounds or to the villages of friendly or unfriendly tribes. Nearly all of the early explorers of Missouri—De Soto, La Salle, Joutel, Nicolet, Bourgmont, Du Tisne—followed early Indian trail and traces. These ancient trails or warpaths often followed the routes made by buffalo, deer, and other wild animals along dividing ridges or down into stream valleys. They were unmarked and usually only wide enough to follow single file, but they were by all odds the easiest routes of travel. Sometimes the trails were so indistinct that they baffled the most intrepid *voyageur des bois.*

It is interesting to note the close association between these early Indian trails and the present system of federal highways. Many of our heavily traveled highways follow ancient trails that connected strategic trading locations which grew to be the largest cities in Missouri.

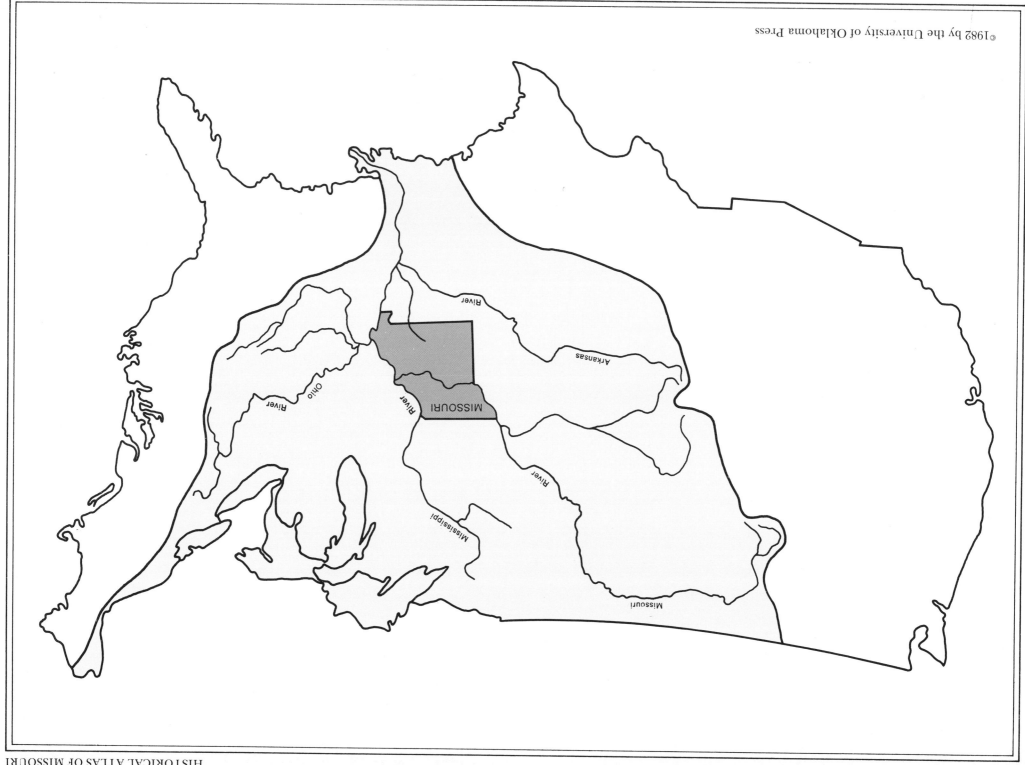

France, like England, started late in the exploration of the New World. The first permanent French settlement in North America at Quebec (1608) was contemporary with English beginnings in Virginia (1606–19). An energetic group of explorers sent out by Henry IV, Louis XIII, and Louis XIV elevated colonial France to a position of rivalry with the British. In the great armed conflicts over possession of America north of the Gulf of Mexico and the Río Grande, the basic struggle was between France and England. Between 1689 and 1763, colonial wars recessed only for recovery of strength and regrouping of allies.

England's claims, based chiefly upon exploration of the Atlantic coast and rising national confidence in sea power, were set down in charters to commercial companies. Vast stretches of unexplored territory all the way from the Atlantic to the Pacific were covered by these charters.

French claims were based upon the great explorations and settlements of such pioneers as Samuel de Champlain and Pierre du Gua, sieur de Monts, founders of Quebec, and their successors. Jean Nicolet explored in the St. Lawrence and Great Lakes basin.

Father Jacques Marquette, intent upon his work as a missionary to the Indians, and Louis Jolliet, primarily interested in expansion of French trade, reached the Mississippi River on June 17, 1673. Robert Cavelier, sieur de La Salle, explored the Mississippi from the Illinois to the Gulf of Mexico in 1682 and became the chief advocate of a vast inland empire for France in North America.

Between the activities of La Salle, who claimed for France all of the territory drained by the Mississippi, and the final colonial struggles of the Seven Years War, the region that is now Missouri was claimed by Spain, France, and England. As a result of the bitterly fought French and Indian War (Seven Years War), French control in North America was ended. Peace was restored in 1763 by the Treaty of Paris. France abandoned all claim to North America except two small islands in the St. Lawrence estuary; Great Britain took over Canada and the eastern half of the Mississippi Valley; Spain, in a separate treaty, received the area west of the great river and New Orleans. Half the continent had changed hands at the scratch of a pen.

Missouri

Mississippi River

River

MISSOURI

Ohio   River

Arkansas

River

Area Claimed by Spain Based on Explorations by De Soto, Coronado, and others

27. SPANISH CLAIMS IN NORTH AMERICA

In 1494, by the Treaty of Tordesillas, Spain and Portugal negotiated an agreement about their exploitation of the new discoveries of Columbus and other adventurers. In effect, Portugal continued to concentrate on Africa, leaving the New World, except for Brazil, to the Spanish. Thereafter, for more than two hundred years, Spain was engaged in the conquest of new lands and the consolidation of her claims. With the rise of English sea power and the growth of privateering during the second half of the sixteenth century, Spain's profits in the New World were threatened. French colonial enterprise early in the seventeenth century established another rival for Spain, particularly in the Mississippi Valley and on the northern coast of the Gulf of Mexico.

Spain's claims to huge tracts of land in North America were based largely on military expeditions. Francisco Vásquez de Coronado marched as far north as Kansas and west to the Grand Canyon, Hernando De Soto discovered the Mississippi River and marched northward as far as southeastern Missouri, and Juan de Oñate explored the American Southwest.

In much of North America the claims of Spain, France, and England overlapped. Spain at various times asserted a strong claim to the West Coast all the way north to Alaska, to the Mississippi Basin, and to the entire Gulf Coast. She held Florida against all rivals until 1819 (with the exception of only twenty years) and in the treaties of 1763 was recognized by France and England as the owner of Louisiana, west of the Mississippi.

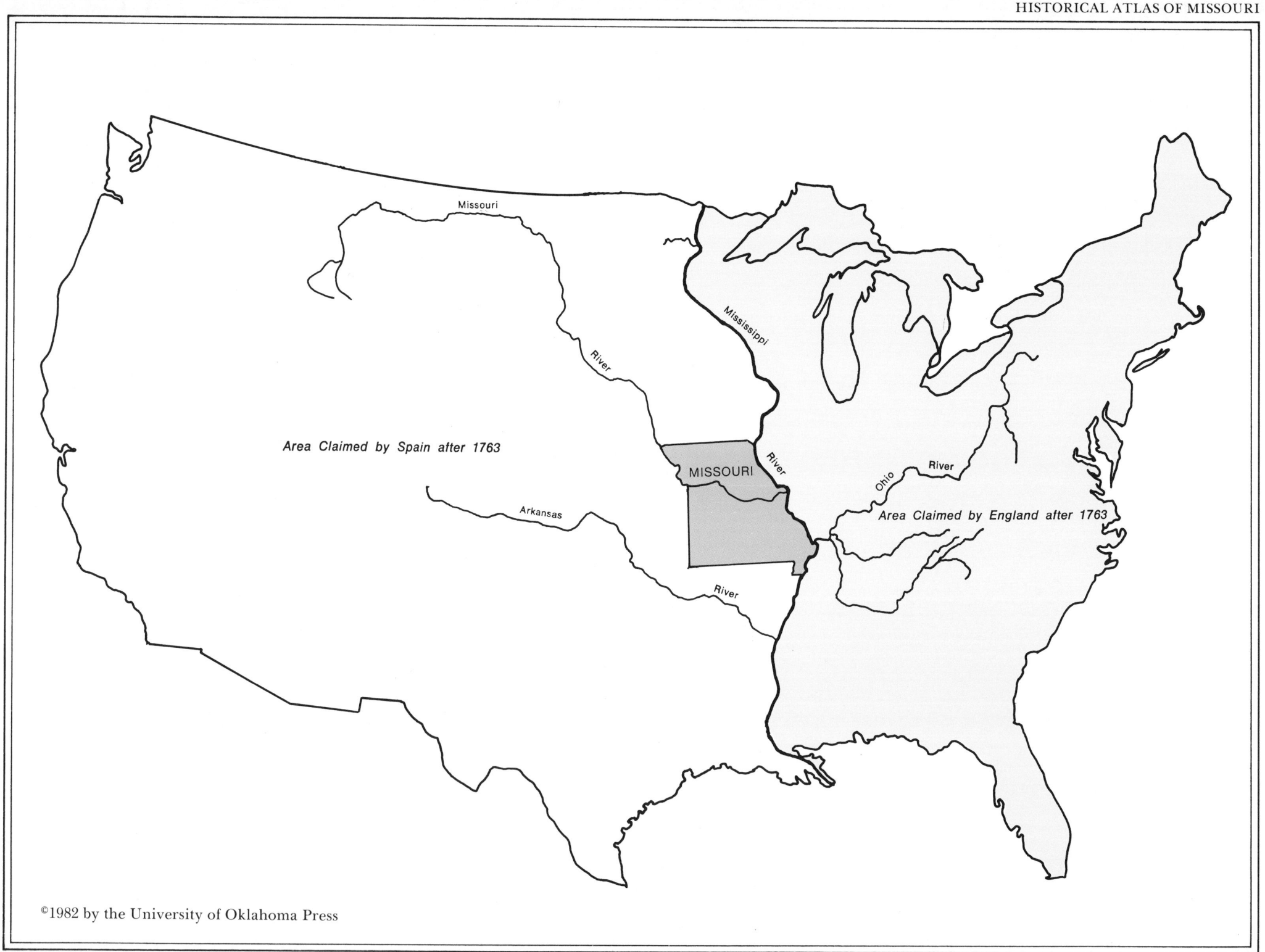

Area Claimed by Spain after 1763

MISSOURI

Area Claimed by England after 1763

Missouri

Mississippi

River

River

Ohio

River

Arkansas

River

28. SPANISH AND BRITISH CLAIMS AFTER 1763

Except for two small islands, St. Pierre and Miquelon, French claims to territory in North America were ended by the Seven Years War, 1756–63. Spain, an ally of France, had lost the Philippine Islands and Cuba to British naval forces, but these possessions were returned to Spanish control by the treaties of 1763. England obtained East and West Florida and all other territory east of the Mississippi, with the exception of the Isle of Orleans.

In the Treaty of Fontainebleau (1762), Louisiana west of the Mississippi and the Isle of Orleans, east of the river, had been ceded to Spain. The Iberville and Amité rivers, together with Lakes Maurepas, Pontchartrain, and Borgne, formed the northern boundary of the Isle of Orleans.

British possession of the Floridas continued until the end of the American Revolution in 1783. By the terms of the Treaty of Paris in that year Spain recovered Florida and retained possession of Louisiana west of Mississippi along with the Isle of Orleans east of it.

Spanish colonial policy was changed to a marked degree by the acquisition of undisputed title to Louisiana in 1762. Previously the Spanish frontier had been at the Red and the Sabine rivers, but the withdrawal of France from the area moved the frontier to the Mississippi and brought Spain into direct contact with England.

The Spanish fortified St. Louis, New Orleans, and other Spanish posts adjacent to the British territories. Upon the outbreak of the American Revolution, Spain disclosed sympathy for the colonists against England and eventually a willingness to join France in promoting American independence.

The establishment of the United States of America as an independent federal republic again changed the situation of Spain in Louisiana Territory. Soon American farmers, miners, and investors were seeking land grants, trading privileges, and even citizenship in Spanish Louisiana. The American insistence upon expansion was the most potent factor in forming a national policy of expansion that was to move American boundaries to the Pacific.

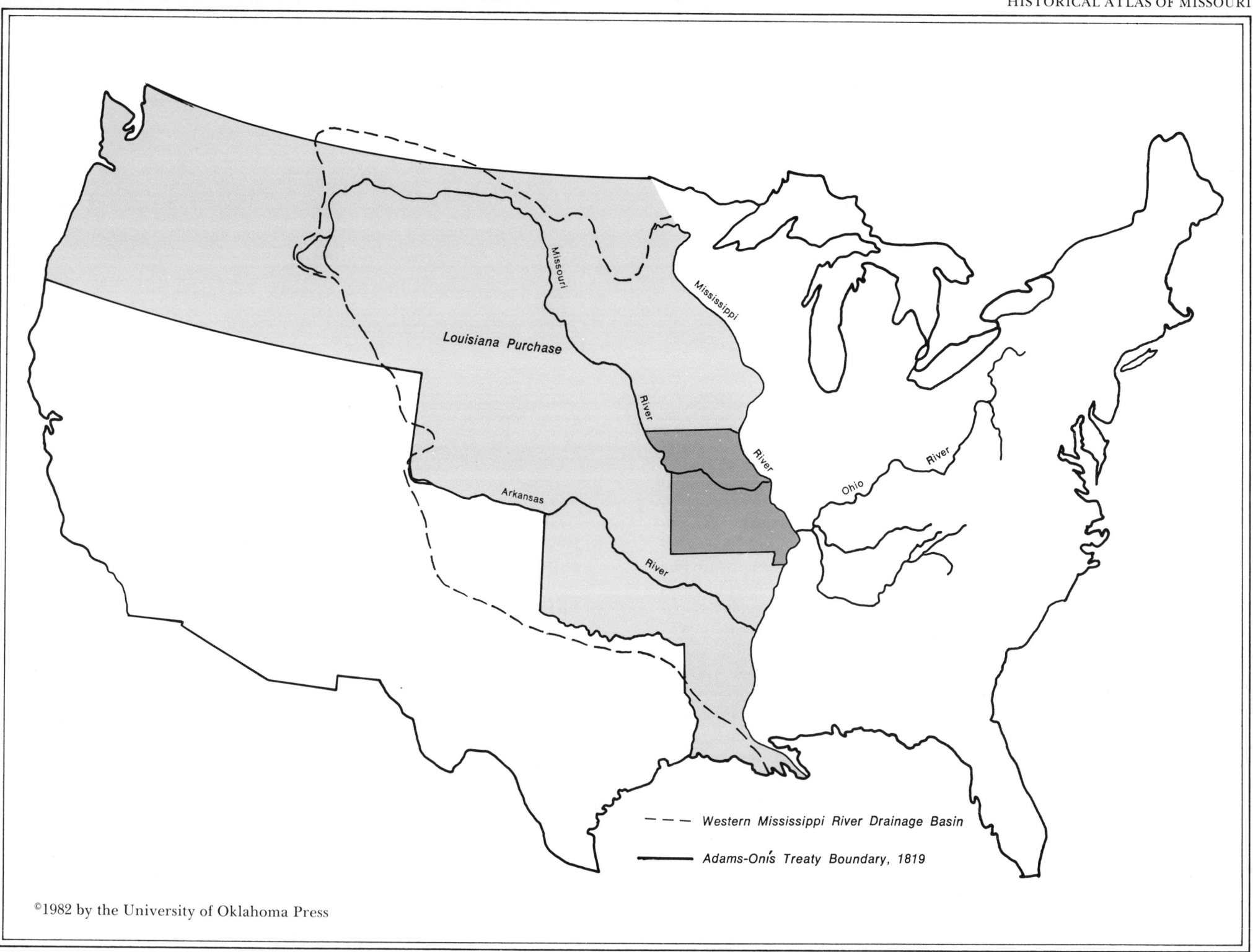

Louisiana Purchase

Missouri

Mississippi

River

Arkansas

River

Ohio River

River

- - - Western Mississippi River Drainage Basin

——— Adams-Onís Treaty Boundary, 1819

The expansion of American population into the West brought an acute need for control of the Mississippi River as a commercial outlet. That need was brought into focus by the treaty of San Ildefonso (1800), which included the transfer of Louisiana's title to France. In 1802, shortly after it was announced that Napoleon had secured Louisiana, the Spanish officers who were still in charge suddenly withdrew the right of deposit at New Orleans. There was much talk of war in the West, and the Spanish ambassador in Washington sent hurried notes of concern to his government.

President Jefferson, who admired French culture and had an affection for the French people, nevertheless adopted a new stern policy toward France. Referring to New Orleans and the stranglehold on Mississippi commerce, he wrote, "There is on the globe one single spot the possessor of which is our natural and habitual enemy." In order to abolish the constant threat to western commerce, Jefferson ordered the American ambassador to France, Robert R. Livingston, and James Monroe, a special diplomat, to attempt to buy New Orleans and West Florida, for which they might pay up to ten million dollars.

It was rare good fortune for the young American republic that President Jefferson's offer to purchase the Isle of Orleans was coincident with Napoleon's need for a substantial sum of money and his recognition of the difficulties inherent in a revival of the French empire in America. The failure of French operations in Haiti tipped the scale in favor of Napoleon's sudden shift in plans.

When Livingston suggested to Bishop Talleyrand that the United States would be willing to pay a good price for the left bank of the Mississippi below Lake Pontchartrain, the French diplomat suddenly offered to sell the entire province of Louisiana. After some bargaining—marked on both sides by nervous haste to close the deal—Livingston and Talleyrand agreed upon terms. The United States Senate ratified the treaty, Congress voted the necessary sum—a total of fifteen million dollars, including claims against France—and November 3, 1803, was set as the date for transfer of Louisiana to the United States.

The purchase of this great area west of the Mississippi was perhaps the most notable achievement of a great administration. At a single stroke President Jefferson acquired for the United States control of the Mississippi River as a commercial artery, got rid of Napoleon Bonaparte as a neighbor, and practically doubled the nation's area.

By the terms of the treaty, Louisiana was to include the same land as that acquired by France in 1880—that is, the "same extent" that it had "in the hands of Spain." The boundaries with Spanish territory to the southwest remained indefinite until John Quincy Adams and Luis Onís agreed upon the terms of the Florida Purchase Treaty in 1819.

The right bank of the Sabine, the right bank of the Red, the right bank of the Arkansas, the 100th meridian, and the 42d parallel were the principal segments of the Spanish boundary. A year earlier, in 1818, a convention with the British had resulted in agreement upon the 49th parallel as the northern boundary of Louisiana from the Lake of the Woods to the Continental Divide in the Great Stony (Rocky) Mountains.

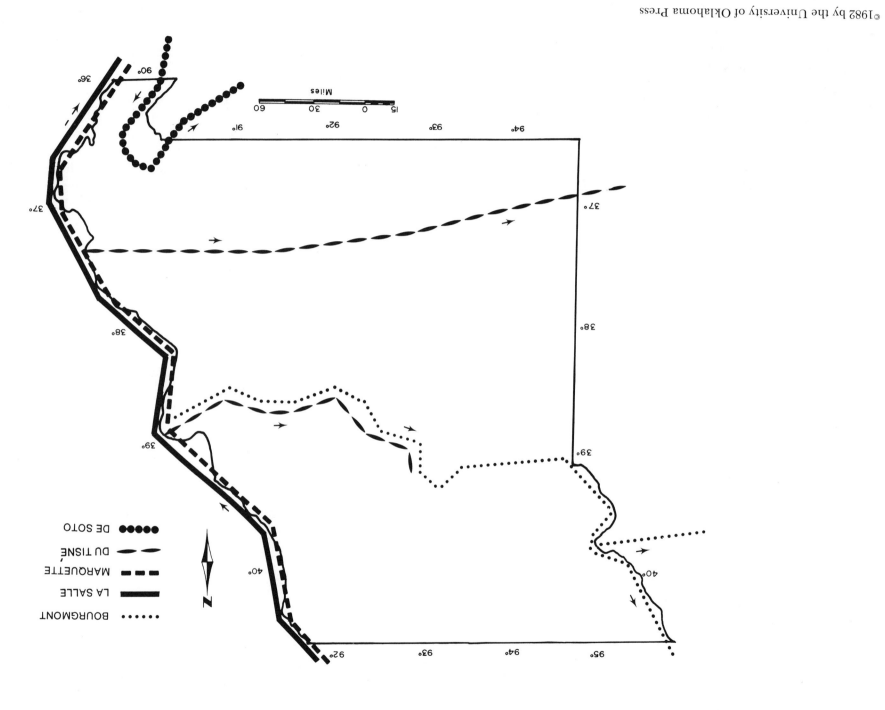

Miles

15   0   30   60

36°
90°
91°
92°
93°
94°
37°
38°
39°
40°
95°
94°
93°
92°

N

BOURGMONT
LA SALLE
MARQUETTE
DU TISNE
DE SOTO

30. SPANISH AND FRENCH EXPLORATIONS

There will always be arguments on the precise identity of the first white men in the territory now known as Missouri. Bolton *(Spanish Explorations in the Southwest, 1542-1706)*, working largely from original data, places De Soto in Dunklin County in 1541. If De Soto did enter Missouri, his stay was certainly brief, and, in all probability, he merely passed through on his way farther west.

Most historians credit the French with the discovery of Missouri. Possibly Radisson and Groseilliers, who in the 1650s discovered a stream they described as flowing toward Mexico, were the first. However, Father Jacques Marquette and Louis Jolliet made the first voyage on the Mississippi River of which there is now a detailed account. They left the mission of St. Ignace on the Straits of Mackinac on May 17, 1673, and reached the mouth of the Arkansas River about the middle of July. The voyage of Marquette and Jolliet did not include an ascension of the Missouri River, although they noted its presence and possible significance as a route to the Pacific Ocean. In 1682, La Salle, also coming from the north, descended all the way to the Gulf of Mexico and in the same year took possession of the Mississippi Valley for France.

Charles Claude Du Tisné was the first to ascend the Missouri River. In 1719 Du Tisné went up the Missouri River to the village of the Little Osage Indians near the mouth of the Grand River. Returning from the village of the Little Osages to Kaskaskia, a settlement founded by the French in 1700 on the east side of the Mississippi River, Du Tisné in the summer and fall of 1719 made a journey overland to the Great Osage and Pawnee Indians. The terminus of his journey was a village of the Pawnees in what is now northeastern Oklahoma.

Étienne Venyard, sieur de Bourgmont, ascended the Missouri River on a number of occasions after 1714 and for a period of five years lived among the Indians in the vicinity of Carroll County. Later, in 1724, he built Fort Orléans under orders from Paris. In the same year Bourgmont set out from Fort Orléans on a trading and exploring expedition terminating in western Kansas. Thus was concluded the initial period of French exploration, to be followed soon after by the establishment of permanent settlements beginning with Ste. Genevieve, probably around 1730.

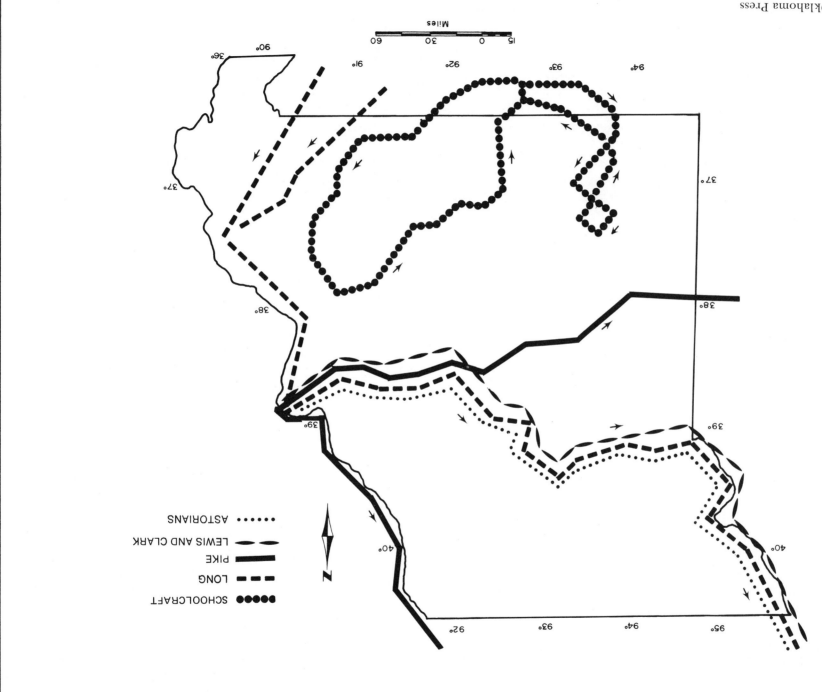

SCHOOLCRAFT ●●●●●
LONG ▬ ▬ ▬
PIKE ▬▬▬▬
LEWIS AND CLARK ▬ ◠ ▬
ASTORIANS • • • • •

Miles
60 30 0 15 60

31. AMERICAN EXPLORATION

St. Louis, at the confluence of the Mississippi and Missouri rivers, was a logical jumping-off point for exploring the western United States, and many of the early expeditions did radiate out from this point. Shortly after Captain Amos Stoddard took possession for the United States of the entire area included in the Louisiana Purchase, the American exploration of the western United States was begun. On May 14, 1804, Captain Meriwether Lewis and Lieutenant William Clark set out from Camp River Dubois (in Illinois near the mouth of the Missouri River) on their famous journey to the Pacific Northwest. Lewis and Clark ascended the Missouri River by boat, recording the character of the lands through which they passed.

In an effort to fix the United States–Canadian boundary, General James Wilkinson, from his headquarters in St. Louis, sent Lieutenant Zebulon Pike in 1805 to explore the headwaters of the Mississippi River. Upon his return, Pike was sent on a longer and more difficult trip, this time to the west. Pike's second venture culminated in the discovery of the mountain peak in Colorado now bearing his name. One of Pike's assignments on his second trip was to visit the Osage Indians. Pike followed a course across Missouri very similar to the one followed by Du Tisné almost a century earlier.

The Astorians, men who went overland to the Northwest Coast and took part in the founding of Astoria and the establishment of the fur trade of John Jacob Astor, set out between 1811 and 1813 from St. Louis. One reason the Missouri River was so widely used was that it connected with Nebraska's Platte Valley— by all odds the natural route to the West. Major Stephen Long followed this very same route when he left in 1819 from St. Louis

to explore the land between the Mississippi River and the Rocky Mountains under orders of Secretary of War James C. Calhoun. Long returned in 1820 by way of the Arkansas River to Fort Smith. Thence the expedition crossed Arkansas and southeastern Missouri, finally arriving at Cape Girardeau. Long had made a previous trip into southeastern Missouri in 1817, when he ascended the Arkansas River to the mouth of the Canadian River.

While trappers, traders, and a few settlers penetrated the interior districts far from navigable streams, they did not record the characteristics of the land. One exception to this rule, Henry Rowe Schoolcraft, distinguished explorer, naturalist, and writer, toured the interior of the Ozarks in 1818 and 1819. Beginning at the mining town of Potosi, Schoolcraft traveled southwest through the rugged interior Ozarks to a point on White River in northern Arkansas. Traveling upstream, he crossed the James River and replenished his supply of ammunition at an Indian lead mine near the present site of Springfield. After a sortie into lush Kickapoo Prairie, he returned to White River, traveled downstream in Arkansas before turning northeast to follow the margin of the Ozark escarpment, and then headed through the St. Francis Mountains to Potosi.

Although the Missouri and Mississippi rivers were not the only routes of importance during this period, they did dominate movement through and around Missouri. Later, during the height of the fur trade, these two rivers became even more important, and although overland routes did exist, they offered little competition to the "natural arteries."

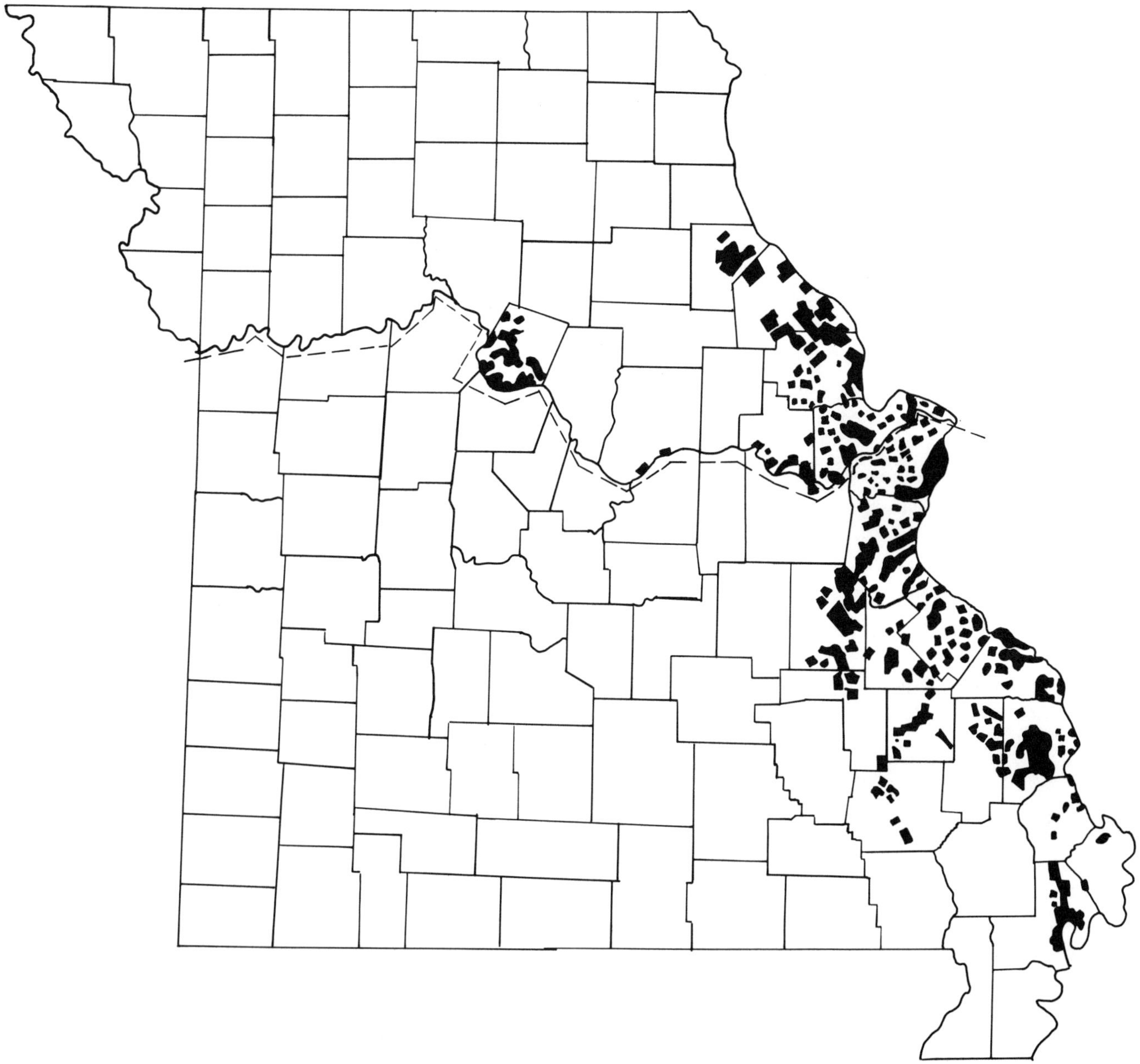

32. SPANISH LAND GRANTS

During the period of Spanish government of the territory west of the Mississippi, uncultivated wild land had no value. Wild land was granted free to all actual settlers and farmers, and it was not possible for land speculators to buy land from the government. To encourage settlement of the lands west of the Mississippi River, the Spanish government sometimes granted large tracts of land to influential people. The Chouteaus, the Valles, Clamorgan, the Cerres, Lorimier, the Prattes, Mackay, Austin, and other large land claimants were regarded by the early American settlers to be something like Spanish grandees. They were good-naturedly called "hildalgos" by the people living on the Ohio River.

The Louisiana Purchase and the change in government as if by magic changed the esteem and value in which land was held. It is reported that just before the transfer of the country, on one flimsy pretense or another, a coterie of French speculators and some Americans who had settled in Upper Louisiana had secured great land concessions. It was openly charged that many of the concessions were antedated, and the truth of that claim was admitted but excused by the easy statement that grants had been promised at the date inserted in the concessions.

Under the Act of 1805, claimants were required to deliver to the recorder of land titles notice in writing, stating the nature and extent of their claims, together with a plat of the tract of land. Additional acts passed by Congress made more liberal provisions for the benefit of claimants. In the period 1814–16 alone, 2,555 claims were presented, and all but 801 were confirmed. William Russell alone filed 309 claims, but of these only 23 were confirmed. In 1836 all claims favorably recommended by the claims board were confirmed by Congress. These claims throughout the whole of Louisiana Territory were near the Mississippi River and its major tributaries. Because of the system of geometric survey without regard to cardinal compass directions, the Spanish grants are easily recognized on topographic and land survey maps.

Among the many grants made by the United State government during the period of active settlement were special grants to replace destroyed property. The New Madrid Land Claims fall into this category. People received certificates to recompense them for lands affected in the New Madrid Earthquake of 1811–12. By act of Congress in 1815 the recorder of land titles in Missouri was authorized to receive evidence of actual damage done by the earthquake and, on being satisfied that material injury had been done to the soil, to issue a certificate authorizing the claimant to locate the like quantity of land on any public realty in the Territory of Missouri. Because the certificates were circulated much like currency and resulted in fraudulent claims, six acts of Congress were required to settle questions which arose from the benevolent Act of 1815.

Altogether, 516 New Madrid claims eventually were made. Definitely known among these claims are those located north of the dashed line on the map in Howard, Boone, Marion, Ralls, and St. Charles counties. Some of the land was measured by the acre and some by the old French measurement of the arpent— 0.85 acre. Some plots were surveyed in conformity with sectional lines, others not. Because of poor and unreported surveys, there were irregular fractions of sections and numerous overlapping claims.

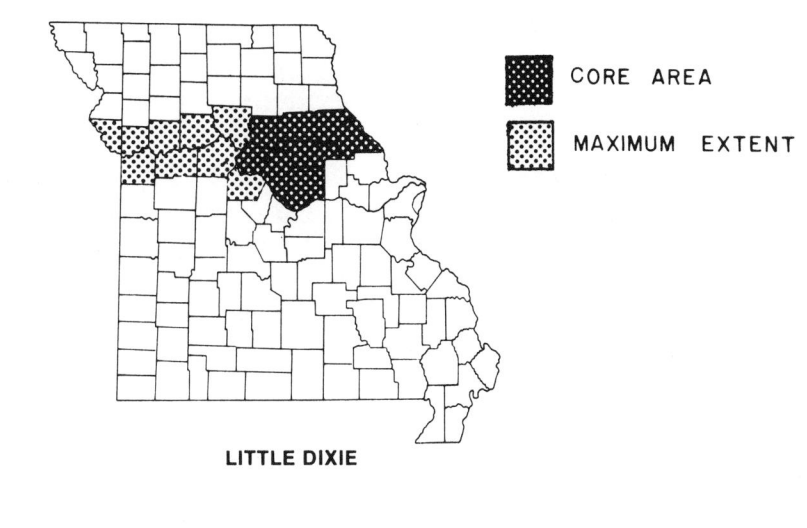

LITTLE DIXIE

CORE AREA

MAXIMUM EXTENT

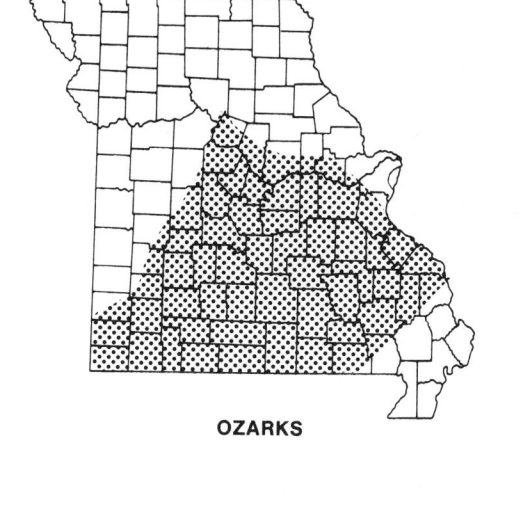

OZARKS

BOONSLICK

IRISH WILDERNESS

Little Dixie. The name "little Dixie" is applied, usually in connection with Missouri politics, to a distinctive section of the state. Apparently the term originated shortly after the Civil War to denote the midsection of Missouri, where Southern sympathies, slavery, and Democratic politics had been prevalent. The name has been popularized through politics. Robert M. Crisler, in an attempt to delimit Little Dixie, found eight counties in east central Missouri that represent the "core" of the region. He also identified nine additional counties that had been at various times included in the "Dixie Belt."

The Ozarks. The Ozarks comprise a historic region of Missouri based on landform and culture. Because of its poverty of resources, the region did not attract heavy agricultural settlement. The lack of roads and railroads was responsible for infrequent contact with areas beyond its borders. As a result, the Ozarks came to be known as an area of poverty, backwardness, and conservatism.

Today, much of the traditional concept of the Ozarks is inaccurate, although not wholly so. Many Ozarkers take pride in their cultural heritage, and with the growing tourist business, Ozark "culture" has attracted numerous visitors to the southern section of the state.

Boonslick Country. After the lower Missouri River valley in St. Charles County and southern Warren County had been settled, the valley in the central part of the state began to attract population. Daniel Boone came here as early as 1807 to make salt. The Boonslick country contained numerous salt springs which, with good water, soil, and timber, attracted settlement. The two leading towns at the outset were Boonville, the major river port, and Franklin, one of the three land offices in the state.

The Irish Wilderness. This name is applied to a sparsely populated area in the eastern Ozarks. The boundaries of the area are rather indefinite, but the name is usually applied to the area between the Eleven Point River and the Current River and between Highway 60 on the north and Highway 14 on the south.

Legend has it that a group of Irish immigrants settled in the area in the early 1800s but were massacred by Indians, possibly with Spanish assistance. However, this colorful legend is not based on fact. Evidence suggests that the name "Irish Wilderness" stems from the fact that about forty Irish families settled in the rugged hill country in the 1850s. They had left Ireland because of the potato famine of the 1840s and found work building railroads in the Midwest. Apparently they became nearly destitute in St. Louis by the mid-1850s. The Catholic Church assisted them by purchasing land on their behalf. Plagued by poor agricultural land and by the troubled times during the Civil War, the settlement virtually ceased to exist a few years after the war ended.

The Missouri Rhineland. The first German settlements in Missouri were along the Mississippi border in Bollinger and Cape Girardeau counties. The next period of German immigration commenced about 1830 and continued until after 1850. This "heterogeneous group of Westphalian hired hands and mottled aristocracy" formed the core of what was to become a heavy concentration of German population. An important factor in directing many of these Germans to Missouri was the circulation in Germany of a book entitled *Reise nach den westlichen Staaten* by Gottfried Duden.

When the Germans arrived, they found the better river bottomlands already occupied by earlier Americans. Thus, while Little Dixie developed in the Missouri Valley and counties to the north, the bluffs and uplands to the south of the river were

MORMON COUNTRY

BOOTHEEL AND SOUTHEAST LOWLANDS

MISSOURI RHINELAND

settled by Germans. By 1860 a large German population had located in St. Louis, Jefferson City, and Boonville. German was taught in the schools of Herman, Washington, and Jefferson City. Also by that time Germans had displaced many of the American settlers in the Missouri River bottoms.

The census of 1870 showed that people of German birth or parentage comprised more than 20 per cent of Gasconade, Warren, and St. Charles counties and more than 15 per cent of Osage, Franklin, and St. Louis counties. These counties, along with the city of St. Louis, which was more than 35 per cent German, made up the Missouri Rhineland. German-born made up more than 10 per cent of the population of Cole, Jefferson, Ste. Genevieve, Perry, and Cape Girardeau counties, but German customs and traditions were stronger and have lasted longer in the counties immediately west of St. Louis.

The Bootheel and Southeast Lowlands. The Bootheel and the larger geographic region encompassing all of the Southeast Lowlands make up a separate historic region largely on the basis of the distinctive agricultural economy practiced there. Its development is both old and of recent times. The area was settled sparsely by planters at an early date, but the New Madrid Earthquake of 1811–12 caused great destruction and considerable emigration.

The more recent settlement has been in connection with drainage projects which opened former swampland to agriculture. Cotton became the chief crop, and a sizable black population lives in the region, most of it connected with cotton culture in some way. More recently soybeans have become important. Today, even though these counties are losing population because of farm mechanization, the acreage under cultivation continues to expand as more land is provided with adequate drainage.

Mormon Country. A people set apart not by foreign cultural traits but by their religion are the Mormons. The Church of Jesus Christ of Latter-Day Saints was founded by Joseph Smith in the religious "shatterbelt" of western New York State about 1830. The group, because of its beliefs and reputed clannishness, was persecuted from the outset. Before finally locating at Salt Lake City and other places in the intermontane plateaus, it settled in Missouri. The first settlement was at Independence, where a form of communal agriculture was practiced (1831). After persecution in Jackson County, the Mormons moved to Clay County and adjacent counties north of the river. Later (1836) they moved to Far West, northwest of Kingston in Ray County. In 1836 the Mormons petitioned to create Caldwell County from a portion of Ray County and were successful. However, by 1838 the troubles had become so great that the main group moved to Illinois.

Today there are relatively few Latter-Day Saints in the old historic Mormon Country. However, there are substantial numbers of the Reorganized Church of Jesus Christ of Latter Day Saints, a separate and distinct religious body.

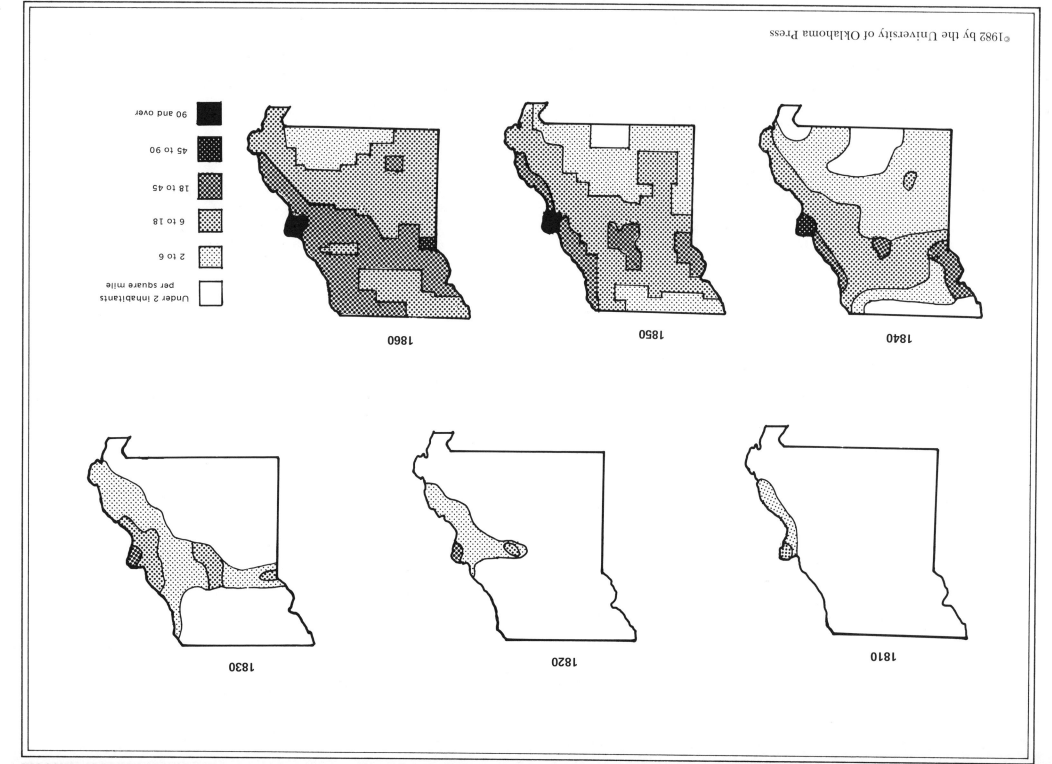

1860

1850

1840

1830

1820

1810

90 and over

45 to 90

18 to 45

6 to 18

2 to 6

Under 2 inhabitants
per square mile

Immigration to Missouri in the years before the Civil War was in large part by way of the Mississippi and Missouri rivers. The most favorable agricultural lands were found in the river bottoms or on nearby uplands where cheaper water transportation permitted practice of commercial agriculture. Also, the eastern Ozark Mineral Area was only fifty miles inland from the Mississippi River.

By 1810 the Mississippi River border inland for ten miles or so was settled with an average density of more than two people per square mile. Settlement progressed up the Missouri River, and by 1820 the Boonslick County in central Missouri rivaled St. Louis as a growth center. The progression of settlement penetrated inland from the Missouri and Mississippi rivers so that by 1850 the state was fairly well settled except for a small area on the extreme southern border. Growth centers and areas of heavy population densities had already become established around St. Louis, Boonslick, Kansas City, St. Joseph, Hannibal, and Springfield. By 1860 the corridor from St. Louis to Kansas City, as well as most of the Mississippi River border, had more than eighteen people per square mile.

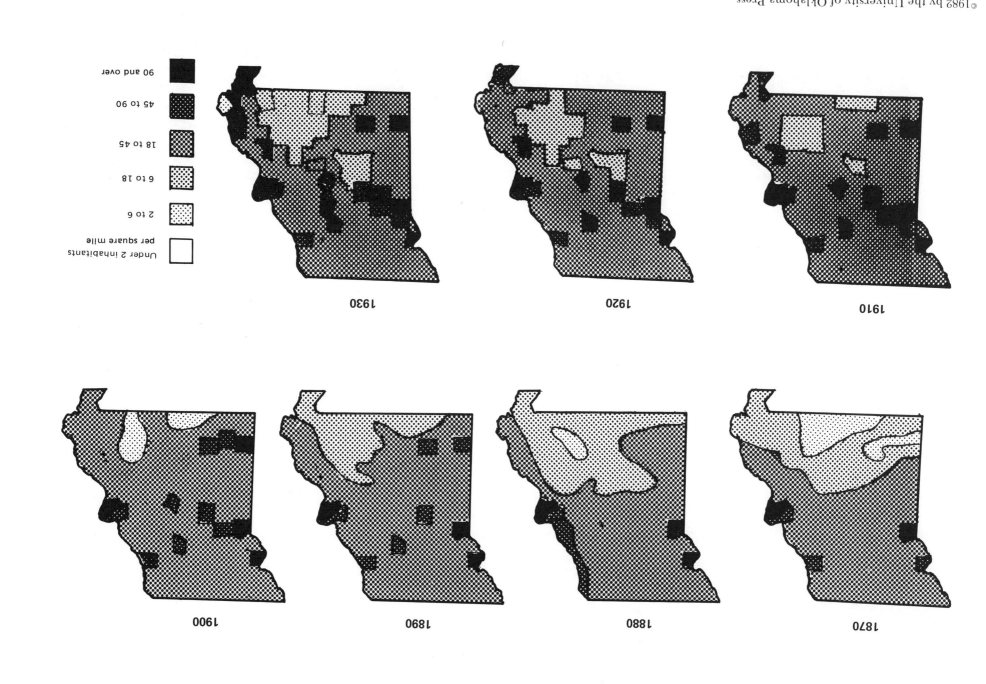

90 and over

45 to 90

18 to 45

6 to 18

2 to 6

Under 2 inhabitants
per square mile

1930

1920

1910

1900

1890

1880

1870

The rapid construction of railroads, particularly in northern Missouri, increased the value of land for agricultural use and led to rapid growth in farm population and the establishment of numerous towns. Through the closing decades of the nineteenth century the rural population density of Missouri continued to increase. By 1890, stimulated by railroad building, lumbering, and mining, the population of the Missouri Ozarks had reached six people per square mile, and that of northern and western Missouri was more than eighteen people per square mile. These densities generally exceed the present rural population densities in both sections of the state.

The first three decades of the twentieth century exhibited the effects of what was to be a long-term trend: rural to urban migration. St. Louis and Kansas City were, by 1930, major metropolitan centers, and St. Joseph, Springfield, and Joplin were prosperous cities in heavily settled counties. Rural densities had begun to decline.

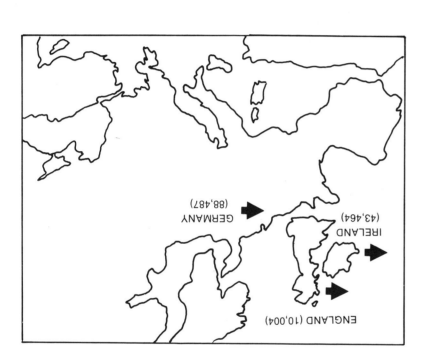

OTHER FOREIGN - BORN (18,586)

GERMANY (88,487)

IRELAND (43,464)

ENGLAND (10,004)

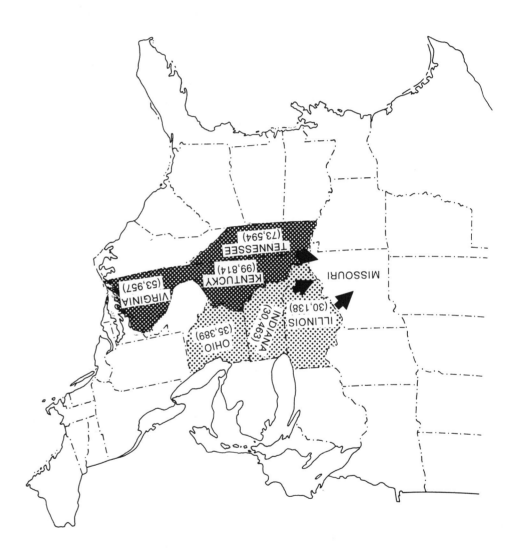

VIRGINIA (53,957)

TENNESSEE (73,594)

KENTUCKY (99,814)

OHIO (35,389)

INDIANA (30,463)

ILLINOIS (30,138)

MISSOURI

36. ORIGIN OF MISSOURI'S POPULATION TO 1860

The French were the first to explore and settle Missouri, and for more than a century they were masters of the region. The first settlement in Missouri may have been St. Louis, but the first settlement along the Mississippi River of which there is certain knowledge was Kaskaskia on the Illinois side across from Ste. Genevieve. The first French were agriculturalists and traders, but the lead deposits of the eastern Ozarks soon attracted American as well as French settlement.

The paths of migration to Missouri followed the established river routes and overland trails. The thrust of pioneer settlement in the United States was essentially east to west, so the majority of settlers in Missouri came from states in the same latitude. The Ohio-Mississippi-Missouri river system was the great migration route to Missouri, and the immigrants were mainly from the Upper South and the Lower Middle West. Many were of Scotch-Irish descent. The rank of states according to the origins of immigrants to Missouri in 1860 was Kentucky (99,814), Tennessee (73,954), Virginia (53,957), Ohio (35,389), Indiana (30,463), and Illinois (30,138). The mountaineer from Middle or East Tennessee was especially attracted to the Ozarks, where land was not only cheaper, but also similar to that in the eastern uplands.

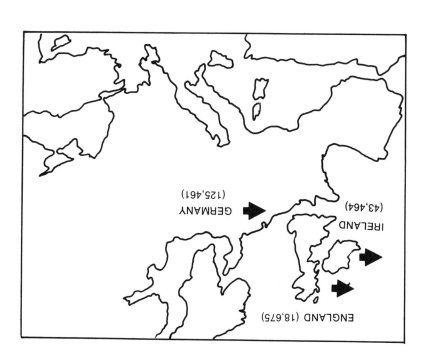

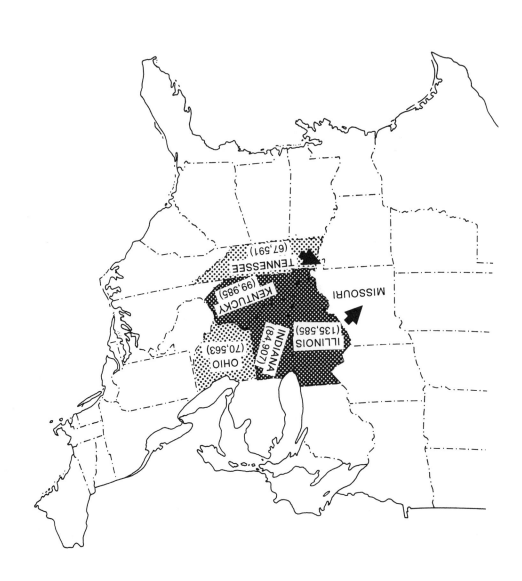

OTHER FOREIGN - BORN (49,767)

GERMANY (125,461)

IRELAND (43,464)

ENGLAND (18,675)

OHIO (70,563)

INDIANA (84,907)

ILLINOIS (135,585)

KENTUCKY (99,985)

TENNESSEE (67,591)

MISSOURI

37. ORIGIN OF MISSOURI'S POPULATION, 1860–90

Following the Civil War and the resumption of peaceful conditions, there began a period of railroad construction which provided much improved connections with the remainder of the Middle West. By 1890 the Lower Middle West had replaced the Upper South as Missouri's leading source of immigrants. Illinois (135,585) was the leading state, followed by Kentucky (99,985), Ohio (84,907), Indiana (70,563), and Tennessee (67,591).

Germans made up the major group whose homeland was outside the British Isles. The Polish and Bohemian settlements of Franklin and Gasconade counties and the Italian communities at Tontitown and Rosati were small by comparison. The larger number of the German farmers located in the Missouri River and Mississippi River border regions, often in compact settlements. Such large numbers of Germans settled in St. Louis that by the turn of the century South St. Louis had become widely known as a German community.

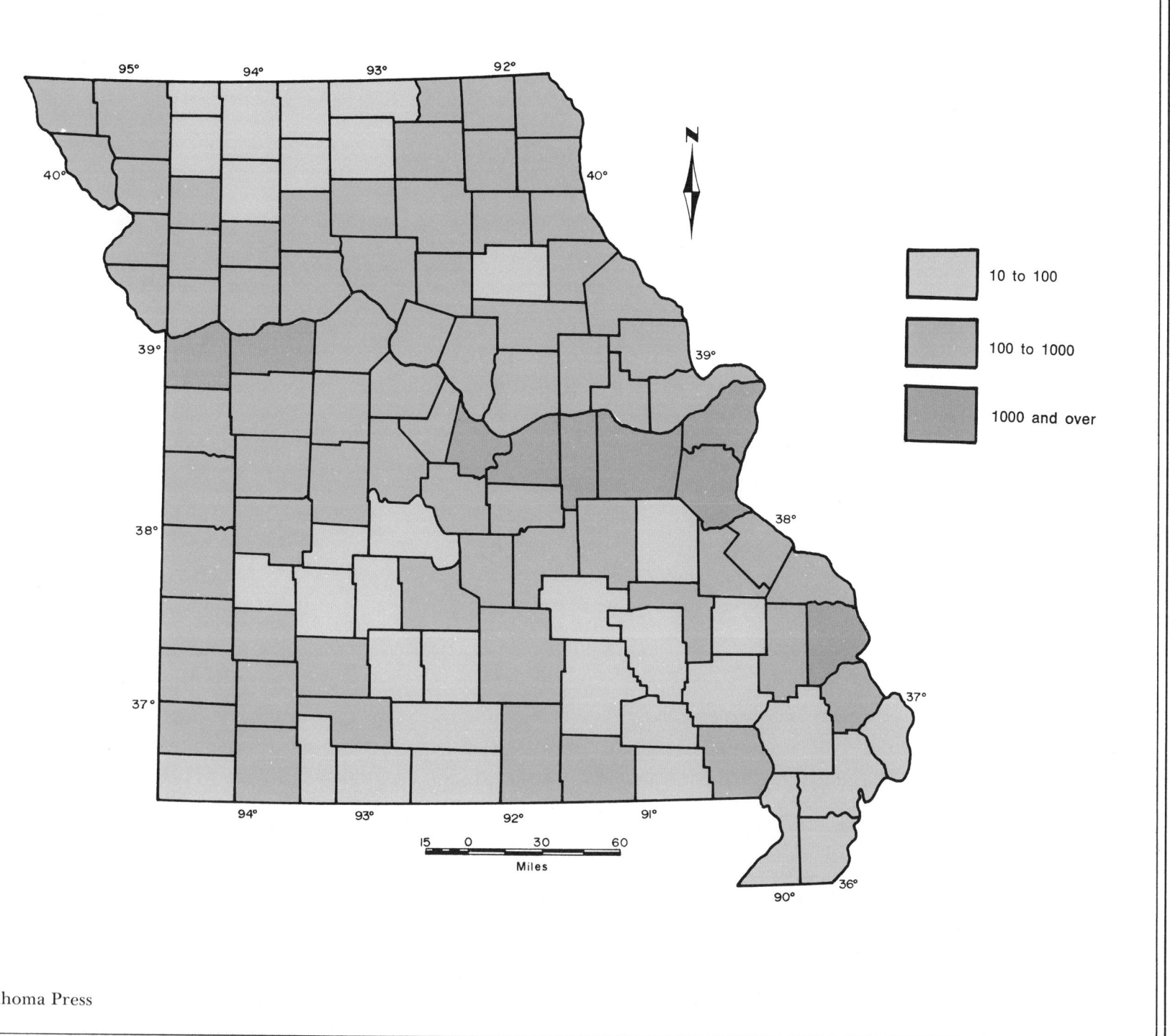

10 to 100

100 to 1000

1000 and over

Most of the stock that settled Missouri came from the British Isles, but Germans were the major immigrant group from the mainland of Europe. The larger number of the German farmers located in the Missouri River and Mississippi River border regions in compact settlements. Also, as part of the general trend of rural-to-urban migration in the United States, many Germans moved from farms in the river border counties and took up residence in St. Louis. By 1900 South St. Louis had become known widely as a German community. Even today many neighborhoods in the city remain strongly German, and the 1976 St. Louis telephone directory lists no fewer than thirty-three pages of names beginning with *Sch.*

The earliest settlement of Germans was that of the so-called Whitewater Dutch, who settled in Bollinger County along the Whitewater River. These colonists did not immigrate directly from Germany, and not being in contact with other German groups, they gradually dropped the use of the German language.

Between 1830 and 1850 large numbers of Germans immigrated to the northern and eastern Ozarks. They were primarily of four types: (1) educated men of the Jungdeutchland movement who had been suppressed by a reactionary government, (2) romanticists who wished to escape a convention-ridden society, (3) religious separatists who sought to escape the repression of the established church, and (4) common men who sought to improve their economic situation.

A book written by Gottfried Duden, *Reise nach den westlichen Staaten,* was circulated widely in Germany, and because of its glowing description of the region along the Missouri River, large numbers of Germans were influenced to immigrate to the lower Missouri Valley. Dutzow was founded in 1834 in Warren County by the Emigration Society of Gressen, Washington was settled by an emigration society from Berlin, and in 1838 the Hermann settlement was established by an emigration society based in Philadelphia. Catholic Germans settled at Westphalia in Osage County and at Taos, Richfountain, Loose Creek, Lustown, and Frankenstein in Cole County. Other Catholic Germans settled at New Offenburg and Zell in Ste. Genevieve County.

The geographic reasons for German settlement, besides Missouri's frontier location, were the accessibility of the region from Europe by way of New Orleans and the Mississippi River, the low cost of land, and the similarity of soil, climate, and vegetation to conditions in their homeland. The Germans were successful farmers, and gradually the German settlements expanded. They were clannish and retained the use of their mother tongue, and as their numbers increased, many of their non-German neighbors, it is reported, sold out because they did not want to live among them.

By 1859 the German settlements of Washington and Hermann had become important towns; Jefferson City was one-half German, and Boonville one-fourth. The census of 1870 showed that people of German birth or parentage composed more than 20 per cent of Osage, Franklin, and St. Louis counties. German-born made up 10 per cent of the populations of Cole, Jefferson, Ste. Genevieve, Perry, and Cape Girardeau counties.

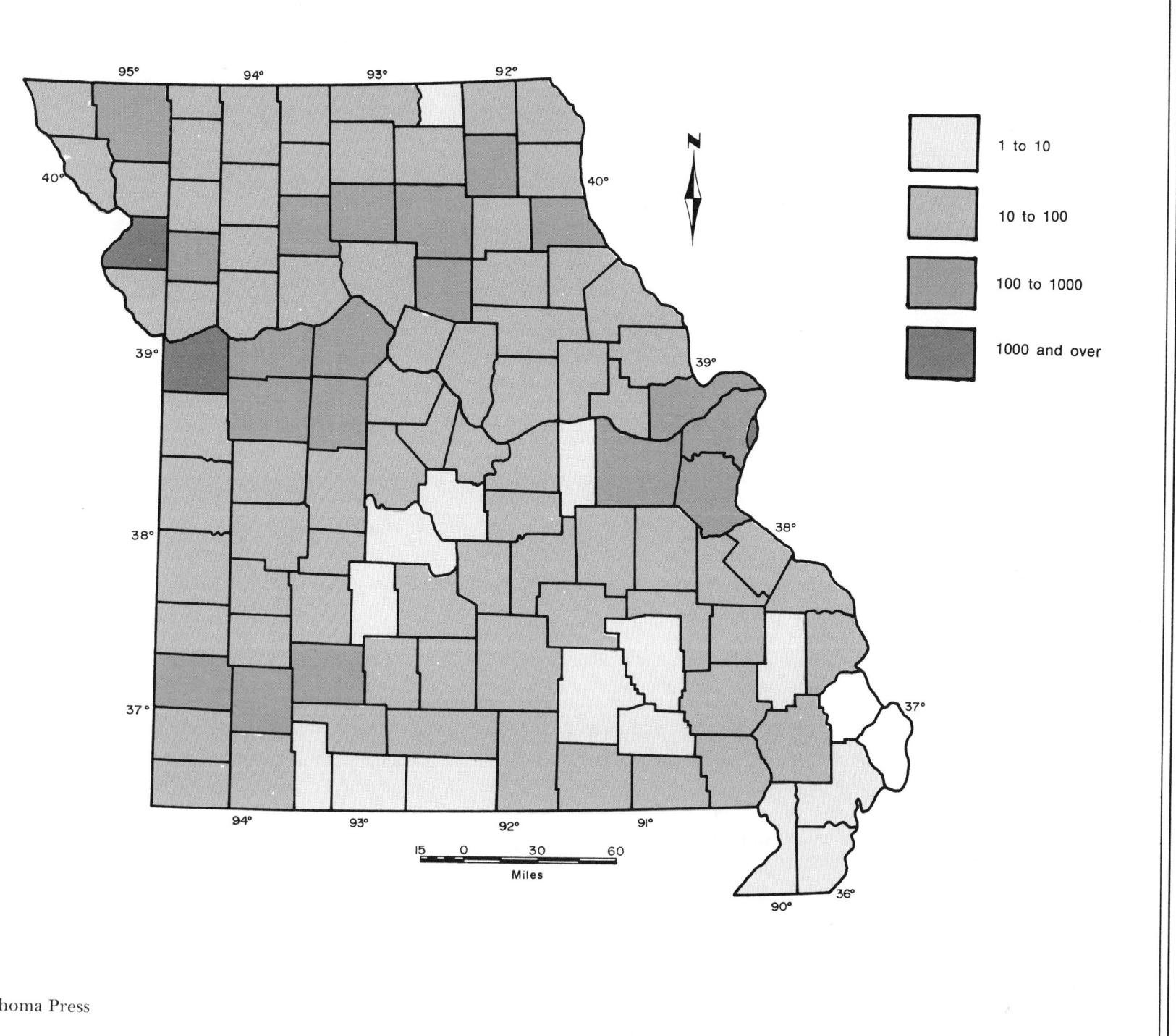

1 to 10

10 to 100

100 to 1000

1000 and over

The second-ranking foreign immigrant group was the Irish. The first settlers of Missouri were strongly Scotch-Irish in descent, and before the beginning of immigration of the Catholic Irish in the 1840s they were known as "the Irish." The old Irish stock were Protestants from Ulster (northern Ireland). Then when Catholic Irish began to immigrate in large numbers in the 1840s as a result of the great potato famine, they were called "the Irish" and the old-stock Protestant Irish were called "the Scotch-Irish."

The map of foreign-born Irish in 1900 does not distinguish between Scotch-Irish (Protestant Irish) and Catholic Irish, although it is reasonable to assume that the largest proportion were from southern Ireland and were Catholics. The period from 1860 to 1910 brought a constant flow of foreign immigrants to the state, and many of them were Catholic Irish. Most of the Irish were poor and of the laboring class. Factors important in attracting Irish immigrants included (1) the burgeoning industries in St. Louis and Kansas City, (2) the numerous mining districts, (3) the rapid expansion of railroad construction, and (4) the fact that the Catholic Church was well established in Missouri's metropolitan centers where it could serve the new immigrants. As early as 1818 an immigrant aid society was established in St. Louis to assist Irish and German settlers.

Unlike the Germans, the Irish tended not to retain their national identity, although for a time they did settle heavily in certain neighborhoods in St. Louis and Kansas City. They were preponderantly urban dwellers who found employment in the packing houses, steel mills, flour mills and grain elevators and in other unskilled jobs.

1 ATCHISON
2 SCHUYLER
3 SCOTLAND
4 WARREN
5 HICKORY
6 MISSISSIPPI
7 STONE
8 REYNOLDS

40. COUNTY AREA DISTRIBUTION PROPORTIONATE TO POPULATION, 1970

This map showing the area of political units proportionate to population was prepared in the Department of Rural Sociology in the University of Missouri-Columbia. It is useful for understanding population densities and distributions. Readers who are familiar with the shape and size of Missouri's counties can readily grasp the subtleties of population patterns in urban and rural areas by studying the map. Those wholly unfamiliar with Missouri's geography can easily grasp the fact that three political units—St. Louis City, St. Louis County, and Jackson County—contain more than half of Missouri's population. Sparsely settled agricultural counties in the northern part of the state and rural Ozark counties are very small by comparison.

Missouri has experienced a long period of rapid population growth. From 1810, when the population was 19,873, until 1890, when the population was 2,679,185, the increase in population averaged 94.5 per cent for each decade. In the period 1890 to 1970, when the population reached 4,687,759, the percentage of growth averaged 9.4 per cent for each decade. This steady increment of population is all the more striking when it is noted that Missouri is a population exporting state; that is, there are more people emigrating than immigrating.

Essentially there have been four significant regional population growth patterns in Missouri since 1890. The Dissected Till Plains and Osage Cuestas have topography, soil, climate, and other conditions conducive to profitable mechanization of farms. Thus, the surplus agricultural labor coupled with rapidly growing economic opportunities in cities have brought significant decreases in population. Many counties in northern Missouri have declined more than one-third in population. Because a larger proportion of the emigrants are young people, the average age of the population is higher in most counties in the western and northern sections of the state. Census estimates in the 1970s indicate that the decline of rural population has nearly ended and that there have been modest increases in population in northern and western Missouri counties.

The Ozark region was never settled very heavily. The Ozarks have many small farms on steep slopes, so as a whole the agriculture there has not been mechanized to the degree that it has in areas better endowed for farming. There the population of most counties has been static or has grown slightly. Because of the construction of large reservoirs, the development of second homes, the growth of the recreation industry, and the increase in manufacturing employment, some Ozark counties are now among the fastest growing in Missouri.

In the Southeast Lowlands there is a high percentage of cultivated land in cash crops, particularly cotton, soybeans, and corn. Until recently the farms remained small, mainly because cotton had not proved to be adapted to mechanical cultivation. Therefore, because of the high labor requirements for cotton culture, the region retained its population. But since 1950 farm mechanization has made great strides, and surplus labor leaving the farms has caused these counties to lose population rapidly.

The counties with large urban centers have experienced rapid growth. Between 1890 and 1970 the percentage of the state's population living in urban centers grew from 32 per cent to 70 per cent. However, in the two large metropolitan areas the population has decreased in the central sections. In St. Louis the population has declined more than 300,000 since 1950.

40. COUNTY AREA DISTRIBUTION PROPORTIONATE TO POPULATION, 1970

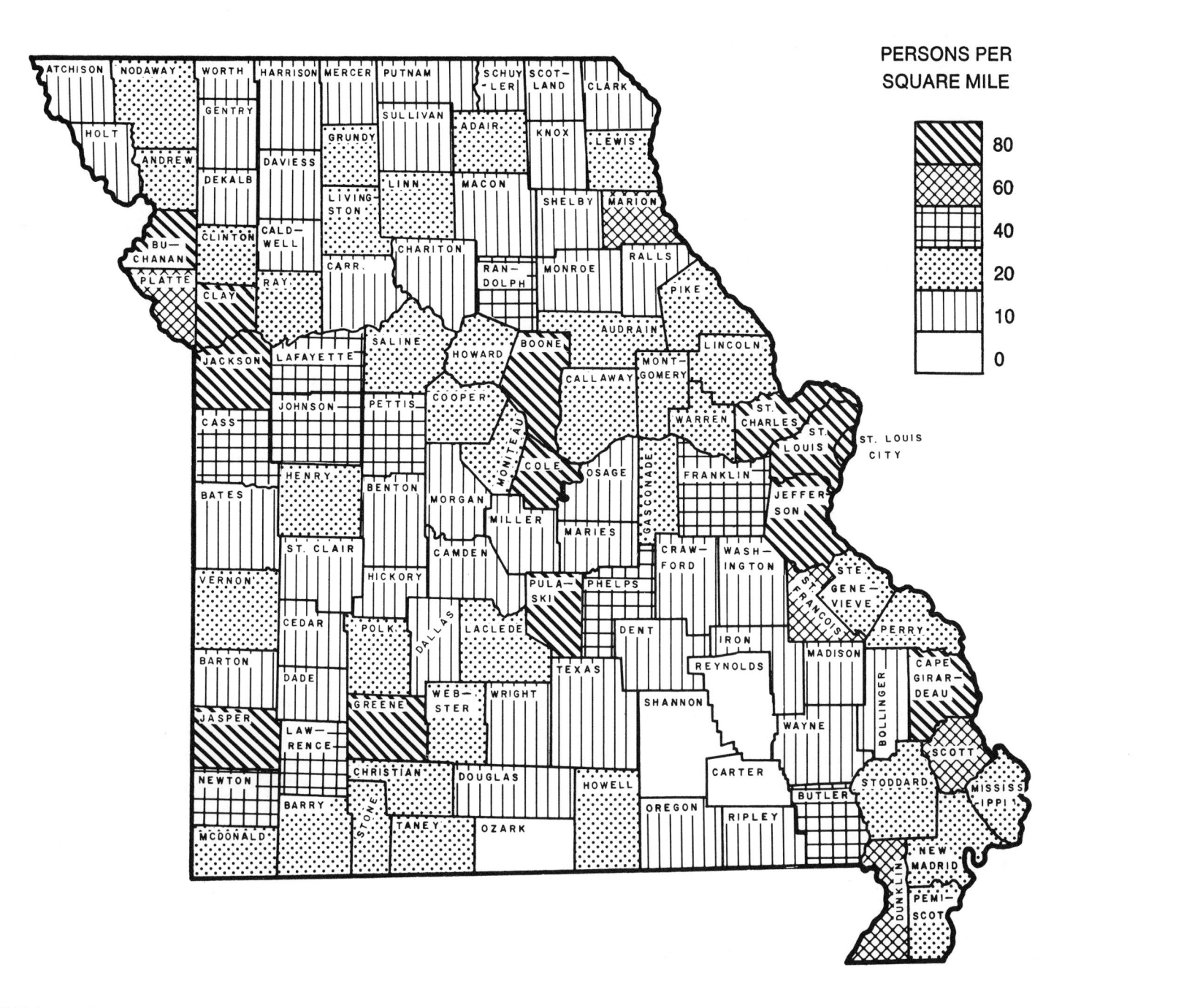

PERSONS PER
SQUARE MILE

80
60
40
20
10
0

41. POPULATION DENSITY BY COUNTY, 1974

The U.S. Bureau of the Census population estimates for 1974 credited Missouri with a total population of 4,772,000, or an average density of 68.4 people per square mile. This average compares to an average density of 67.7 per square mile in 1970, 62.3 per square mile in 1960, and 54.6 per square mile in 1940. The average density for the United States as a whole in 1970 was approximately 55 per square mile.

Within the state the density of population varies significantly from region to region. Densities within the state range from a high of almost ten thousand people per square mile in St. Louis City to a low of seven people per square mile in Shannon County. This is an extreme example of the urban-rural dichotomy in population density evident throughout the United States.

The majority of Missourians reside in a relatively small number of urban centers. They are, so to speak, once removed from direct dependence upon the land for their sustenance. Six of every ten Missourians are concentrated in only five urban areas: St. Louis City and County, Jackson County, Greene County, Clay County, and Buchanan County. In total, nearly three-fourths of Missouri's population is classed as urban (living in towns of twenty-five hundred or more).

In all urban centers, population densities are high, albeit the densities are much greater in metropolitan St. Louis and Kansas City, where there are more large apartment buildings than in the smaller urban centers of the state. Although cities tend to be scattered about the state, a band of counties stretching from Kansas City to St. Louis, and including Columbia and Jefferson City, stands out as having higher than average densities. A second corridor of counties with greater than average densities extends across the Ozarks from St. Louis to Joplin. This corridor includes Rolla, Lebanon, and Springfield.

The remainder of Missouri's population is classified as either "rural non-farm" or "rural farm," depending upon whether or not they are actually engaged in agriculture. In both cases densities are much lower than in urban areas. Fifty-two counties in the state reported a rural farm population exceeding 35 per cent of the county's total population. These counties are located along the Iowa border, where good agricultural land has led to large farms and low population densities, and in the Ozarks, where much of the land is in forest and, therefore, not capable of supporting high densities of farm population. A smaller area with a large rural farm population is the Southeast Lowlands. Although the farm population in this region has dropped rapidly since about 1950, the high labor requirements for agriculture when cotton was the chief crop led to a very heavy rural farm population.

Forty-six counties in the state are completely rural; that is, they have no towns exceeding twenty-five hundred in population. These counties have the highest proportion of rural non-farm inhabitants. For the most part, these counties are located in the more rugged sections of the Ozarks where Missouri's lowest population densities occur. For example, more than 80 per cent of Iron County's population is classified as rural non-farm.

SLAVES, 1820

SLAVES, 1840

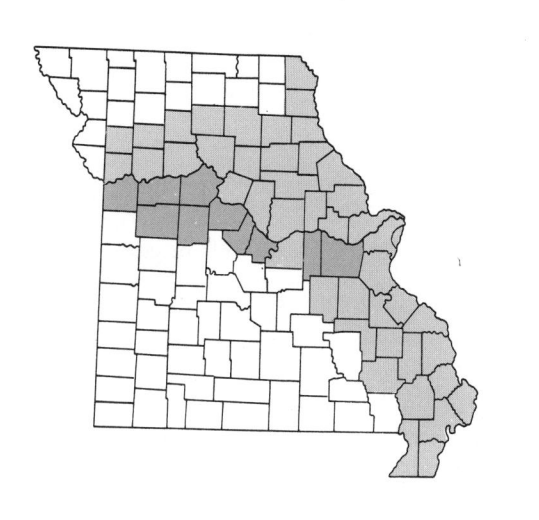

SLAVES, 1860

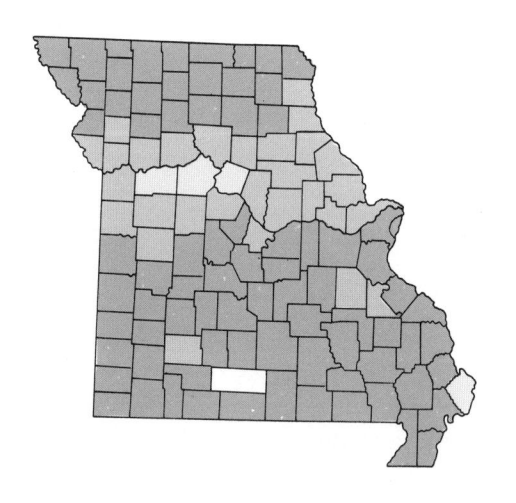

No non-white population

10 to 30 percent

Under 10 percent

30 to 50 percent

42. SLAVE POPULATION, 1860

The distribution and density of slave population in Missouri followed closely the distribution and density of the white population. The main immigration route to Missouri was along the Mississippi and Missouri rivers, and it was there that slave population was concentrated. Slaves were used mainly for agricultural labor and domestic servants. The productive agricultural land close by the two major rivers was used for commercial crops of tobacco and hemp. Slaves were used to cultivate, harvest, and process these crops.

The greatest concentration of slaves in rural Missouri was in the Little Dixie region in the central part of the state along the Missouri River, because it was settled by Southerners before the Civil War, and a plantation economy based on slavery was installed there.

BLACK POPULATION, 1880

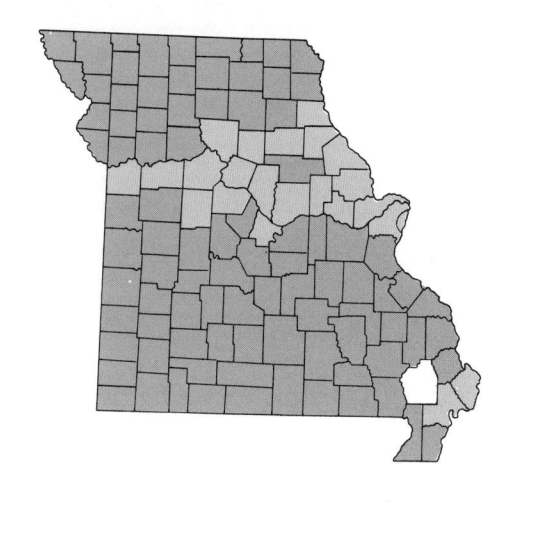

BLACK POPULATION, 1900

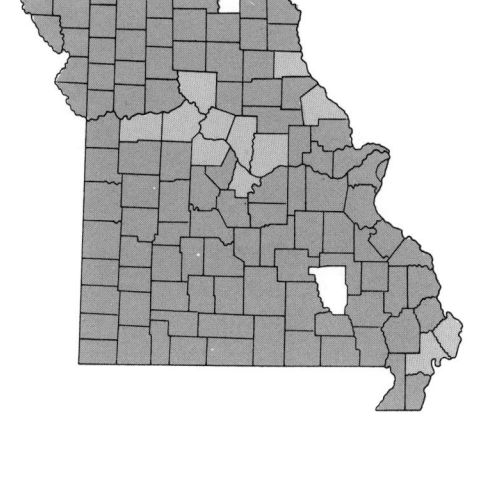

BLACK POPULATION, 1930

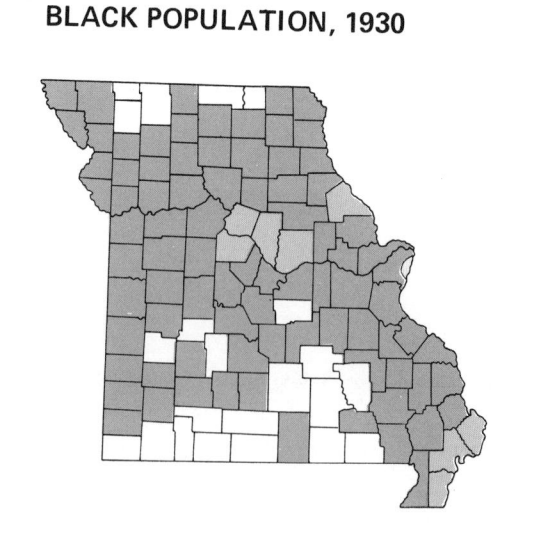

BLACK POPULATION, 1970

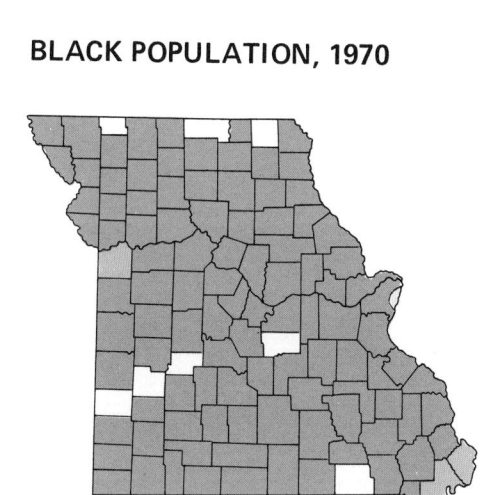

☐ No non-white population

▨ 10 to 30 percent

▨ Under 10 percent

☐ 30 to 50 percent

The past several decades have been characterized by unprecedented shifts in the population of the United States. The migration of thousands of blacks away from the rural South and into the urban North has been one of the major shifts, and Missouri has been very much affected by it.

Missouri's urban areas, like most urban areas, have experienced an increase in black population relative to the white population. Between 1940 and 1970 the white population of the state increased only 11 per cent, while the nonwhite population increased 62 per cent. (Although *nonwhite* is a broader category than *black,* 99.8 per cent of Missouri's nonwhite population is black.) The increase in nonwhite population was mostly in the cities. In 1970 only 9.4 per cent of the nonwhites residing in Missouri were in rural areas as compared to 21.9 per cent in 1940.

In the two largest cities, the proportion of the nonwhite population was significantly increased. In St. Louis City, nonwhites constituted 30.1 per cent of the population in 1960 as compared to 13.4 per cent in 1940. By 1970 the nonwhite population constituted 46 per cent of the population in St. Louis. In Kansas City nonwhites constituted 18.0 per cent of the population in 1960 as compared to 10.5 per cent in 1940. In both cases nonwhites are concentrated in the central city. By 1970 the nonwhite population had increased to 30 per cent of the total population of Kansas City. (The percentages for Kansas City and St. Louis refer to the central cities only, and not to the metropolitan areas.)

Outside of the major urban centers blacks in Missouri are found in significant numbers in two widely separated parts of the state. One concentration is in the counties of east central Missouri near the Missouri River, the region referred to as Little Dixie. It was there that most of the slaves in Missouri were located before the Civil War. The other concentration of blacks in Missouri is in the Southeast Lowlands. The movement of blacks into this region is largely a post–Civil War occurrence. When the fertile bottom soils were provided with artificial drainage, an extension of the Southern cotton economy moved into this region, bringing with it large numbers of blacks. However, the delta region has experienced a significant emigration of blacks in the decade from 1960 to 1970.

The Missouri portion of the Corn Belt and the Ozarks are conspicuous by the absence of blacks there. In both cases, settlement was primarily by whites not involved in the slave economy of the South. The Corn Belt of northern Missouri was populated from the northeast. The Ozark region was settled largely by yeomen farmers from the hill country of Appalachia, few of whom held slaves.

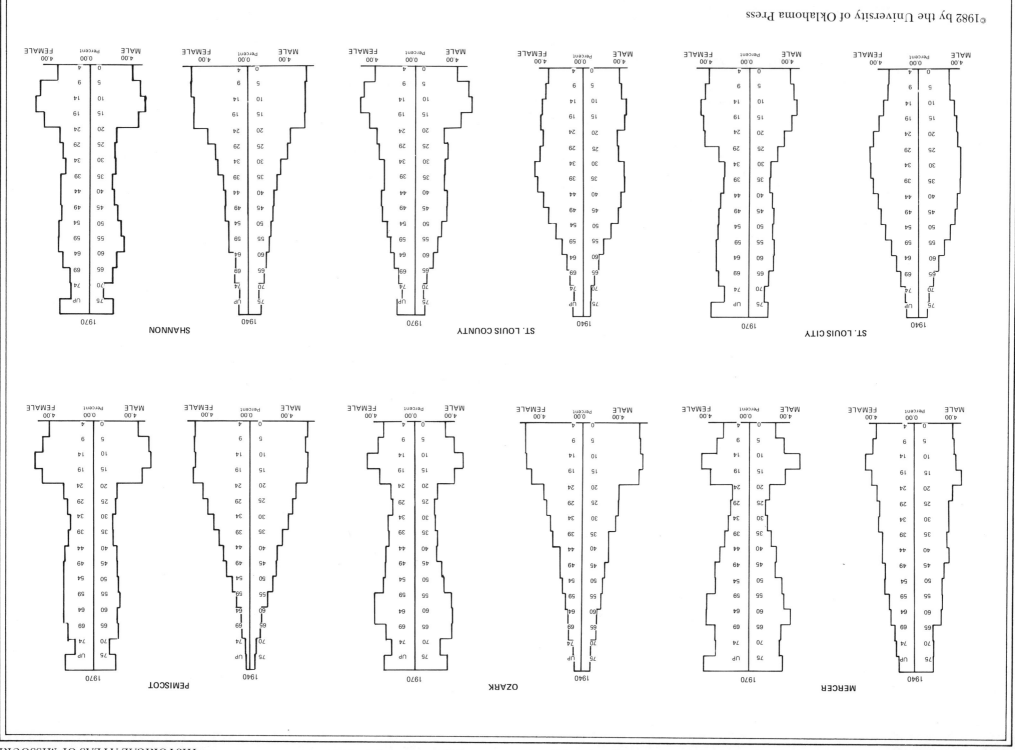

HISTORICAL ATLAS OF MISSOURI

©1982 by the University of Oklahoma Press

44. POPULATION PYRAMIDS FOR SELECTED COUNTIES

The age structure of the population is very important to people preparing plans for hospitals, schools, and other public facilities and to private organizations and groups planning future activities. In Missouri the age structure varies widely from county to county. Many counties have populations with relatively large proportions of older people, while others have more younger people.

The age structure in many counties has changed considerably over time. The population pyramids presented show the 1970 age structure and that for 1940 for selected counties. The pyramids present a graphic description of the changes that have occurred over time. A population pyramid can be interpreted as being two bar graphs back to back. One side of the graph indicates the percentage of males in the various age groups, while the other side indicates the percentage of females. The percentage is figured by dividing the number of persons in a specific age group by the total population for the county.

Some of the causes of changes in the age structures are fluctuations in the birth rates and migration in or out of the county. Generally speaking, northern Missouri has an older population as a result of a long-continuing trend of out-migration. Southern Missouri has varying patterns of age structure, with an aging trend in most counties. Southeastern Missouri has had some dramatic changes from a predominantly younger age population to an increasingly older population. The metropolitan areas of the state have remained relatively stable in their age structure, with some increase in the older age groups. The population pyramids presented here were selected as representative examples of each type.

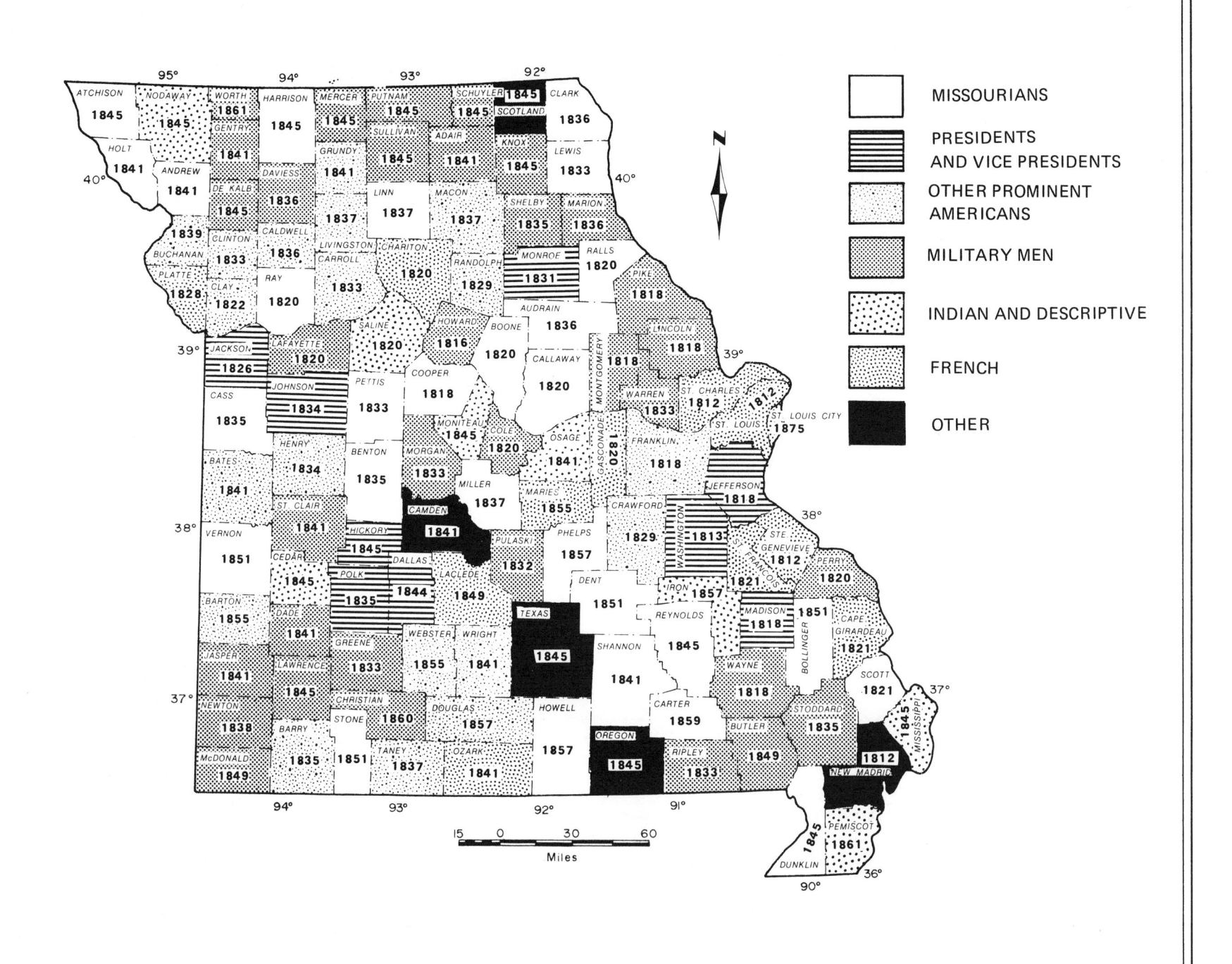

MISSOURIANS

PRESIDENTS
AND VICE PRESIDENTS

OTHER PROMINENT
AMERICANS

MILITARY MEN

INDIAN AND DESCRIPTIVE

FRENCH

OTHER

45. ORIGIN OF COUNTY NAMES

The first counties in Missouri were organized in 1812 under the auspices of the territorial government. After 1821 the counties were organized by the state legislature. The years in which the 114 counties were organized are designated on the map. The city of St. Louis was detached from St. Louis County in 1875 and given independent status with the same standing as Missouri's counties.

The American Revolution provided twenty-four Missouri counties with names—more than any other single event. Contributors ranged from famous generals such as Anthony Wayne to less famous generals such as Benjamin Lincoln and sergeants such as McDonald and Jasper. Foreign contributors to the American Revolution are also represented by Count Pulaski, a Polish general who served with American forces, and by the Marquis de Lafayette of France, whose contributions are well known. Camden County derives its name from Charles Pratt, the Earl of Camden, who was an English statesman opposed in Parliament to "taxation without representation."

Lawrence County owes its name to Captain James Lawrence, commander of the *Chesapeake* in the War of 1812, who when wounded and dying cried out, "Don't give up the ship." Daviess County derives its name from a colonel who had the distinction of dying in the Battle of Tippecanoe.

The office of president of the United States has provided its share of county names. Andrew Jackson has the distinction of having two counties named for him: Jackson County and Hickory County after his nickname "Old Hickory." Polk County was named for James Polk before he became president. A number of vice-presidents are also represented.

Political figures of national prominence other than presidents and vice-presidents are also among the namesakes. Chief Justice Roger B. Taney's name was fixed to Taney County when, in 1856, he rendered the famous Dred Scott decision. Nathaniel Macon, a U.S. senator from North Carolina, was admired for the undying faith he had in the ability of the people to govern themselves. His favorite saying was, "If left alone they will always do what is right." Charles Carroll had the distinction of being the last surviving signer of the Declaration of Independence at the time his name was chosen for Carroll County.

Twenty-eight counties were named after Missourians, although one could argue that Lewis, Clark, and Boone were not native Missourians. Reynolds County chose the name of a former governor of Missouri, Thomas Reynolds, who committed suicide while in office. Ralls County owes its name to Daniel Ralls, a member of the state legislature who died while the legislature was in session. His vote, when he was carried from the sick chamber into the legislative hall, elected Senator Thomas Hart Benton in 1820. Callaway County is named for Daniel Boone's grandson. Some, such as Stone, who was an early settler in that county from eastern Tennessee, had little claim to fame.

The French provided county names in a variety of ways. Girardeau and Chariton were both fur traders. Saints of France, including one female, Ste. Genevieve, are well represented in the areas of early French settlement. Gasconade derives from the French word *Gascon*, meaning an inhabitant of Gascony in France; the French pioneers thought the Indians of the area were much like the people of Gascony.

The Indians of Missouri provided names for a number of counties. Mississippi County derives its name from the Algonquin words *missi* and *seepee*, meaning "great river." Moniteau and Nodaway are Indian names for streams; Pemiscot is an Indian word for liquid mud, applied to the bayous.

The principle of local self-government is strongly entrenched in Missouri. It is this fact which largely accounts for the multiplicity as well as the complexity of the state's local government units. There are 114 counties and 329 townships. The township as a unit of local government is of minor importance.

The most important units of local government in Missouri are the county and the city. Although the county is considered to be essentially a local government to serve the rural areas, the activities of many of its officers affect urban as well as rural inhabitants. Actually the county is an administrative area for state as well as local governmental programs. Also, many federal programs are administered at the county level. Incorporated municipalities such as cities and villages are subject to the government of the county within which they are located. An important exception in Missouri is St. Louis City, which is not governed by any county, and in fact the people of St. Louis, under authority granted by the Constitution of 1875, elect their own officers to perform county government functions.

Analysis of population data gathered in the U.S. census of 1970 reveals several interesting facts regarding Missouri's counties and county seats. Thirty-four counties contained less than 10,000 people. Eighteen of the counties with less than 10,000 population were north of the Missouri River, and sixteen lay to the south of the river in the Ozark region. Four counties had less than 5,000 people: Wright (3,359), Carter (3,878), Hickory (4,481), and Mercer (4,910). Five counties, in addition to the city of St. Louis, exceeded 100,000 population: St. Louis (951,685), Jackson (654,178), Greene (152,929), Clay (123,702), and Jefferson (105,647). The disparity in governmental responsibilities, extent of services, and per capita cost of government are apparent from the population data for the foregoing counties.

While the county seat is ordinarily the largest town in the county, there are numerous exceptions to this rule. The majority of the county seats are in the range of 1,000 to 3,000 in population. Disregarding the city of St. Louis, there were only fourteen county seats with more than 10,000 population. On the other hand, there were twenty-four county seats which have fewer than 1,000 people. Only two county seats exceeded 100,000 population: Springfield (120,096) and Independence (111,662). Nine of the county seats were small villages under 500: Monticello (157), Centerville (209), Hermitage (284), Kingston (291), Greenville (328), Galena (391), Linneus (400), Hillsboro (432), and Pineville (444). While most of the small county seats are in sparsely settled counties, there are a few exceptions, the most striking of which is Hillsboro, the seat of populous Jefferson County (105,647).

Missouri's county seats are remarkably centrally located within the counties. Only about 15 of the 114 county seats may be said to be asymmetrically located within the counties. Of these, nine are towns founded on the Mississippi and Missouri rivers as ports and trading centers. The explanation for the central location for county seats is related to the fact that all of the county seats were founded before the development of the automobile. A central location was desirable when travel by horse-drawn wagon was at a rate of six or seven miles per hour. Many of the county seat towns were established at the time the counties were founded, and the locations were determined by a committee appointed specifically for that purpose. As new counties were carved from older counties, the competition between existing towns for the new county seat often was bitter. Once a town was designated as the seat of county government, it tended to be permanent, and in only a few cases were the political forces strong enough to move the county government to a larger town.

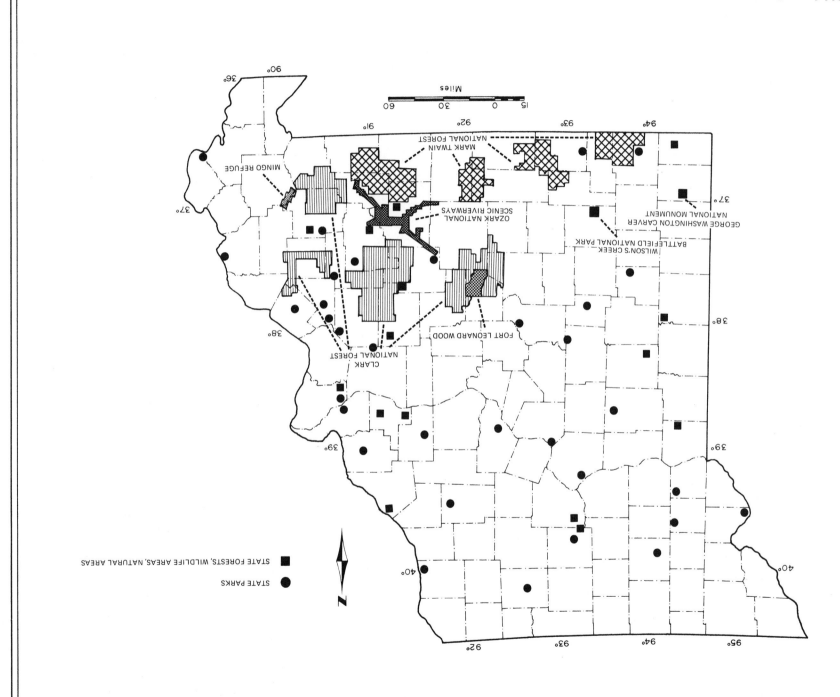

47. PUBLIC LANDS

The federal lands of the United States of America date back to the time of the union's formation. Then, and soon afterward, seven of the original states ceded to the central government some 233.4 million acres of land lying westward to the Mississippi River. This land was the foundation of the public domain. Thereafter, through treaty and purchase, the United States acquired additional public domain, the last acquisition being the purchase of Alaska from Russia in 1867.

All of Missouri, except the small amount of land that was granted by the Spanish government of Louisiana, was once part of the public domain. Thousands of acres were given as grants to railroad companies to finance construction of railroads, and thousands more were given for public education, but most of Missouri's 41 million acres of land was either sold or given to individuals under the various laws for disposal of land.

The largest acreage of public land in Missouri is held by the federal government in the Mark Twain and former Clark national forests, recently consolidated under the name Mark Twain National Forest. This land was purchased from private individuals under provisions of the Weeks Act, which provided funds for the purchase of cut-over forest land and eroded agricultural land for purposes of conservation and the public good. Purchase of land for inclusion in the national forests has progressed since its inception in the 1930s. A small amount of federally owned land is included in the Ozark National Scenic Riverways on the Current and Jacks Fork rivers and in the Wilson's Creek National Battlefield, George Washington Carver National Monument, and Jefferson National Expansion Monument in St. Louis.

State-held property is mainly in the state park system. Legislation passed in 1976 established a special sales tax to provide funds to acquire land for conservation and recreational use.

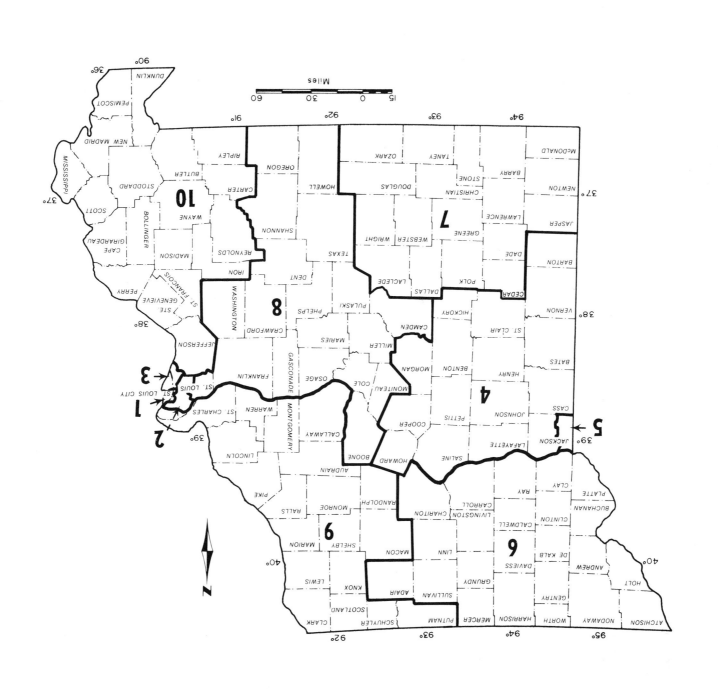

Miles
60 30 15 0

N

48. U.S. CONGRESSIONAL DISTRICTS

This map shows the boundaries of the congressional districts of Missouri for the Ninety-fifth Congress of the United States. The boundaries shown are those specified in the laws and/or court orders establishing the congressional districts within Missouri and reflect the number of representatives apportioned to the state based on the results of the 1970 census of population in accordance with provisions of Title 2, United States Code, Section 2a.

Congress must meet annually on January 3 unless it has, by law, appointed a different day. Members of the House of Representatives are elected November 2 in even-numbered years to serve two-year terms beginning January 3 in the odd-numbered year following election.

Eight of Missouri's ten representatives in the Ninety-fifth Congress are Democrats. Republican representatives serve the sixth and seventh districts. The seventh district is the only district that is considered solidly Republican.

Miles

15 0 30 60

N

1-3, 6, 7, 13-15, 24-26

49. STATE SENATORIAL DISTRICTS

Legislative power in Missouri is vested by Section 1, Article III of the Constitution of 1945 in the General Assembly, more commonly known as the legislature, composed of the Senate and the House of Representatives.

The Senate consists of thirty-four members who are elected for four-year terms. Senators from odd-numbered districts are elected in presidential election years. Senators from even-numbered districts are chosen in the "off-year" elections. Each senator must be at least thirty years of age, a qualified voter of the state for three years and of the district he represents for one year. The lieutenant governor is president and presiding officer of the Senate. In his absence, the president pro tem, who is elected by the Senate members, presides. The Missouri constitution provides that new senatorial and representative districts be established after each federal decennial census. The last redistricting was in 1971.

Senators receive a salary of $8,400 per year, a weekly allowance for miles traveled going to and returning from their place of meeting, and necessary expenses not to exceed $25 per diem. The General Assembly convenes annually on the first Wednesday after the first Monday of January. In odd-numbered years it adjourns on June 30, with no consideration of bills after June 15. In even-numbered years adjournment is on May 15, with no consideration of bills after April 30. If the governor returns a bill with his objections after adjournment sine die in even-numbered years, the assembly is automatically reconvened on the first Wednesday in September for a period not to exceed ten days to consider vetoed bills.

The governor may convene the General Assembly in special session for a maximum of sixty calendar days at any time. Only subjects recommended by the governor in his call or a special message may be considered.

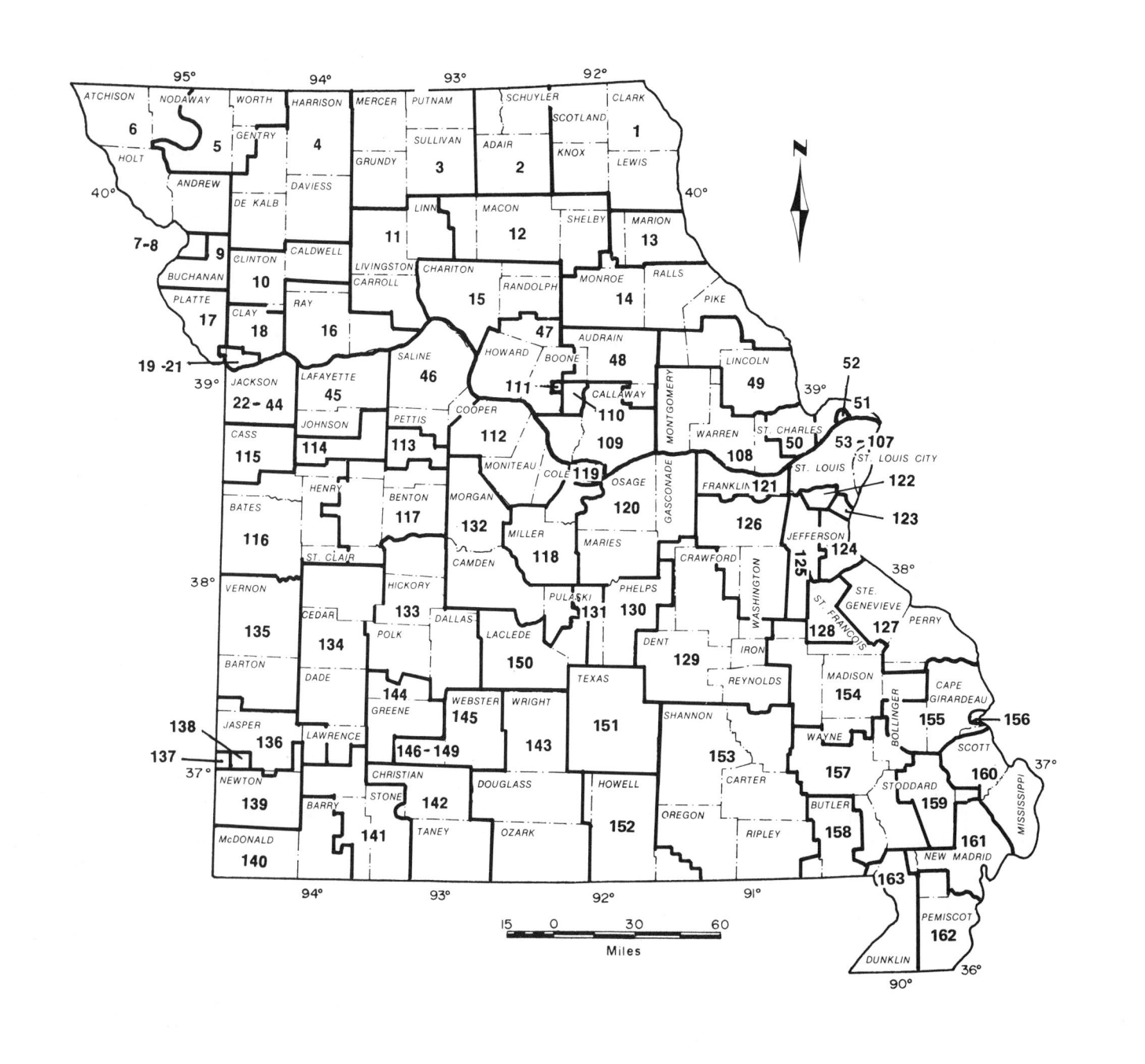

The Missouri House of Representatives consists of 163 members elected at each general election for two-year terms. A representative must be at least twenty-four years of age, a qualified voter of the state for two years and of the district he represents for one year. The House of Representatives is presided over by the speaker, who is chosen by the members, and in his absence by the speaker pro tem. The Missouri Constitution provides that new senatorial and representative districts be established after each federal decennial census. The last redistricting was in 1971.

Like senators, representatives receive a salary of $8,400 per year, a weekly allowance for miles traveled going to and returning from their place of meeting, and necessary expenses not to exceed $25 per diem.

No law is passed except by bill. Bills are designated as Senate bills or House bills depending on the house in which they originate. Bills truly agreed to and finally passed in their typed form are then signed in open session by the House speaker and the Senate president or president pro tem. A bill signed by the governor takes effect ninety days after the end of the session at which it was enacted.

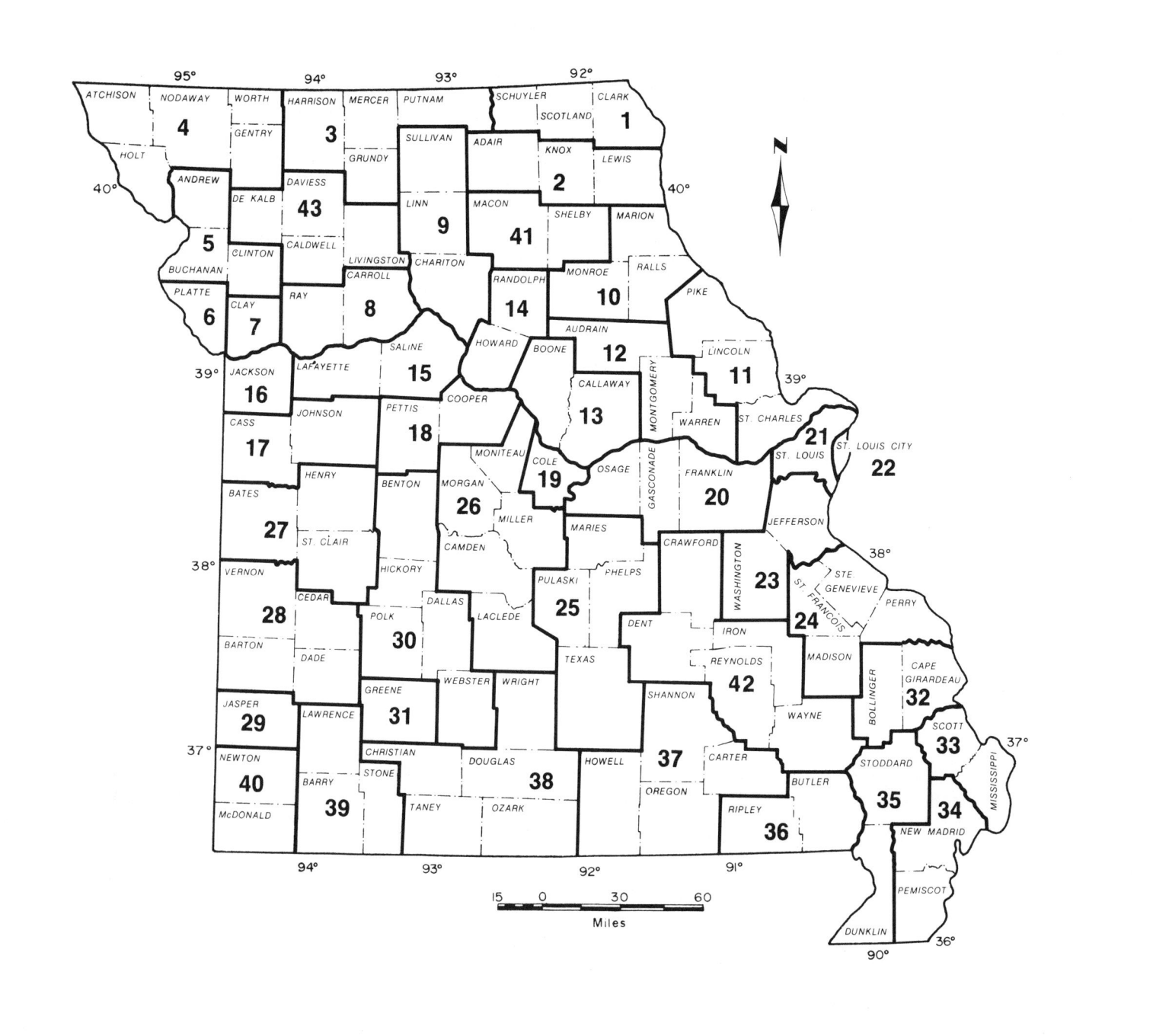

51. JUDICIAL REGIONS

Missouri's first two circuit courts were established in 1815. The Constitution of 1820 provided for the creation of four circuits, each consisting of from four to eight counties. In 1831 the number of circuits was increased to five, and over the years additional circuits have been created, bringing the number to forty-three today.

The first circuit judges were appointed by the governor with the advice and consent of the Senate. However, the life term of the judges and their method of appointment proved unpopular, and in 1849 the constitution was amended to provide for their popular election. That is the way in which most circuit judges are selected today, although judges in some circuits are selected under provisions of the Nonpartisan Court Plan.

The circuit courts are courts of general jurisdiction, meaning that they have jurisdiction generally over all criminal and civil matters not exclusively within the jurisdiction of another court, such as the magistrate or probate courts. The circuit courts have concurrent original jurisdiction with magistrates in all civil actions for the recovery of money when the sum demanded exceeds fifty dollars and also have appellate jurisdiction from the judgment and orders of county courts, probate courts, and magistrate courts in all cases not expressly prohibited by law.

Circuit court judges receive an annual salary of $45,000 paid by the state.

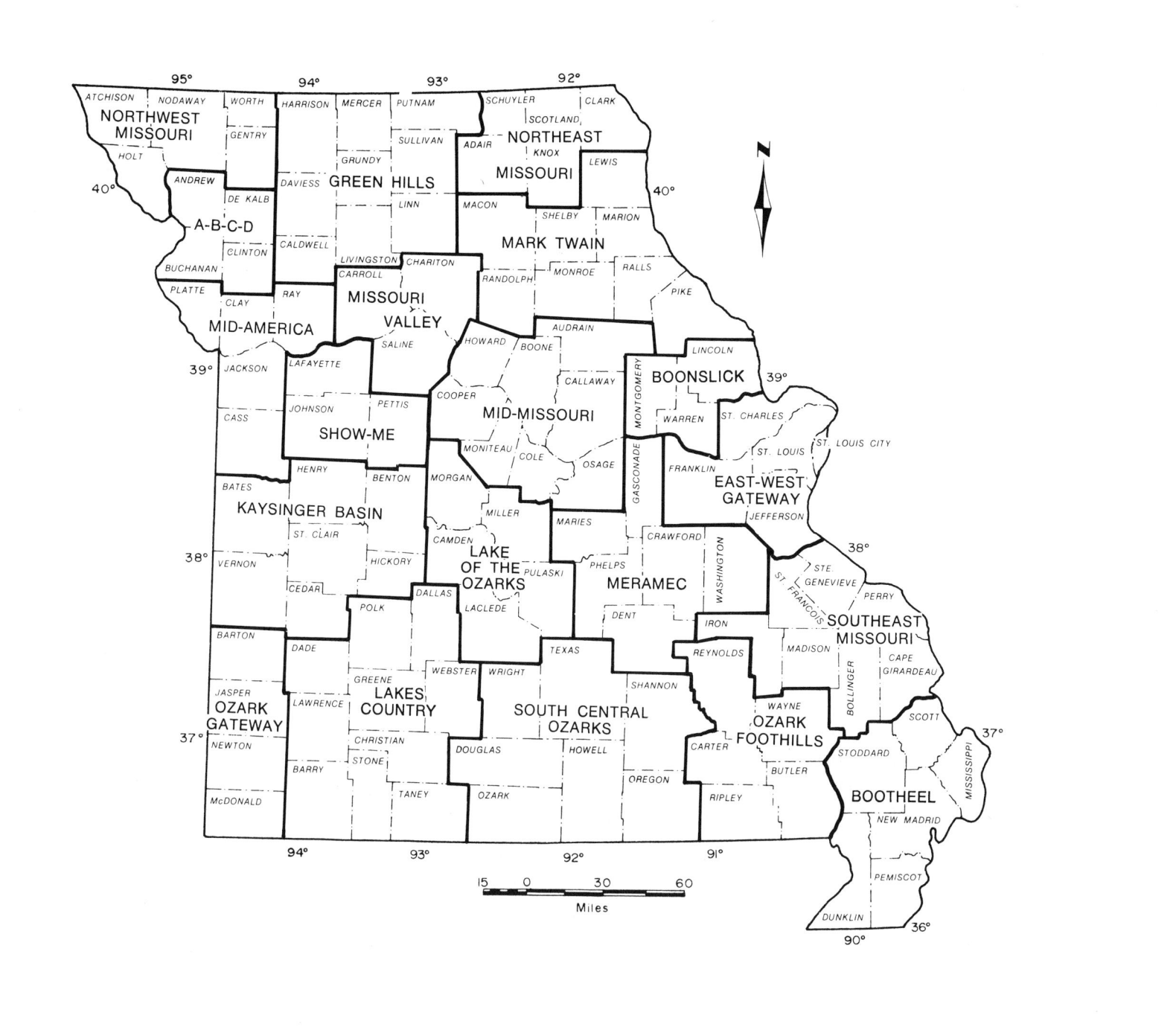

Missouri Revised Statutes, section 251, 1969, authorized the establishment of the Department of Community Affairs for planning and development. Twenty regional planning districts were delineated. The membership composition of a regional planning commission is in accordance with resolutions passed by the governing bodies of the local units in the region, representing in aggregate at least half of the population of the region. For purposes of this determination, a county is one unit and the population of each member county is based upon the inhabitants residing in the unincorporated area of such county as determined by the last decennial census of the United States.

The functions of the various substate planning districts, as outlined in the Missouri Revised Statutes, include comprehensive planning for the following:

1. Public water systems
2. Storm water drainage and flood control systems
3. Sanitary sewerage systems
4. Integrated transportation systems
5. Orderly land-use arrangements for residential, commercial, industrial, and public and other purposes
6. Local, area-wide, and state governmental services coordinated with federal governmental services insofar as may be feasible
7. Solid waste disposal systems or facilities
8. Educational facilities
9. Open space, park, and recreational areas
10. Improved standards of community aesthetics and facilities design
11. General living conditions and environmental health
12. Community health and hospital needs and related facilities
13. The coordination of planning activities for all federal assistance and grant-in-aid programs which require comprehensive planning as prerequisites for eligibility.

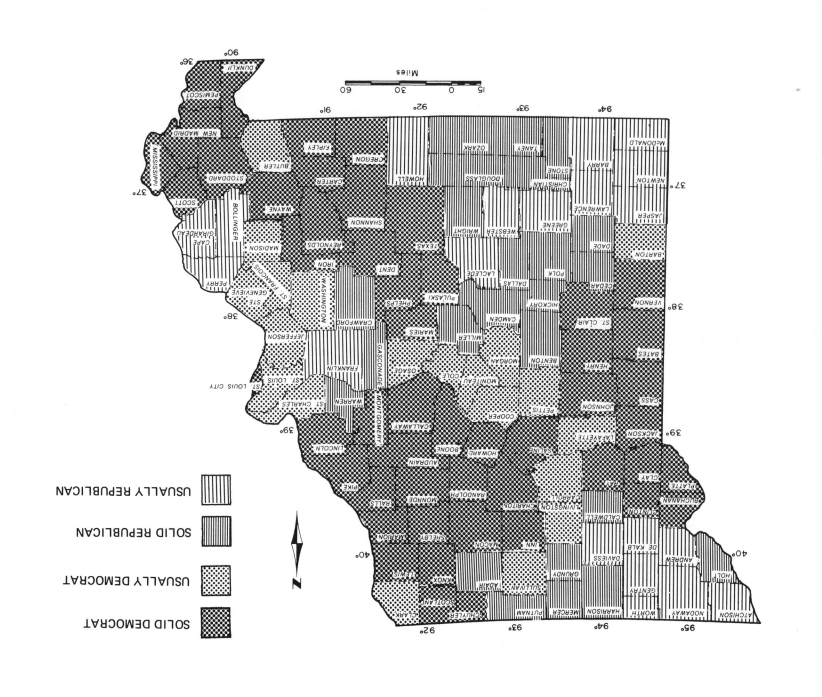

USUALLY REPUBLICAN

SOLID REPUBLICAN

USUALLY DEMOCRAT

SOLID DEMOCRAT

Regional voting patterns in Missouri trace their origins to the time of the Civil War or before it, at least in a general way. Southern stock has meant Democratic allegiance; Northern stock has been Republican. The Little Dixie region of the Missouri Valley was settled primarily by Southerners and is, to this day, the stronghold of the Democratic party in Missouri. In the 1880s German immigrants settled the lower Missouri Valley, largely displacing the earlier settlers. The Germans were strongly anti-slavery and pro-Northern, and as a result the counties where the German element is strong are today the strongest Republican districts in the state. The largely Republican character of Northwestern Missouri is analogous to the Republican character of the rural Corn Belt as a whole.

Population of the Southeast Lowlands came primarily from areas farther south, including a substantial black population to fulfill the heavy labor requirements for growing cotton. The Democratic character of the region is unmistakable, reflecting the origin of its population.

The Republican character of the major part of the Ozarks is analogous to the Republican character of the hill districts of Kentucky and Tennessee, and the settlement of that region was affected mainly by the same stock, reinforced later by small farmers from the northern states. In the eastern Ozarks, the Democratic party dominates. There, small tracts of land were settled at an early date by people of Southern origin.

Because voting patterns are influenced by national political issues, votes cast in primary elections were used to map political preferences in the state. This map shows that while there is a Democratic preponderance statewide in primary voting, as there is in general voting, approximately 40 per cent of Missouri counties vote predominantly Republican; most of these counties are in the southwestern Ozark area of the state. There is remarkable consistency in county voting in the 1908–72 period—counties that voted heavily Republican in the earlier years are still doing so today, and the same is true for the heavily Democratic and more evenly balanced counties.

In only 3 counties out of 115 has there been a clear-cut shift in primary voting behavior over the years. They are the three contiguous units of St. Louis City, St. Louis County, and St. Charles County—all densely populated areas. St. Louis City, once marginally Republican, has become strongly Democratic, especially since the 1950s, while St. Charles and St. Louis counties have changed from overwhelmingly Republican to marginally Democratic in primary voting. The dramatic changes in these counties are probably because of major changes in the composition of the population of these areas and the effect of the New Deal on the voting of minority groups such as blacks, Jews, Catholics, and labor union members.

The gross data indicate that in the 1908–72 period the Republican primary vote has increasingly become more of an "outstate" vote (meaning outside the St. Louis and Kansas City metropolitan areas), whereas the Democratic vote has changed from one that was primarily outstate to one that is concentrated in the urban-suburban Kansas City and St. Louis areas. This is not to say that there are no longer outstate areas that vote heavily Democratic, for there still are (for example, the eastern Ozarks and Little Dixie) but these outstate areas have declined in population over the years and are less important in statewide elections.

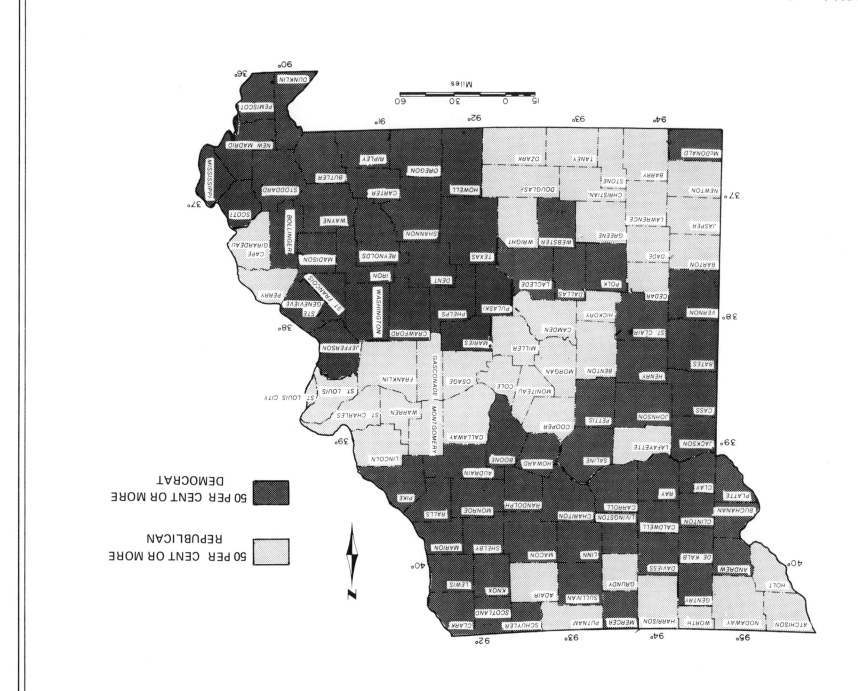

50 PER CENT OR MORE
DEMOCRAT

50 PER CENT OR MORE
REPUBLICAN

Miles

DUNKLIN

PEMISCOT

NEW MADRID

MISSISSIPPI

SCOTT

STODDARD

RIPLEY

BUTLER

OREGON

CARTER

WAYNE

BOLLINGER

CAPE GIRARDEAU

PERRY

STE. GENEVIEVE

ST. FRANCOIS

MADISON

SHANNON

HOWELL

OZARK

TANEY

STONE

BARRY

NEWTON

McDONALD

DOUGLAS

CHRISTIAN

WEBSTER WRIGHT

GREENE

LAWRENCE

JASPER

REYNOLDS

TEXAS

IRON

DENT

LACLEDE

DADE

BARTON

POLK

DALLAS

CEDAR

VERNON

PHELPS

PULASKI

HICKORY

ST. CLAIR

WASHINGTON

CRAWFORD

MARIES

MILLER

CAMDEN

BENTON

HENRY

BATES

JEFFERSON

ST. LOUIS

ST. LOUIS CITY

FRANKLIN

GASCONADE

OSAGE

COLE

MONITEAU

MORGAN

JOHNSON

CASS

WARREN

ST. CHARLES

MONTGOMERY

CALLAWAY

COOPER

PETTIS

SALINE

LAFAYETTE

JACKSON

LINCOLN

BOONE

HOWARD

AUDRAIN

RAY

CLAY

PLATTE

PIKE

RALLS

MONROE

RANDOLPH

CHARITON

CARROLL

LIVINGSTON

CLINTON

CALDWELL

BUCHANAN

MARION

SHELBY

MACON

LINN

DE KALB

ANDREW

GENTRY

HOLT

LEWIS

KNOX

ADAIR

SULLIVAN

GRUNDY

DAVIESS

CLARK

SCOTLAND

SCHUYLER

PUTNAM

MERCER

HARRISON

WORTH

NODAWAY

ATCHISON

54. 1976 PRESIDENTIAL ELECTION

Missouri, traditionally a Democratic state, cast its electoral votes for the Jimmy Carter–Walter F. Mondale ticket in the 1976 elections. The total vote was 998, 387 Democratic, 927,443 Republican, and 24,029 Independent (Eugene J. McCarthy and Marlene K. Barrett).

There were few surprises in the voting patterns except that a few of the northern and western counties that traditionally vote Republican went Democratic. Jimmy Carter, a Georgia peanut farmer, demonstrated wide appeal in agricultural areas. The western Ozarks and the lower Missouri Valley counties, two Republican strongholds, voted in the usual pattern. Likewise, the Bootheel counties, the eastern Ozarks, and Little Dixie voted strongly Democratic as expected. St. Louis City and Kansas City voted strongly Democratic.

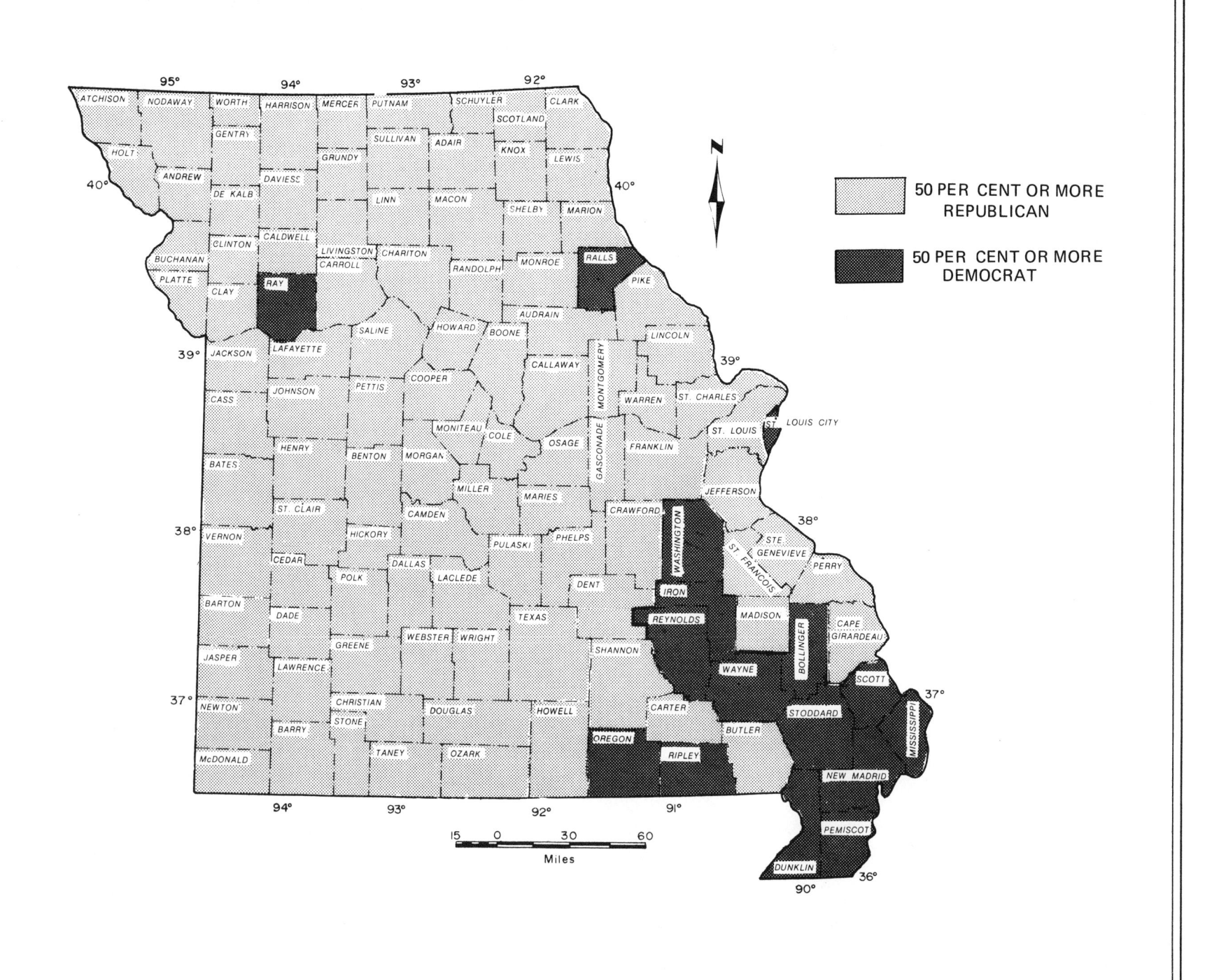

50 PER CENT OR MORE
REPUBLICAN

50 PER CENT OR MORE
DEMOCRAT

55. 1976 U.S. SENATORIAL ELECTION

The 1976 election for the U.S. Senate was unusual in many respects. Republican John C. Danforth defeated Democrat Warren E. Hearnes 1,090,067 votes to 813,571. This strong showing by a Republican senatorial candidate in a traditionally Democratic state is surprising, and all the more so when one considers that it was a year when the Democratic party regained both the White House and the Missouri governor's mansion.

Several extraordinary factors probably influenced the normal voting patterns. First, John Danforth, a wealthy and popular candidate, had a commendable record as Missouri attorney general. Having previously run unsuccessfully in a close race for the U.S. Senate, Danforth was well known to Missouri voters. Second, the tragic death in an airplane crash on August 3, 1976, of Jerry Litton, the winner of the Democratic nomination, left the Democratic party stunned and divided. Because of the unfortunate accident, the replacement on the Democratic ticket, Warren E. Hearnes, had little time to organize his campaign. As a result, most of the counties except those in southeastern Missouri and the city of St. Louis voted Republican.

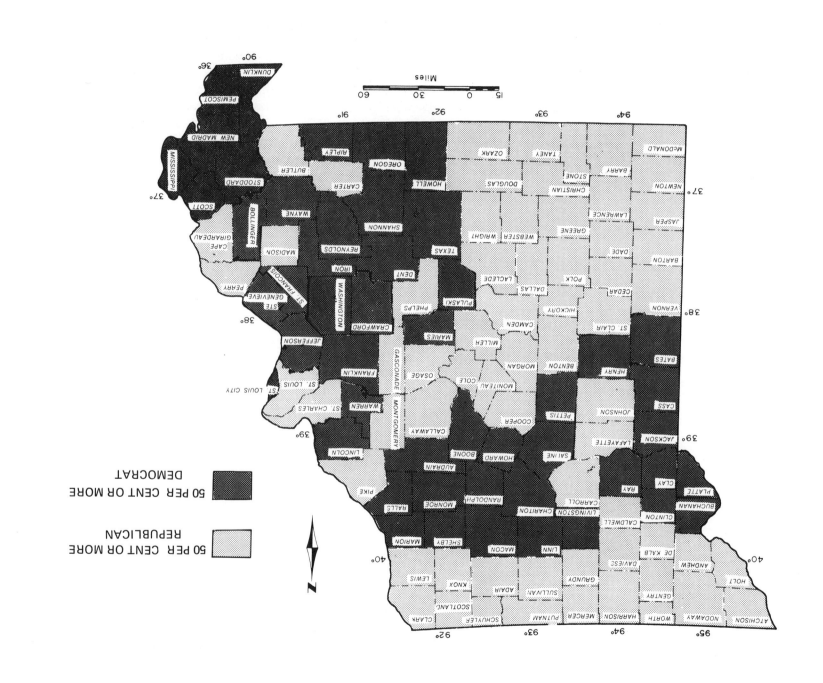

DEMOCRAT
50 PER CENT OR MORE

REPUBLICAN
50 PER CENT OR MORE

Miles
15 0 30 60

The truest measure of the relative strength of the two major political parties can best be assessed by viewing the results of gubernatorial elections. Congressional elections are sectional, and frequently, discouraged minorities do not vote in them. Presidential elections bring to the fore issues of foreign policy. Gubernatorial elections come the closest to presenting the political character of the state without these distorting influences.

The 1976 Missouri gubernatorial election resulted in an upset victory by Democrat Joseph P. Teasdale over incumbent Republican governor Christopher ("Kit") Bond. The race was close: 971,124 votes for Teasdale and 958,110 votes for Bond.

The map of voting returns is very similar to the traditional voting patterns in Missouri. The eastern Ozarks, the Southeast Lowlands, Little Dixie, and the cities of St. Louis and Kansas City voted Democratic. The western Ozarks, lower Missouri Valley, and rural counties of northern Missouri voted Republican. The importance of Democratic strength in the heavily populated urban centers and, at the same time, the fact that Republican strength is concentrated particularly in rural counties are demonstrated by the map of election returns. Kit Bond carried sixty-six counties, well more than half, but the plurality of Democratic votes in the large urban centers enabled Teasdale to win the election.

1 THE FIRST CONFLICTS

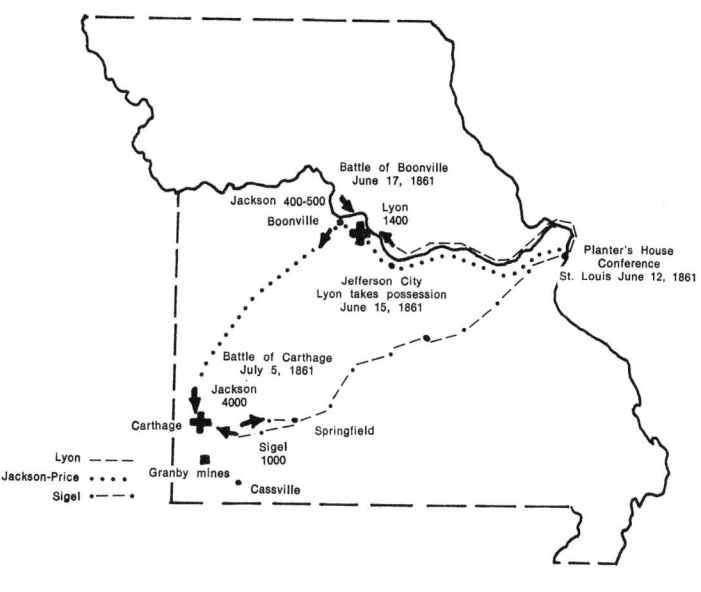

Battle of Boonville
June 17, 1861

Jackson 400-500
Boonville

Lyon
1400

Planter's House
Conference
St. Louis June 12, 1861

Jefferson City
Lyon takes possession
June 15, 1861

Battle of Carthage
July 5, 1861

Jackson
4000

Carthage

Springfield

Sigel
1000

Granby mines

Cassville

Lyon –––––
Jackson-Price ••••
Sigel —•—•—

2 EARLY CONFEDERATE VICTORIES

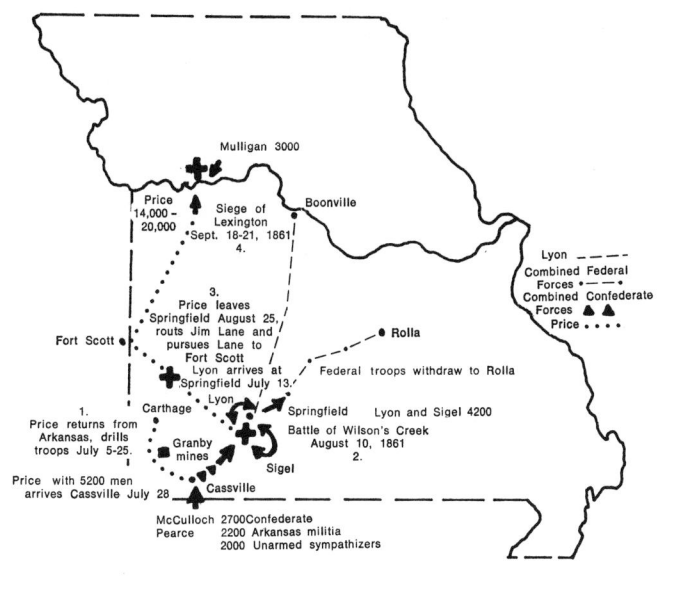

Mulligan 3000

Price
14,000 –
20,000

Boonville

Siege of
Lexington
Sept. 18-21, 1861
4.

3.
Price leaves
Springfield August 25,
routs Jim Lane and
pursues Lane to
Fort Scott

Rolla

Fort Scott

Lyon arrives at
Springfield July 13.

Federal troops withdraw to Rolla

1.
Price returns from
Arkansas, drills
troops July 5-25.

Carthage

Lyon

Springfield   Lyon and Sigel 4200

Granby
mines

Battle of Wilson's Creek
August 10, 1861
2.

Sigel

Price with 5200 men
arrives Cassville July 28

Cassville

McCulloch 2700 Confederate
Pearce   2200 Arkansas militia
2000 Unarmed sympathizers

Lyon –––––
Combined Federal
Forces ••––••
Combined Confederate
Forces ▲▲
Price ••••

3 FEDERAL ADVANCES

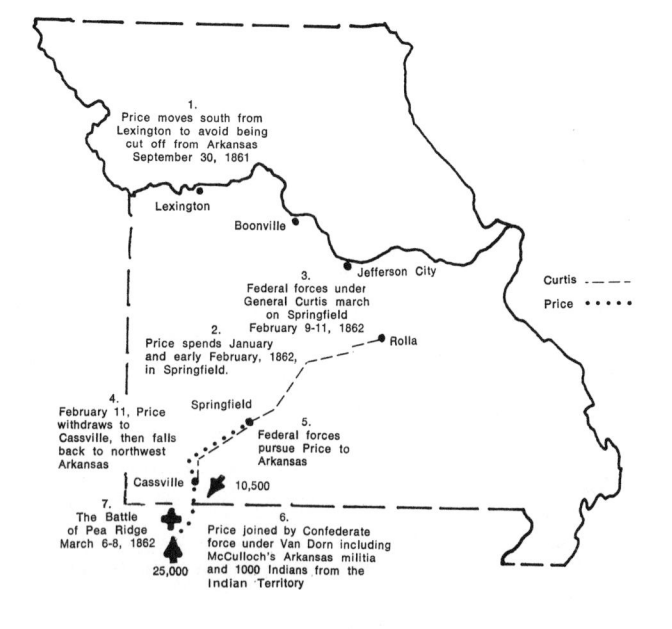

1.
Price moves south from
Lexington to avoid being
cut off from Arkansas
September 30, 1861

Lexington

Boonville

3.
Jefferson City
Federal forces under
General Curtis march
on Springfield
February 9-11, 1862

Rolla

2.
Price spends January
and early February, 1862,
in Springfield.

4.
February 11, Price
withdraws to
Cassville, then falls
back to northwest
Arkansas

Springfield

5.
Federal forces
pursue Price to
Arkansas

Cassville   10,500

7.
The Battle
of Pea Ridge
March 6-8, 1862

6.
Price joined by Confederate
force under Van Dorn including
McCulloch's Arkansas militia
and 1000 Indians from the
Indian Territory

25,000

Curtis –––––
Price •••••

4 BATTLES IN THE HEARTLAND

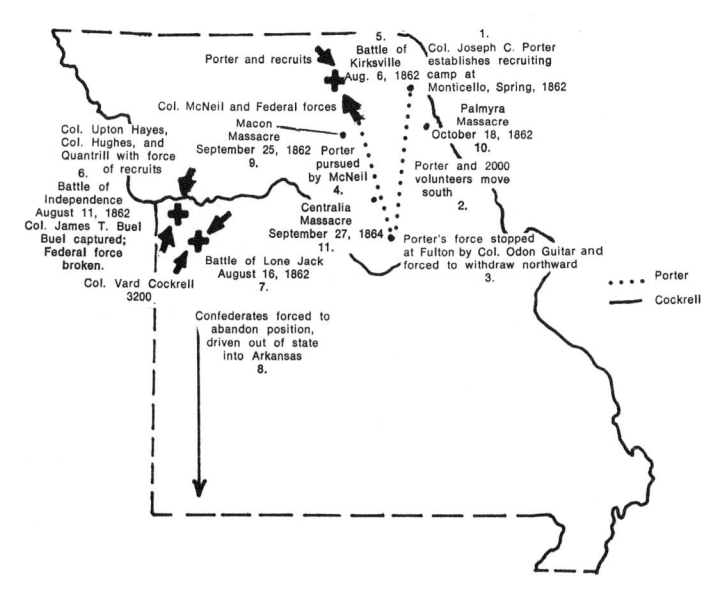

5.
Battle of
Kirksville
Aug. 6, 1862

Porter and recruits

1.
Col. Joseph C. Porter
establishes recruiting
camp at
Monticello, Spring, 1862

Col. McNeil and Federal forces

Col. Upton Hayes,
Col. Hughes, and
Quantrill with force
of recruits

Macon
Massacre
September 25, 1862

Palmyra
Massacre
October 18, 1862
10.

Porter
pursued
by McNeil
4.

Porter and 2000
volunteers move
south
2.

6.
Battle of
Independence
August 11, 1862
Col. James T. Buel
Buel captured;
Federal force
broken.

Centralia
Massacre
September 27, 1864
11.

Porter's force stopped
at Fulton by Col. Odon Guitar and
forced to withdraw northward
3.

Col. Vard Cockrell
3200

Battle of Lone Jack
August 16, 1862
7.

Confederates forced to
abandon position,
driven out of state
into Arkansas
8.

Porter ••••
Cockrell ——

While neither the Confederate nor the Union government considered the military acitvities west of the Mississippi River crucial, the battles fought in Missouri were of strategic importance. Missouri's location on the Missouri and Mississippi rivers made control of the state essential to the maintenance of communication with the West and to the use of the rivers for transportation.

The first battles in Missouri were fought to determine whether Union or Confederate forces would control the heartland in the Missouri Valley. General Nathaniel Lyon's Union forces marched west from St. Louis in the summer of 1861 to drive the Missouri Militia, under the command of Sterling Price and Governor Jackson, from Jefferson City and Boonville. The militia proved more effective when, moving southward, they drove off the forces of Colonel Franz Sigel.

At the Battle of Wilson's Creek, fought on August 10, 1861, the Confederate army under General McCulloch drove Union forces from southwestern Missouri and gained control of Springfield. During the six-hour battle the total casualty list reached 2,330, including the leader of the Union army, General Lyon. Following the victory at Wilson's Creek, "Old Pap" Price led the state militia north to the Missouri Valley, where, on September 20, they captured Lexington.

Following a brief interval when General John C. Fremont commanded the Army of the West, the Union forces were placed under the command of General Samuel R. Curtis, an intelligent, aggressive commander. Curtis recaptured Springfield in February, 1862, and pressed on into Arkansas, where, at the Battle of Pea Ridge fought March 6–8, 1862, he led the Union army in a decisive victory over the confederate forces of General McCulloch. The victory excluded the state militia from Missouri and gave control of the state to the federal government.

Between the conflict at Pea Ridge in March, 1862, and the beginning of a short-lived invasion by General Price in September, 1864, the battles in Missouri resulted either from recruiting operations on the part of the Confederacy or from the hit-and-run raids of Confederate guerrillas. The term *bushwhacking* is descriptive of the kind of war fought in Missouri during that period. Confederate forces, after raiding a settlement or sabotaging telegraph wires or railroad bridges, would ride off into the woods and then resume their normal agricultural occupations when federal forces arrived to put down the trouble. Because Southern sympathy was strongest in Little Dixie, the more important encounters occurred in the Missouri Valley heartland.

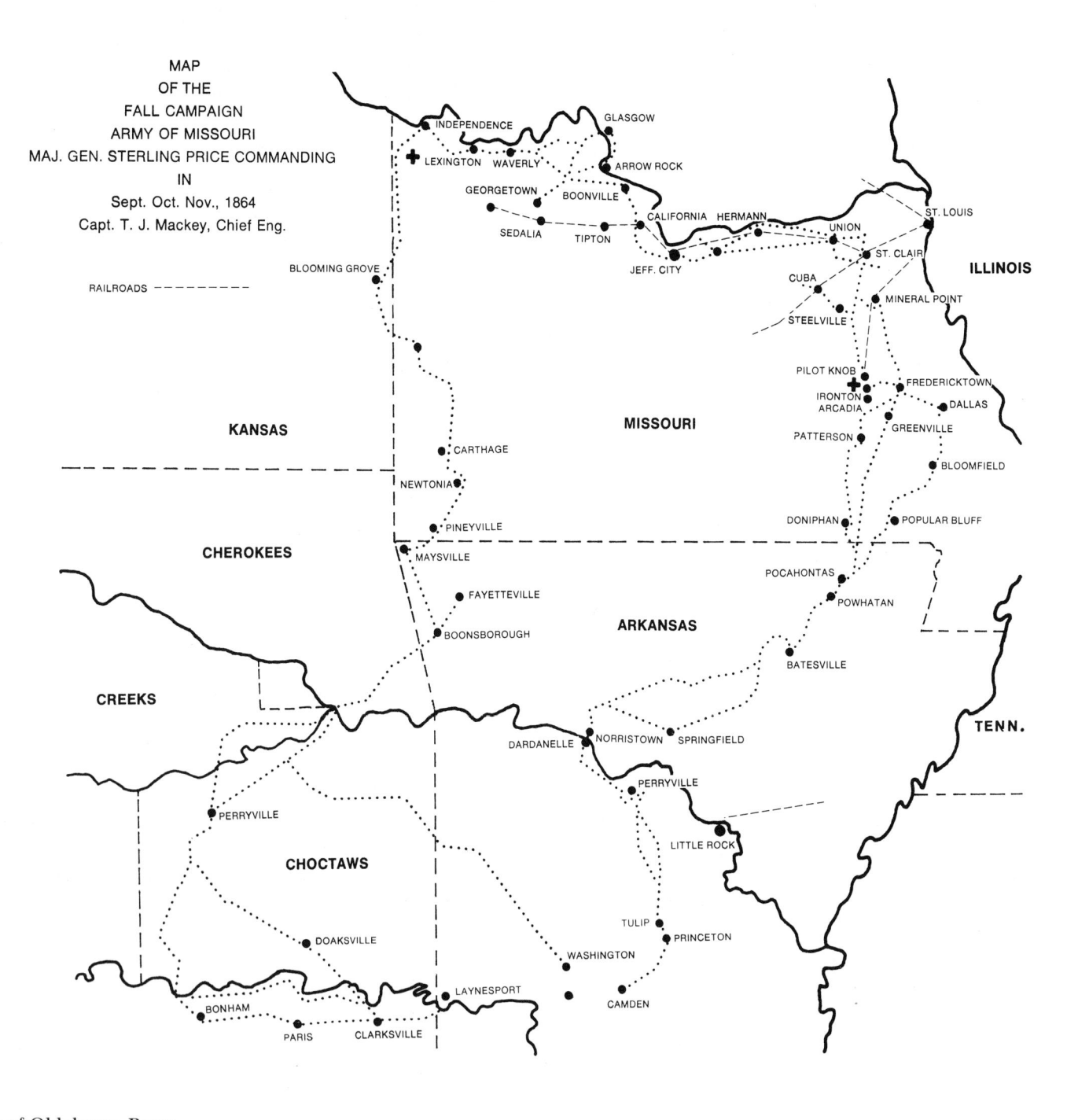

MAP
OF THE
FALL CAMPAIGN
ARMY OF MISSOURI
MAJ. GEN. STERLING PRICE COMMANDING
IN
Sept. Oct. Nov., 1864
Capt. T. J. Mackey, Chief Eng.

RAILROADS --------

INDEPENDENCE
GLASGOW
LEXINGTON   WAVERLY   ARROW ROCK
GEORGETOWN   BOONVILLE
SEDALIA   TIPTON   CALIFORNIA   HERMANN   UNION   ST. LOUIS
JEFF. CITY   ST. CLAIR   ILLINOIS
CUBA   MINERAL POINT
STEELVILLE
BLOOMING GROVE

KANSAS   MISSOURI

PILOT KNOB   FREDERICKTOWN
IRONTON   DALLAS
ARCADIA   GREENVILLE
PATTERSON
BLOOMFIELD

CARTHAGE
NEWTONIA   DONIPHAN   POPULAR BLUFF

PINEYVILLE
CHEROKEES   MAYSVILLE   POCAHONTAS
FAYETTEVILLE   POWHATAN
ARKANSAS
BOONSBOROUGH
BATESVILLE

CREEKS
NORRISTOWN   SPRINGFIELD   TENN.
DARDANELLE
PERRYVILLE

PERRYVILLE   LITTLE ROCK
CHOCTAWS

DOAKSVILLE   TULIP
PRINCETON
WASHINGTON
LAYNESPORT
BONHAM   CAMDEN
PARIS   CLARKSVILLE

The last major episode in Missouri during the Civil War was the raid by General Sterling Price in the fall of 1864. After the Battle of Pea Ridge (March, 1862) in northwest Arkansas, the Confederate military effort was shifted east of the Mississippi. Nevertheless, "Old Pap" Price, believing that an army could be raised from Southern sympathizers in the Missouri Valley and aware that many Union troops had been moved to the eastern theatre, decided to make one more invasion of Missouri. In his five-week raid in the state, Price aided the Confederacy by forcing the Union officers in the state to recall some six thousand men from the Georgia campaign.

Price's Confederate force of twelve thousand mounted and unmounted infantry entered the state in Riply County in the southeast in September, 1864, intent upon an attack on St. Louis. A force of approximately twelve hundred federal troops under General Thomas Ewing defending Fort Davidson at Pilot Knob inflicted over one thousand rebel casualties before retreating toward St. Louis.

Price abandoned his planned attack on St. Louis but marched north toward Jefferson City, burning bridges and ripping up railroad tracks on his way. Skirting Jefferson City, where a large Union force had gathered, Price fought skirmishes at Glasgow and Lexington as he marched westward. Vicious rebel guerrilla groups, such as those of Quantrill, "Bloody Bill" Anderson, and George Todd, plundered the countryside.

The key battle of the campaign, sometimes called the "Gettysburg of the West," occurred at Westport (present-day Kansas City) on October 21–23, 1864. At Westport, Price fought one army led by Major General Samuel R. Curtis and another commanded by General Alfred S. Pleasonton. Faced by superior forces, Price broke away, marching south into the safety of southern Arkansas. Price's army had marched 1,434 miles in the campaign and had fought forty-three skirmishes.

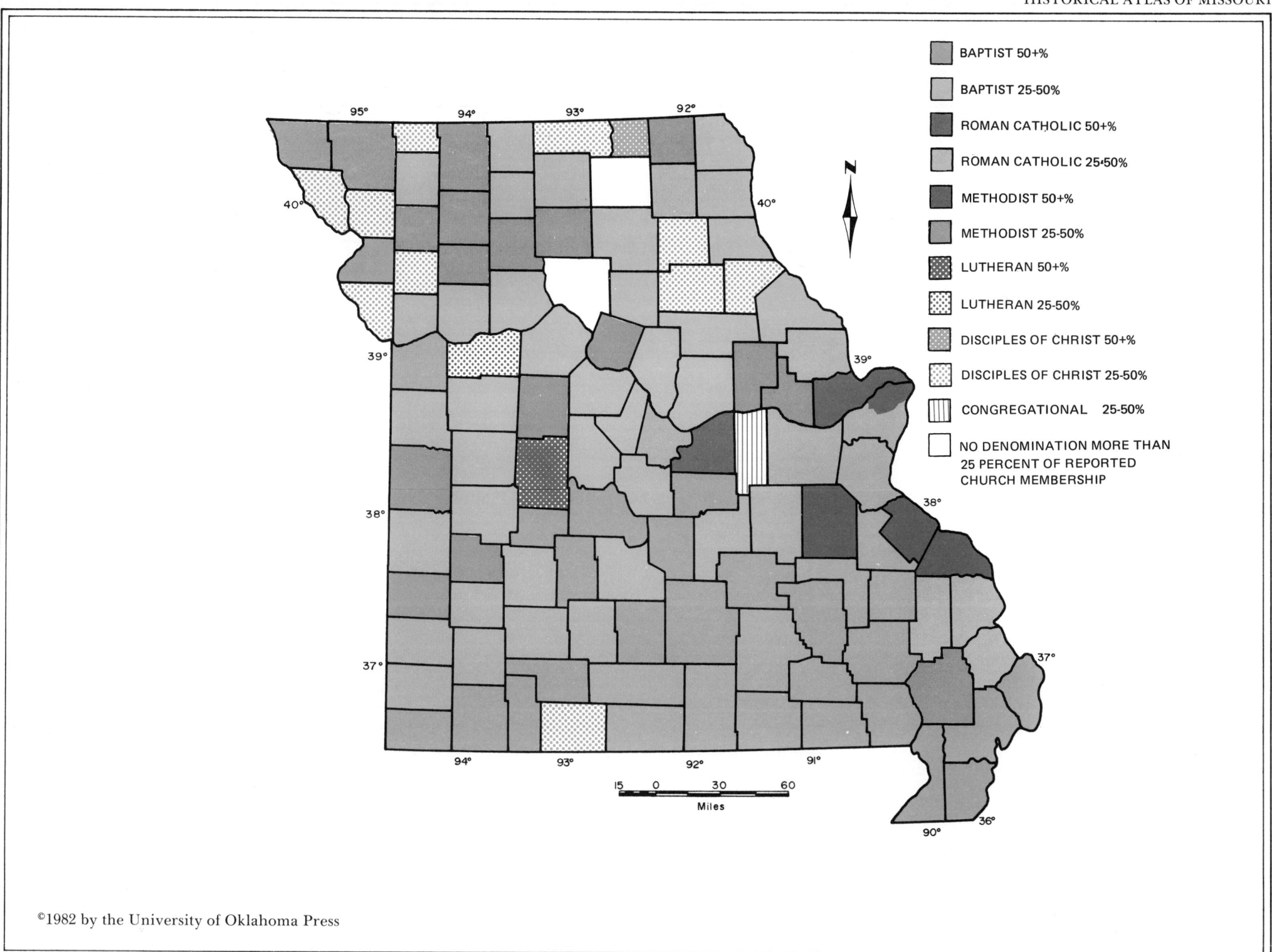

BAPTIST 50+%

BAPTIST 25-50%

ROMAN CATHOLIC 50+%

ROMAN CATHOLIC 25-50%

METHODIST 50+%

METHODIST 25-50%

LUTHERAN 50+%

LUTHERAN 25-50%

DISCIPLES OF CHRIST 50+%

DISCIPLES OF CHRIST 25-50%

CONGREGATIONAL   25-50%

NO DENOMINATION MORE THAN
25 PERCENT OF REPORTED
CHURCH MEMBERSHIP

The principal source of data on religious denominations is the National Council of Churches. The most recent study conducted by the council is based upon 1952 data collected for 114 religious bodies in the coterminous states. The reporting organizations accounted for 49 per cent of the total population of the United States, whereas the total church membership is estimated to be about 60 per cent of the population.

A basic characteristic of religious affiliation in Missouri is the multiplicity of denominations, which is matched by the heterogeneity of religious composition within smaller areas. The four leading denominations in the country by membership—Roman Catholic, Baptist, Methodist, and Lutheran—are well represented in Missouri, as are most other denominations of lesser membership.

Next to Methodists, Roman Catholics are the most ubiquitous of religious groups in the United States. Although more heavily concentrated in the northeastern quarter of the nation than elsewhere, they are well represented in all states. In Missouri, Roman Catholic concentrations in Kansas City and St. Louis stand out conspicuously. The influx of Roman Catholics into the state was primarily in response to a growing demand during the nineteenth century for an industrial labor supply which existed primarily in urban areas. This pattern of concentration in cities is characteristic of Roman Catholics. Seventy-five per cent of all Roman Catholics in the United States are urban. A second cluster of Roman Catholics in Missouri originated with pioneer settlement. Those in east central Missouri, south of the Missouri River, trace their origin back to the period of French pioneer settlement. As late as 1925 the use of the French language in some outlying settlements in that area was still being reported.

Methodists are found in Missouri primarily north of the Missouri River, with lesser concentrations in the southeastern and southwestern corners of the state. The growth of both Methodists and Baptists over other Protestant denominations in Missouri was largely a matter of the widespread practice by Baptists and Methodists of converting the unchurched and members of other denominations. Baptists have been the more successful of the two in this venture in Missouri and now dominate, especially in rural areas, most of the state.

Lutherans are the least numerous of the four major U.S. denominations in Missouri. Very few came into Missouri during the period of pioneer settlement. Most went farther north where conditions very similar to those they had left in Europe prevailed. Those who did come into Missouri did not attempt to expand their numbers by the use of conversion.

Two other groups deserve mention, although neither is found in large numbers in Missouri. Jewish communities in the state are restricted primarily to St. Louis and Kansas City. Nationally, 97.5 per cent of the Jewish congregations are located in metropolitan areas, a pattern which carries over into Missouri.

Mormons, a group well represented in Missouri's history, are not a major denomination in Missouri. The main body of the membership of the Church of Jesus Christ of Latter-Day Saints migrated from Missouri and eventually to Utah in the 1840s. There is, however, in the vicinity of Kansas City, a fairly large number of people who belong to the Reorganized Church of Jesus Christ of Latter Day Saints.

Miles

60   30   0   15

30 — 40.0

25 — 29.9

19 — 24.9

13 — 18.9

3 — 12.9 %

N

Over the past forty years, per capita personal income in Missouri grew faster than the nation's. However, the growth was greatest in the counties which include large towns and cities where there are jobs in manufacturing, commerce, and finance.

The lowest rates of family income in 1970 were found in counties in southern Missouri. In seventeen counties in the Ozarks and Southeast Lowlands, more than 25 per cent of families reported incomes under three thousand dollars in 1970. In five other Ozark counties and Pemiscot County in the Bootheel, more than one out of three families had incomes below three thousand dollars. The Ozarks have long been plagued by poverty of agricultural resources and lack of roads and railroads; the counties in the Southeast Lowlands depend heavily on agriculture and have histories of high rates of farm tenancy. Low rates of personal income are also reported in northern Missouri counties. These counties have populations with high median age due to prolonged emigration, and they are mainly agricultural.

It is important to note that in agriculture a certain degree of self-sufficiency combined with payment in kind (such as free rent for agricultural laborers) tend to reduce the reported levels of income. Therefore, counties that rely heavily on agricultural support tend to report more families with low incomes.

60. FAMILIES WITH INCOMES UNDER
THREE THOUSAND DOLLARS

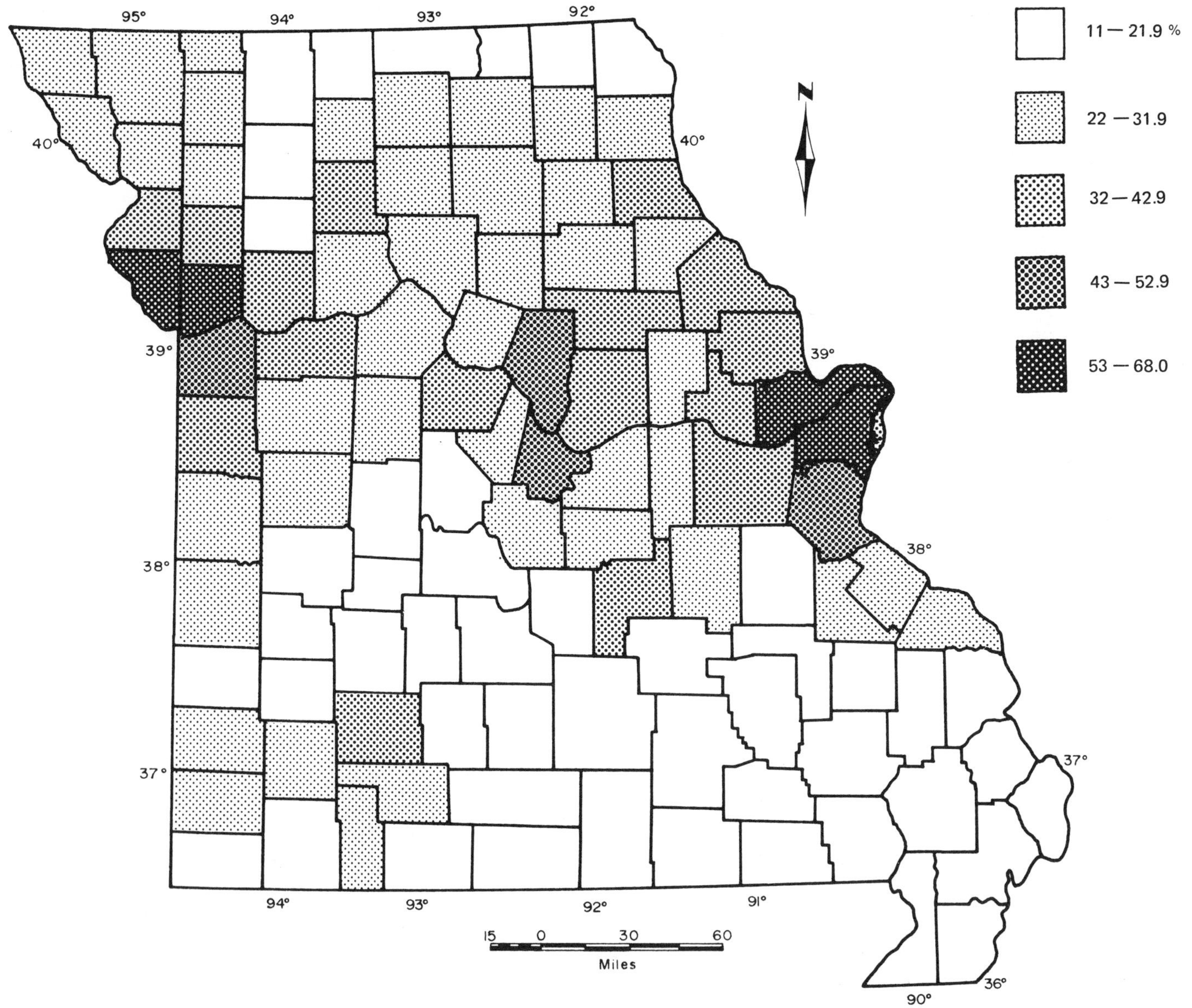

Miles

15   0   30   60

53 — 68.0

43 — 52.9

32 — 42.9

22 — 31.9

11 — 21.9 %

N

The median family income for Missouri in 1970 was $8,908. Median incomes for counties range from $3,973 in Ozark County to $12,372 in St. Louis County.

The percentage of families with incomes over ten thousand dollars is a measure of general affluence and indirect evidence of potential spendable income. There is close geographic re- lationship between income levels and urbanization, commerce, and manufacturing. It is in larger cities that there are oppor- tunities for employment for more than one member of the family. In four counties—Clay, Platte, St. Charles, and St. Louis —more than half the families had over ten thousand dollars in income in 1970.

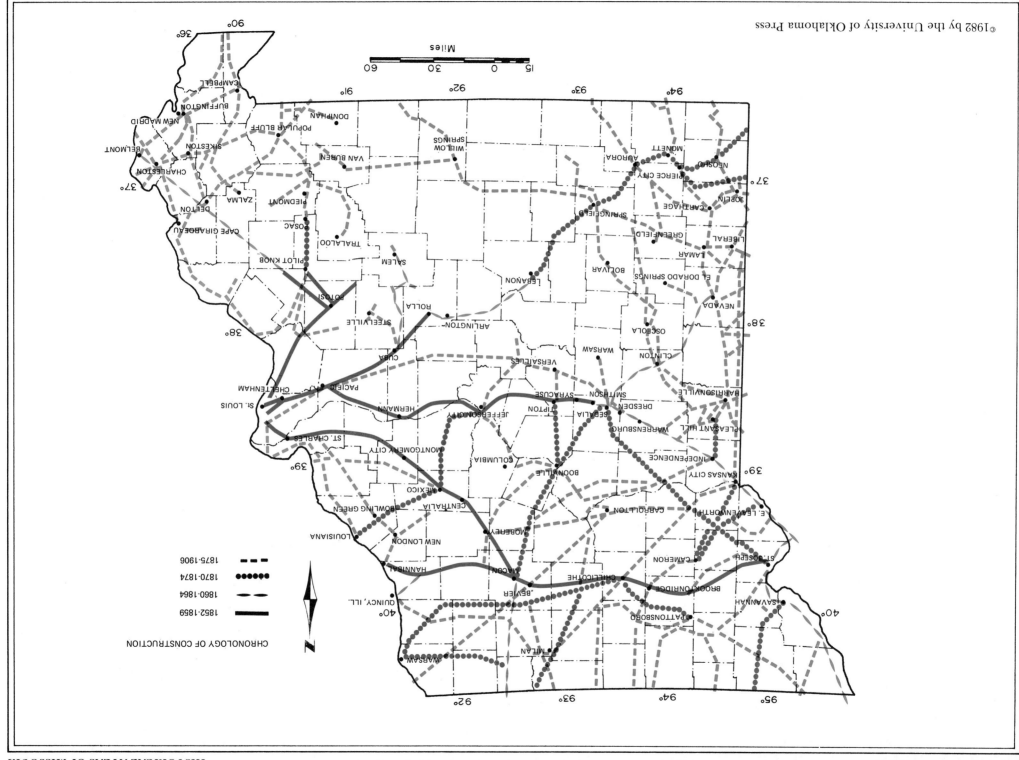

CHRONOLOGY OF CONSTRUCTION

————	1852-1859
– – –	1860-1864
●●●●●	1870-1874
- - - -	1875-1906

N

Miles

60 30 0 15

The historical geography of railroads has long been of interest to students of American development. The importance of railroads in the settlement and development of regions through which they were constructed, in changing the social and economic life of the people in their vicinity, and, often, in altering the political attitudes of the districts which they served can hardly be overestimated. Very often the onset of rail service brought changes in the composition of the population, which in turn brought changes in economy and culture.

The first railroad construction in Missouri was in 1851 in what is St. Louis today. The earliest railroad construction was by the Pacific Railroad westward from St. Louis in the Missouri Valley Transportation Corridor. However, because of better financing and more generous land grants, the Hannibal and St. Joseph Railroad was the first to traverse the state. The Hannibal to St. Joseph link was completed in 1859, but it was not until 1865 that the Pacific Railroad reached Kansas City. By 1870, northern Missouri had been linked with Iowa, and branch and feeder lines were under construction. However, the Ozarks remained largely untouched by railroads except for the Southwest Branch of the Pacific Railroad, which reached Springfield, and the St. Louis and Iron Mountain spur line to mining districts in the vicinity of Pilot Knob.

Major extensions of main lines after 1870 include the Springfield-to-Memphis line of the Kansas City, Springfield, and Memphis Railroad in 1881–83 and the railroad system developed around the turn of the century by Louis Houck in southeastern Missouri which included a network of railroads in the eastern Ozarks and Southeast Lowlands connecting to St. Louis by way of Cape Girardeau.

Miles

60 30 0 15

ST. L. & H. — ST. LOUIS AND HANNIBAL
I. & ST. L. — IOWA AND ST. LOUIS
C. B. & Q. — CHICAGO, BURLINGTON AND QUINCY
S.H.C. & RY — SHELBY COUNTY RY CO.
R. L. & N. — ROCKPORT, LANGDON & NORTHERN
MO. N. ARK. — MISSOURI AND NORTH ARKANSAS
M.V. — MISSISSIPPI VALLEY
M. K. & T. — MISSOURI, KANSAS AND TEXAS
WAB. — WABASH
C. R.I. & P. — CHICAGO, ROCK ISLAND AND PACIFIC
Q. O. & K.C. — QUINCY, OMAHA AND KANSAS CITY
ST. J. & G.I. — ST. JOSEPH AND GRAND ISLAND
N.G. — NARROW GAGE
C. & A. — CHICAGO AND ALTON
C.G. & C. — CAPE GIRARDEAU AND CHESTER
K.C. C. & S. — KANSAS CITY, CLINTON AND SPRINGFIELD
MO. PAC. — MISSOURI PACIFIC
MO. SOU. — MISSOURI SOUTHERN
ST. L. & S.F. — ST. LOUIS AND SAN FRANCISCO
S. W. & S. — SALEM, WINONA AND SOUTHERN
SLIG EAST — SLIGO EASTERN
W. G. & STL — WILLIAMSVILLE, GREENVILLE AND ST. LOUIS
M. R. & B. T. — MISSISSIPPI RIVER & BONNE TERRE
ST. L. MT. & S. — ST. LOUIS, IRON MOUNTAIN & SOUTHERN

Much of the economic and cultural geography of Missouri is closely related to the development of a railroad network. Railroads were first built to tap the mineral and timber resources and to supply and haul products from farms. After about 1830 the people of the United States were railroad-minded; they thought and acted in terms of railroads. Politics, legislation, newspapers, public meetings, industry, and invention were made to serve this new means of transportation. Nearly every town had aspirations of being connected to distant markets by railroads, and ambitious schemes were hatched in nearly every community. Railroad construction, stimulated by federal grants and local financial support, progressed at a furious pace.

Around the turn of the century there came the recognition that not all of the lines that had been built could be operated at a profit. The sheer complexity of management and transfer of goods worked toward consolidation of the numerous short lines. Since 1910 there has been considerable reduction of railroad mileage in the state. The map shows the railroad lines that have been abandoned in the period from 1910 to 1970. They tend to be of three types. The first type is lines that ran parallel to other lines and competed for traffic. The Kansas City, Clinton, and Springfield is an example. It was abandoned after it was purchased by the Frisco System, which already had a line between Springfield and Kansas City. The second type is short spur lines that were designed to serve a major town, such as the Missouri Pacific branch line from Crane to Springfield, and the third is short lines built by mining and lumber companies to exploit raw materials. There are many abandoned lines in the Ozarks that were built to serve mines or to serve small sawmill towns. For example, several spur lines in Phelps, Crawford, and Dent counties were built to tap iron ore deposits and were abandoned when the ores were depleted or when the charcoal-fueled furnaces shut down. The Missouri Southern Railroad was an extensive logging railroad built between 1886 and 1910. By 1930 the timber was cut out, and ten years later the system was completely abandoned.

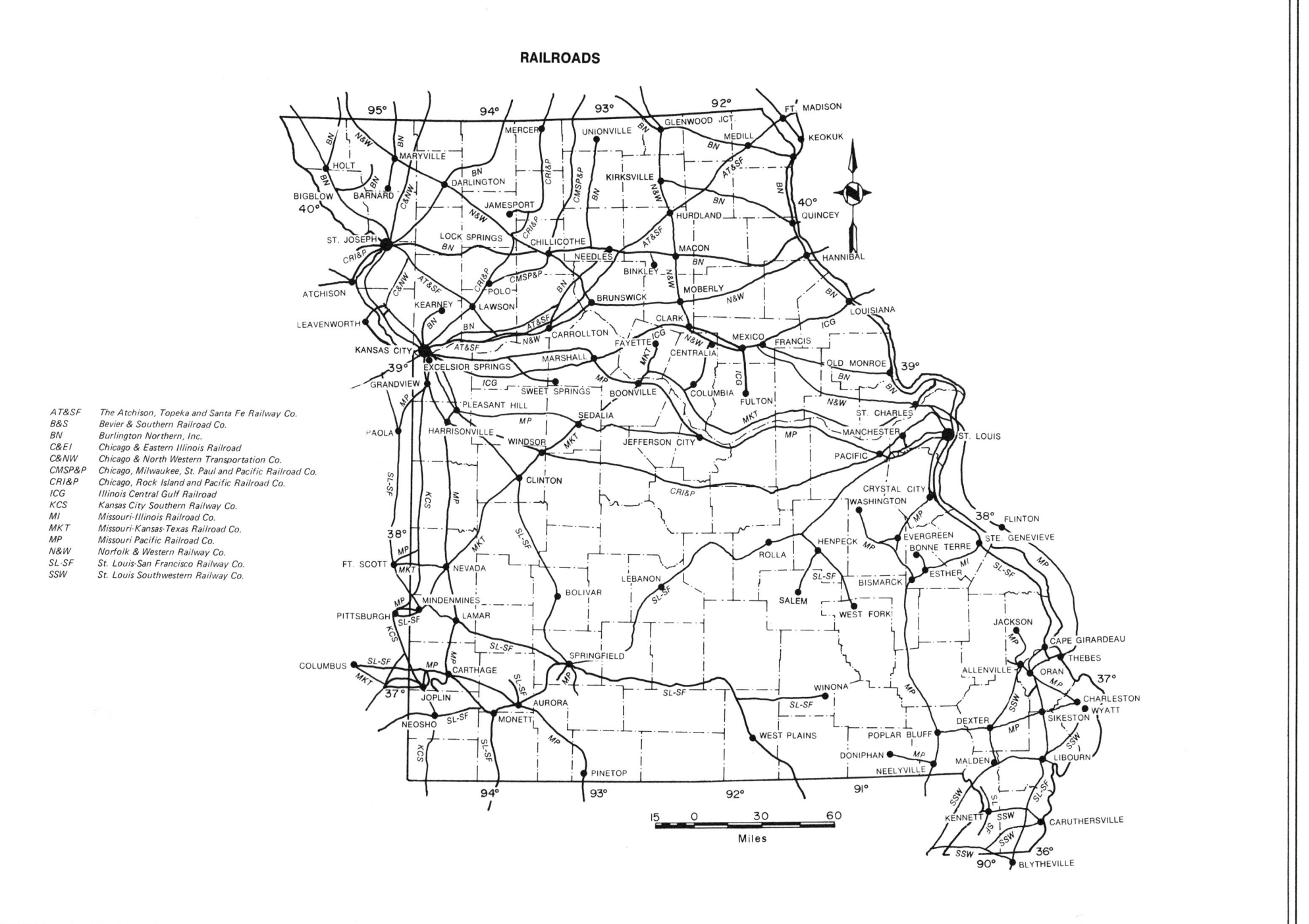

RAILROADS

AT&SF   The Atchison, Topeka and Santa Fe Railway Co.
B&S   Bevier & Southern Railroad Co.
BN   Burlington Northern, Inc.
C&EI   Chicago & Eastern Illinois Railroad
C&NW   Chicago & North Western Transportation Co.
CMSP&P   Chicago, Milwaukee, St. Paul and Pacific Railroad Co.
CRI&P   Chicago, Rock Island and Pacific Railroad Co.
ICG   Illinois Central Gulf Railroad
KCS   Kansas City Southern Railway Co.
MI   Missouri-Illinois Railroad Co.
MKT   Missouri-Kansas-Texas Railroad Co.
MP   Missouri Pacific Railroad Co.
N&W   Norfolk & Western Railway Co.
SL-SF   St. Louis-San Francisco Railway Co.
SSW   St. Louis Southwestern Railway Co.

Miles
15 0   30   60

Today in Missouri there are approximately 6,700 miles of railroad track operated by twelve Class I railroad companies. Class I railroads are defined as those with over ten million dollars in revenue per year. There are also nine switching and terminal companies maintaining 308 miles of rail line within the state. Five additional Class I railroads enter the state solely to serve large metropolitan areas. Three of the twelve rail carriers, Burlington Northern, Missouri Pacific, and the St. Louis–San Francisco Railroad, account for 3,825 miles, or almost 57 per cent of the total railroad mileage within the state.

The sixty-seven hundred miles of Class I rail lines include fourteen hundred miles with low weight-carrying capacity. Because of physical limitations, this low-capacity trackage will not withstand heavy loads such as the one-hundred-ton hopper cars now being used with increasing frequency to haul volume shipments of bulk farm commodities.

Food and farm products account for more than 35 per cent of the total freight hauled by Missouri railroads. This proportion emphasizes Missouri's role as a major producer and processor of agricultural products. Other important rail cargoes originating in the state include stone and refractory products, metallic ores, nonmetallic minerals, chemical products, transportation equipment, and primary metal products. Nearly one-third of the rail shipments terminating in Missouri are coal, mainly from the Illinois and Kansas fields. Other important in-state shipments include food and farm products, chemical products, stone and refractory products, transportation of equipment, metallic ores, pulp and paper products, nonmetallic minerals, lumber and wood products, and primary metal products.

Truck trailers or containers mounted on flat cars, commonly referred to as "piggyback" cars, have become increasingly important in the last decade, generally for long-haul freight movements.

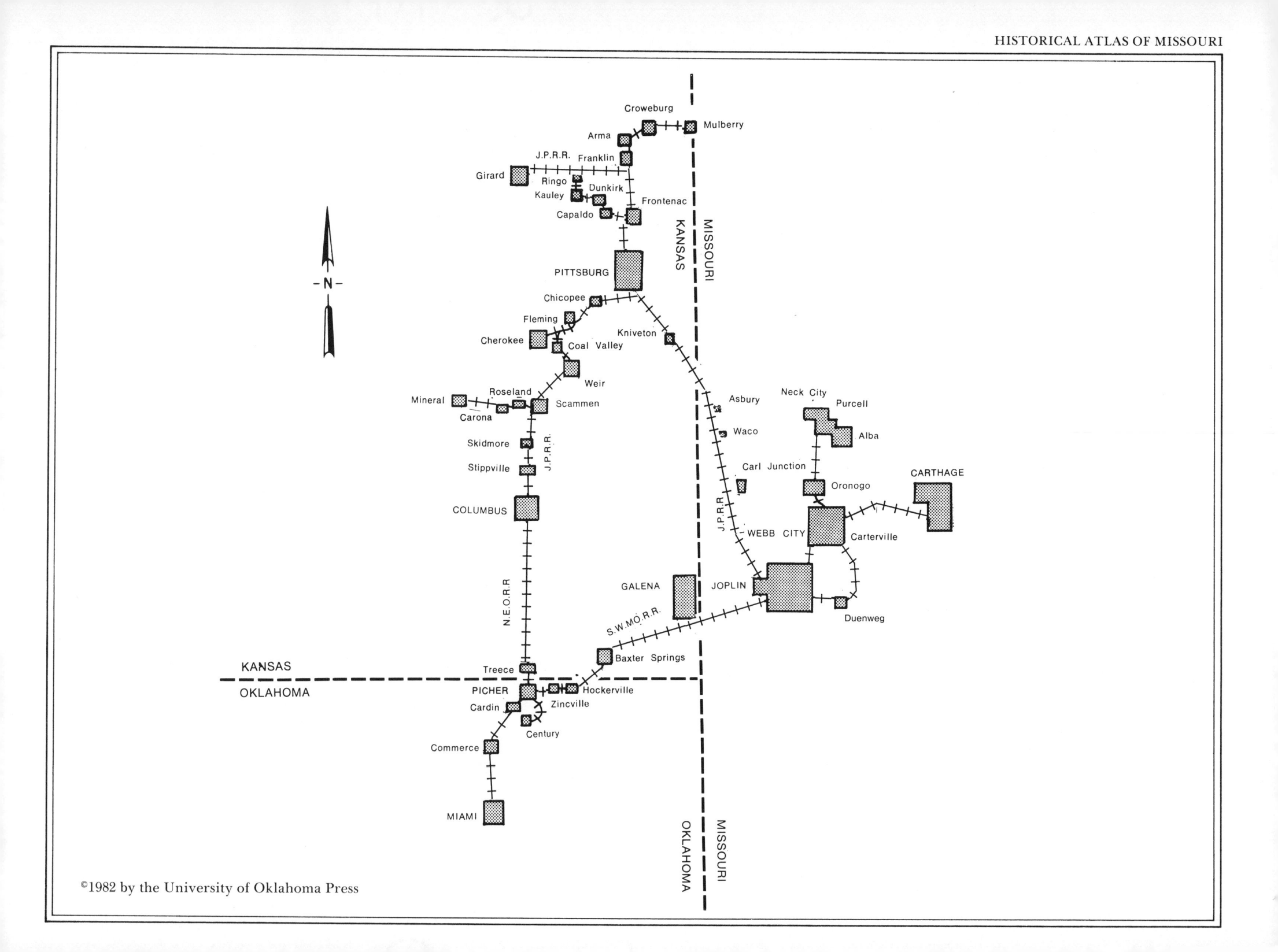

- N -

Croweburg
Mulberry
Arma
J.P.R.R. Franklin
Girard
Ringo
Kauley Dunkirk
Capaldo
Frontenac

KANSAS
MISSOURI

PITTSBURG

Chicopee
Fleming
Cherokee
Coal Valley
Kniveton
Weir
Mineral
Roseland
Scammen
Carona

Asbury
Neck City
Purcell
Waco
Alba

Skidmore
J.P.R.R.
Stippville

Carl Junction

CARTHAGE

COLUMBUS

Oronogo

J.P.R.R.
WEBB CITY
Carterville

GALENA
JOPLIN

N.E.O.R.R.

Duenweg

S.W.MO.R.R.

KANSAS
OKLAHOMA

Treece
Baxter Springs

PICHER
Cardin
Hockerville
Zincville

Century
Commerce

MIAMI

OKLAHOMA
MISSOURI

©1982 by the University of Oklahoma Press

One of the largest interurban electric trolley systems in the United States was constructed in the lead, zinc, and coal mining districts of southwestern Missouri, southeastern Kansas and northeastern Oklahoma during the span of two generations about the turn of the century. The lines were built to serve the numerous mining camps that grew up in the lead and zinc fields of Missouri, Kansas, and Oklahoma and the coal mining towns adjacent to parts of southeastern Kansas. The numerous horse car and electric trolley companies were eventually consolidated into three main interurban railway companies: the Southwest Missouri Railroad, the Northeast Oklahoma Railroad, and the Joplin and Pittsburg Railway Company.

The Southwest Missouri Electric Railway Company, the original name of the Southwest Missouri Railroad, was the brain child of Alfred H. Rogers of Springfield. Rogers was the line's promoter and its head well over a quarter of a century, and the system continued to be affectionately known as the "Rogers Line" long after his death. The system began as a two-mile mule-car line connecting Webb City with its neighbor to the east, Carterville. In 1893, Rogers organized the Southwest Missouri Electric Railway with the help of Pennsylvania capital. Between 1893 and 1929 the electric system was extended to communities in Jasper County, Missouri; Cherokee County, Kansas; and Ottawa County, Oklahoma. The Southwest Missouri Railroad linked Joplin with towns to the northeast—Webb City, Carterville, Carthage, Duenweg, Oronogo, Neck City, Alba, and Purcell—and to the southwest—Galena and Baxter Springs in Kansas and Hockerville, Zincville, and Picher in Oklahoma. The final electric trolley runs of the Southwest Missouri Railroad were made between Galena and Picher on Saturday, May 7, 1938.

It took twenty years to build the Joplin and Pittsburg Railway Company from its first predecessors to the finished product. The original unit, a streetcar line in Pittsburg, founded in 1890, was eventually extended through track construction and purchase of other trolley companies so that the network extended north to Mulberry, Franklin, and Gerard; southeast to Joplin; and southwest to Weir, Mineral, and Columbus. The final run on the Joplin and Pittsburg Railway Company lines was on Saturday, February 27, 1954, when a gasoline-propelled locomotive made its final stop at Pittsburg.

The Northeast Oklahoma Railroad was founded in 1919 at a time when the lead and zinc deposits of Missouri were being depleted and the mines of Oklahoma and Kansas were increasing in production. The company began in 1908 as a steam railroad, the Oklahoma, Kansas, and Missouri Interurban Railway Company. Eventually the line was extended north from Miami to Picher, Columbus, Mineral, Cherokee, Weir, and Chicopee. Another line between Columbus and Miami passed through Baxter Springs. Gradually, as passenger traffic declined because of increased use of motor vehicles and the Northeast Oklahoma Railroad depended increasingly on revenues from the hauling of ore, the system became known as the "Ore Line." Its final year of operation was 1963.

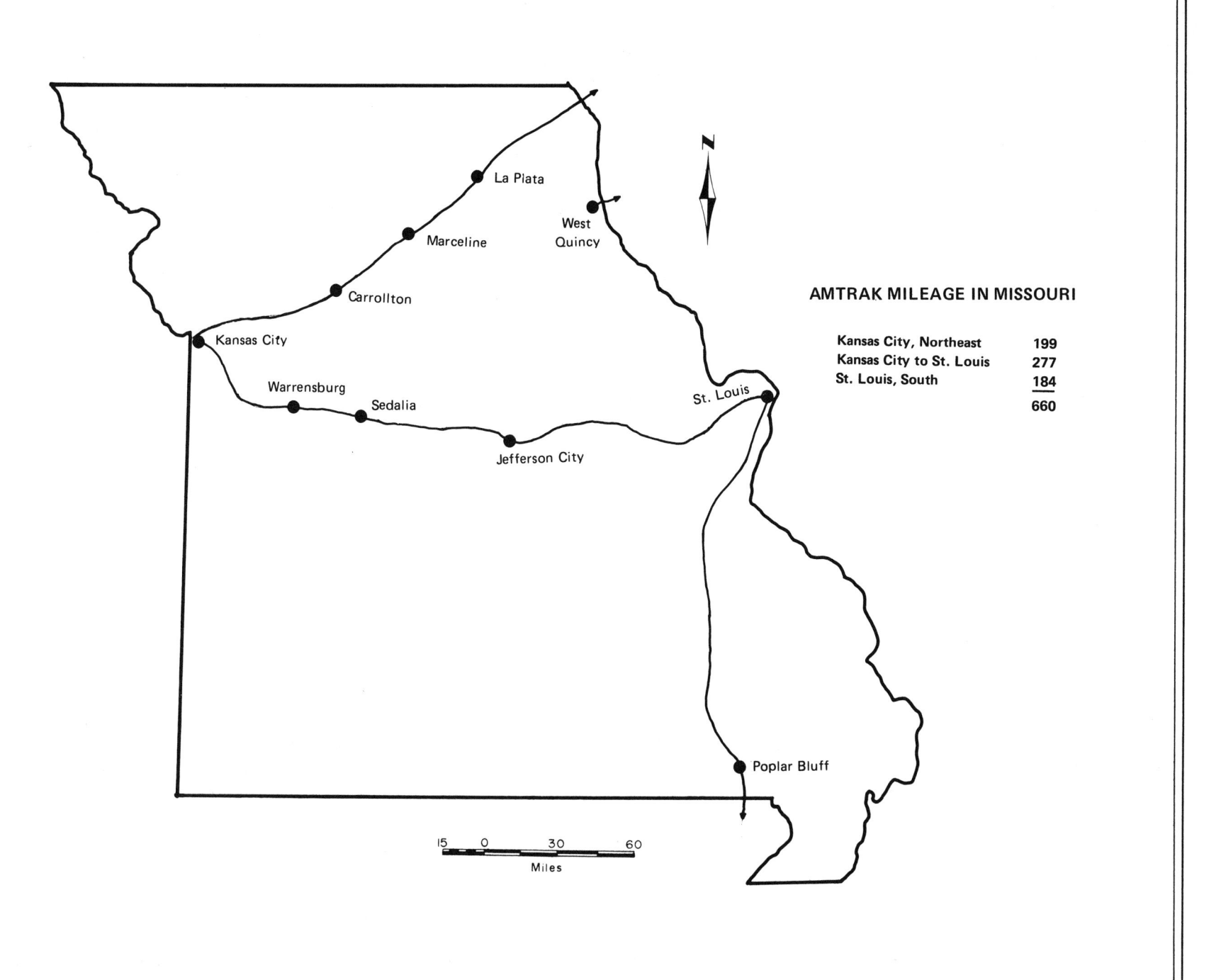

La Piata

West
Quincy

Marceline

Carrollton

Kansas City

Warrensburg

Sedalia

Jefferson City

St. Louis

AMTRAK MILEAGE IN MISSOURI

Kansas City, Northeast	199
Kansas City to St. Louis	277
St. Louis, South	184
	660

Poplar Bluff

15 0 30 60
Miles

66. PASSENGER RAIL TRANSPORTATION (AMTRACK)

Passenger transportation by rail has undergone a transformation in this country during the past half-century. At one time the most prevalent form of personal transportation over long distances, the railroads have given ground to other modes until today the automobile is the dominant personal transporter and the airlines are the leading public carriers of passengers.

In an attempt to revitalize passenger transportation by rail throughout the United States, the National Railroad Passenger Corporation (AMTRAK) was formed in 1970 and began operating trains in May, 1971. The purpose of this reorganization was to combine the passenger services of many separate rail lines into a simplified and federally financed national network. In the process, thousands of rail stations were closed, and millions of citizens found themselves more than fifty miles from AMTRAK passenger depots.

Missouri had a total of 660 miles of AMTRAK routes in 1976. These routes connected Chicago and Kansas City; Los Angeles and Kansas City; Houston and Kansas City; Chicago and West Quincy, Missouri; St. Louis and Kansas City; and St. Louis and Little Rock. Intermediate passenger stops were made at La Plata, Marceline, Carrollton, Warrensburg, Sedalia, Jefferson City, Kirkwood, and Poplar Bluff.

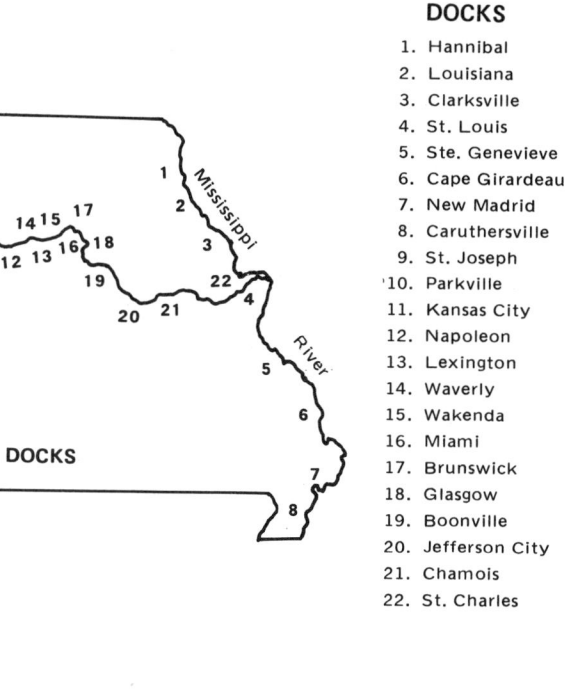

DOCKS

1. Hannibal
2. Louisiana
3. Clarksville
4. St. Louis
5. Ste. Genevieve
6. Cape Girardeau
7. New Madrid
8. Caruthersville
9. St. Joseph
'10. Parkville
11. Kansas City
12. Napoleon
13. Lexington
14. Waverly
15. Wakenda
16. Miami
17. Brunswick
18. Glasgow
19. Boonville
20. Jefferson City
21. Chamois
22. St. Charles

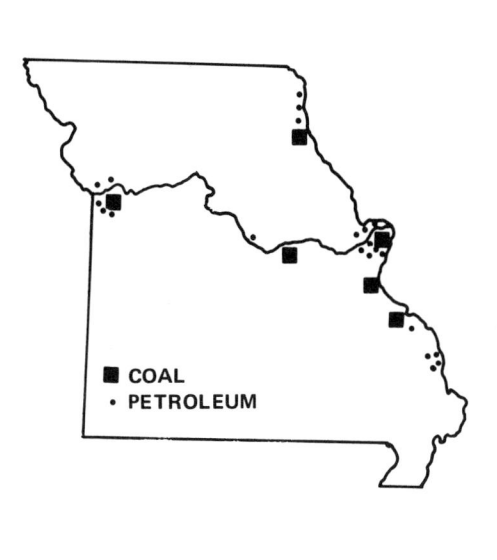

COAL
PETROLEUM

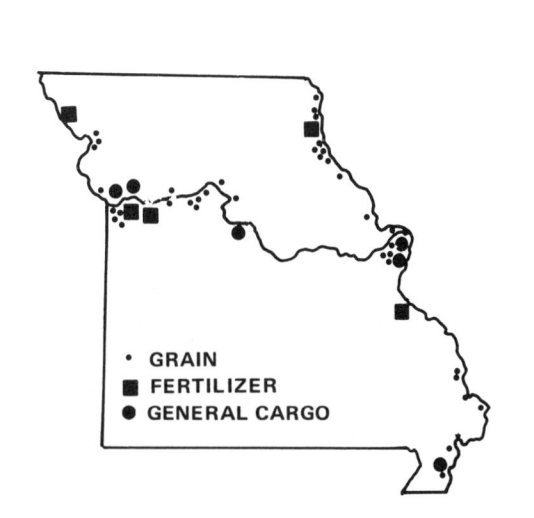

GRAIN
FERTILIZER
GENERAL CARGO

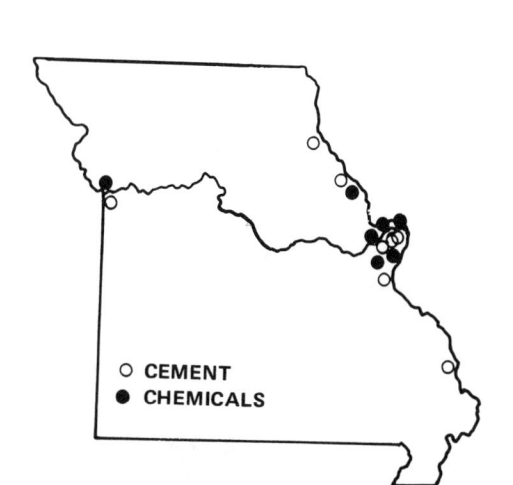

○ CEMENT
● CHEMICALS

A total of 25,380 miles of improved and unimproved waterways in the United States are usable for commercial navigation. The Mississippi River system includes 8,538 miles or about one-fourth of the nation's total inland waterways.

Geographically, the state of Missouri occupies a key position in the Mississippi River system. As a result of this strategic position, a sizable portion of the state's economy is related to or dependent upon water transportation. A 1972 U.S. Department of Commerce survey showed twenty-seven hundred people employed directly by the water transportation industry in Missouri.

The U.S. Army Corps of Engineers plays the major role in the planning of inland waterway transportation. Since 1824, at the direction of Congress, the Corps of Engineers has been responsible for planning, constructing, operating, and maintaining improvements on the nation's waterways. The U.S. Coast Guard is responsible for safety and navigation regulations.

Modern navigation is by diesel-powered towboats, which push instead of pull as their name implies. They are built to various specifications from one thousand to ten thousand horsepower. Several types of barges are used for handling particular types of commodities. Covered dry-cargo barges are built in three basic sizes: one-thousand-, fifteen-hundred-, and three-thousand-ton capacities.

The Mississippi River has an improved nine-foot channel throughout its course in Missouri. It is open to navigation from St. Louis to New Orleans for twelve months of the year and on the upper portion from early March to mid-December. Navigation to Chicago by way of the Illinois River is open the full year. The Missouri River has a seven-and-one-half-foot channel and is normally open to navigation from late March to the end of November.

There are ten common-carrier barge lines serving Missouri. St. Louis is the largest river port, with two public docks and thirty-seven private docks, while Kansas City has nineteen private docks. Other important river ports include Cape Girardeau (twelve docks), Caruthersville (eleven docks), New Madrid (five docks), and Hannibal (five docks).

More and more businesses are discovering that when the element of speed is removed from transportation needs, commodities and products can be moved much less expensively by water. The coal and steel industries have particularly profited from cheap water transportation.

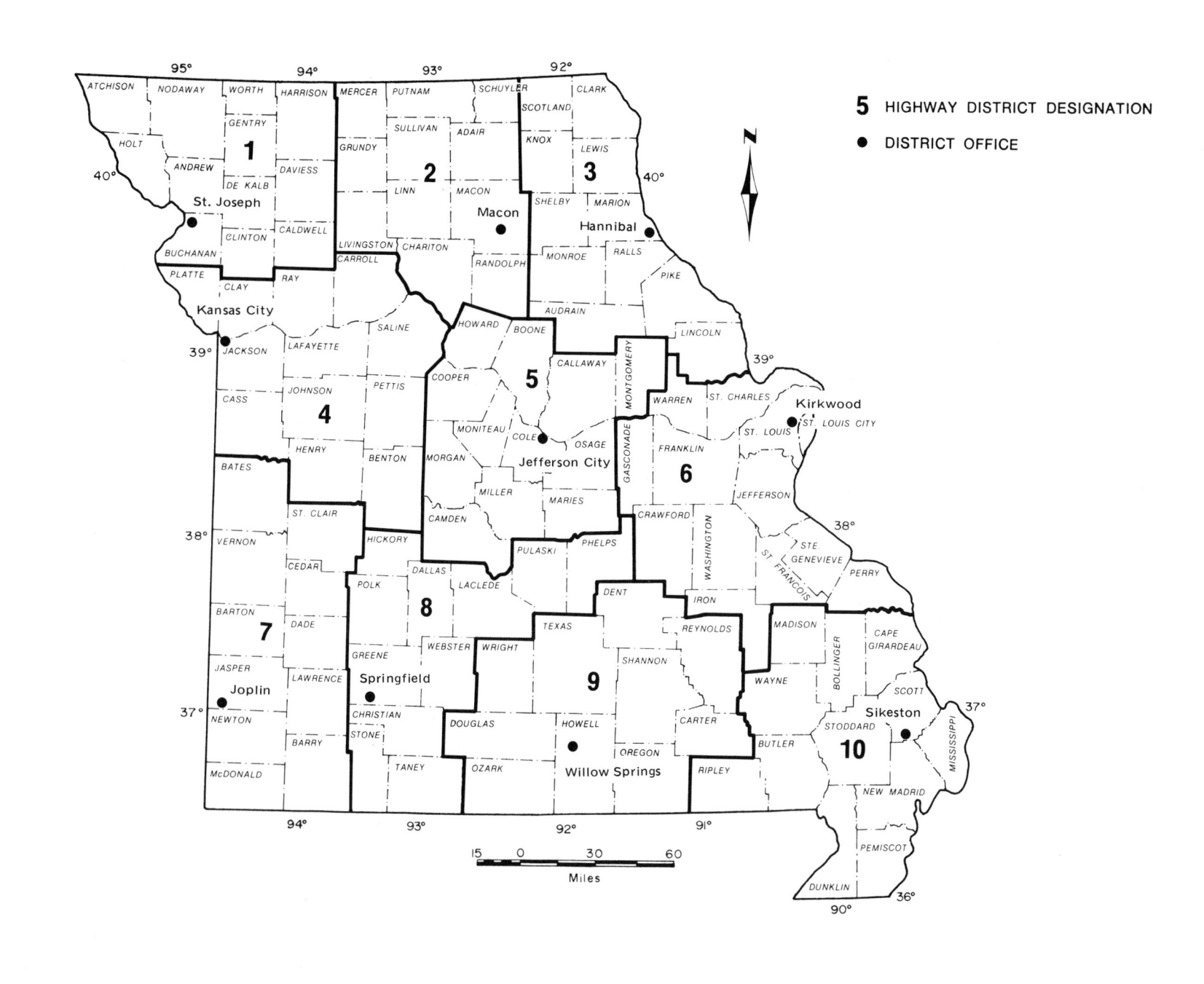

5 HIGHWAY DISTRICT DESIGNATION

● DISTRICT OFFICE

The Missouri State Highway Commission was created in 1921 by legislation which empowered the commission to locate, design, construct, and maintain a state highway system which then comprised about seventy-five hundred miles of roads. The new Constitution of 1945 provided that all highway user taxes, less cost of collection, would be used for the highways of the state. In 1965 the legislature increased the membership of the highway commission from four to six.

By 1976 the highway commission employed about sixty-six hundred people engaged in administration, planning, construction, and maintenance. The state is divided into ten geographic areas, or districts, each of which is headed by a district engineer. The boundaries of the districts are shown on the map.

In addition to the revenues received from road use taxes (licenses), the commission has at its disposal revenues generated by the state's seven-cents motor fuel tax, less 5 per cent that is distributed to counties and 15 per cent distributed to cities. Another program in which the highway commission is involved entails the distribution of approximately five million dollars of off-system federal funds to the counties for capital improvements.

The January 1, 1976, inventory of state-administered highways totaled 32,065 miles, broken down as follows:

System	Miles	Percentage of Total
Interstate	1,033	3.2
Primary	6,764	21.1
Supplementary	24,268	75.7

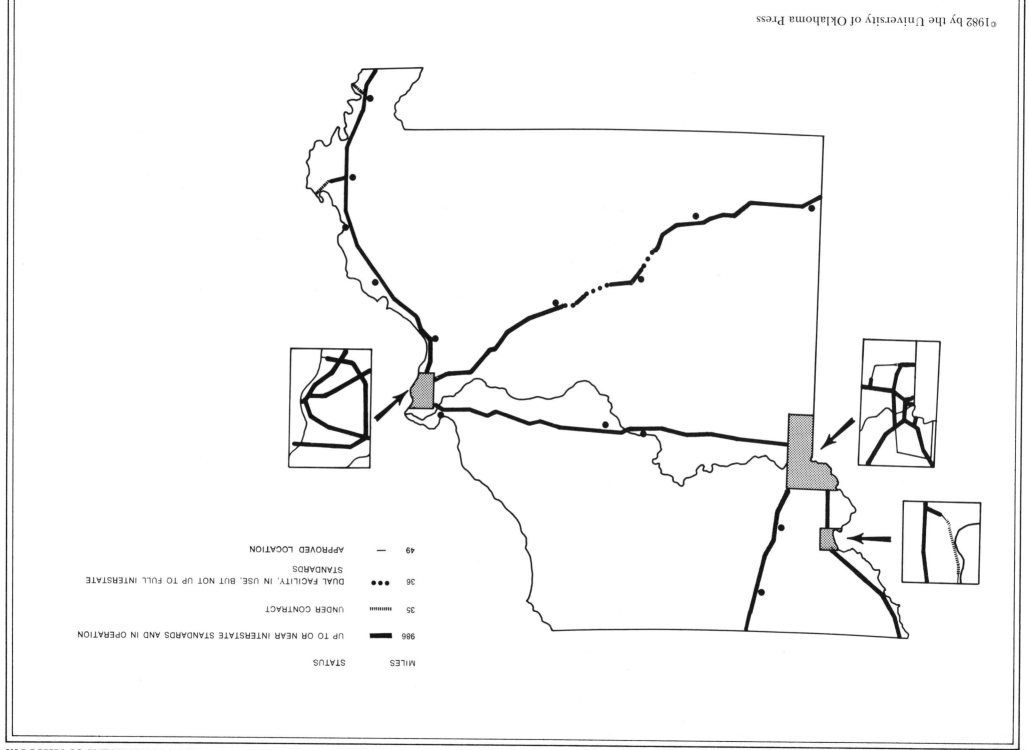

MILES   STATUS

986 ——— UP TO OR NEAR INTERSTATE STANDARDS AND IN OPERATION

35 ⊔⊔⊔⊔ UNDER CONTRACT

36 ••• DUAL FACILITY, IN USE, BUT NOT UP TO FULL INTERSTATE
STANDARDS

49 — APPROVED LOCATION

The 117,000 miles of roads, streets, and highways link Missouri's cities, farms, and industries and fulfill essential personal and freight transportation requirements. Roads and highways have helped shape the state's social and economic institutions by providing a transportation system fundamental to Missouri's growth and vitality. Needless to say, the roads and highways have played a paramount role in shaping human and cultural geographic patterns within the state.

The Interstate Highway System, first authorized during the Eisenhower administration as a comprehensive national system of interstate and defense highways exceeding forty-two thousand total miles, is now authorized for funding and construction into the 1990s. Constructed as modern freeways, the interstate highways connect most cities of greater than fifty thousand population.

The interstate highways in Missouri maintain a pivotal position within the national transportation system. Missouri's interstate highways focus on St. Louis and Kansas City. The greatest volume of vehicular traffic is on Interstate 70 between Kansas City and St. Louis. Interstate 29 links Kansas City with cities northward in the Missouri Valley, while Interstate 35 connects northeastward to Des Moines and southwestward to Kansas and Oklahoma cities. Interstate 55 links St. Louis with Chicago and with Memphis and New Orleans. Interstate 44 links St. Louis with Springfield, Joplin, and the Will Rogers Turnpike in Oklahoma.

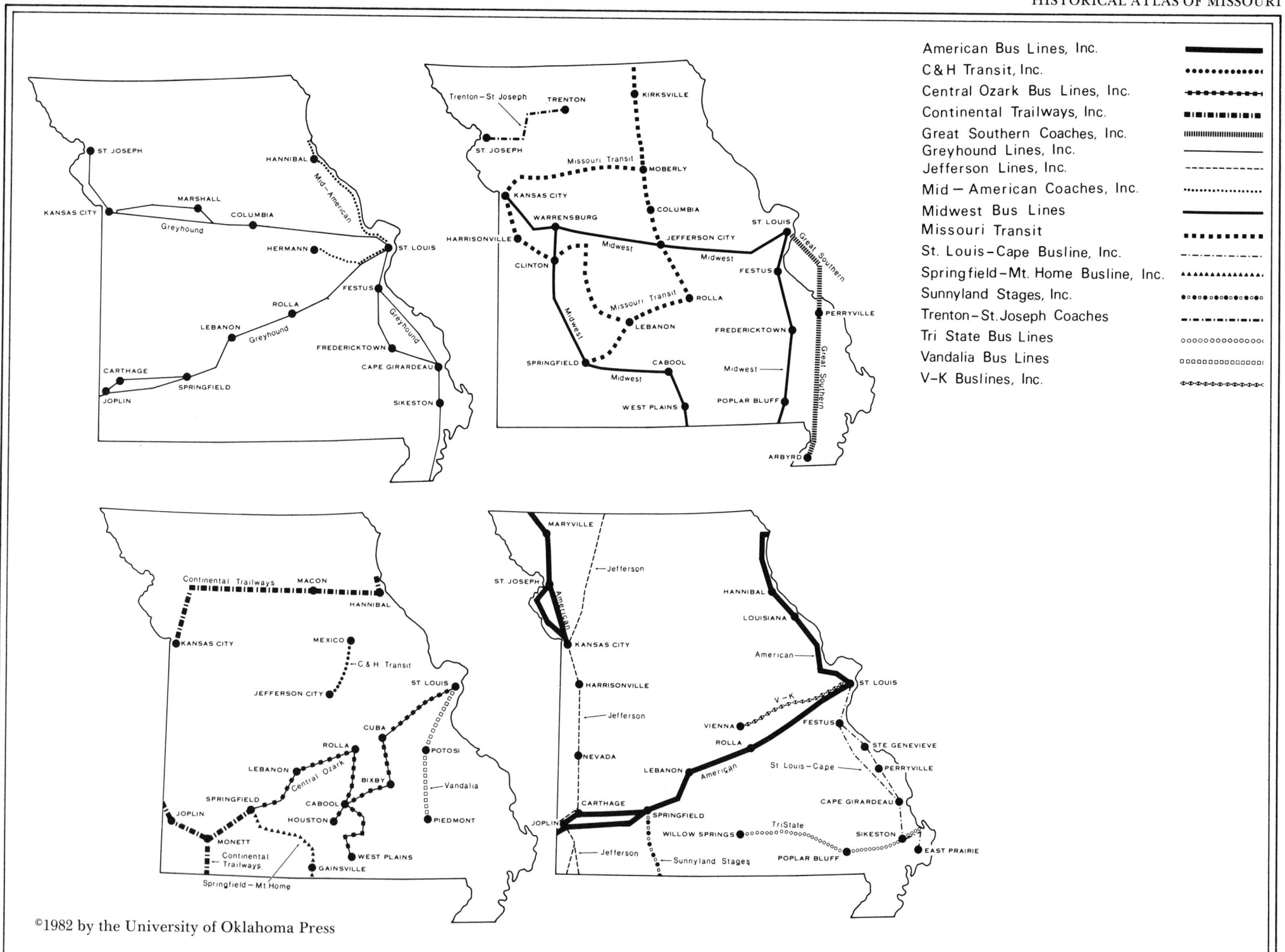

American Bus Lines, Inc.
C & H Transit, Inc.
Central Ozark Bus Lines, Inc.
Continental Trailways, Inc.
Great Southern Coaches, Inc.
Greyhound Lines, Inc.
Jefferson Lines, Inc.
Mid — American Coaches, Inc.
Midwest Bus Lines
Missouri Transit
St. Louis—Cape Busline, Inc.
Springfield—Mt. Home Busline, Inc.
Sunnyland Stages, Inc.
Trenton—St. Joseph Coaches
Tri State Bus Lines
Vandalia Bus Lines
V-K Buslines, Inc.

Intercity scheduled buses provide an essential service to Missouri towns and cities. Often buses are the only public transportation service to small cities and rural areas. Low-income groups and the elderly rely on this mode of travel for social, recreational, and business purposes.

While bus transportation is of critical importance to many Missourians, the number of certified bus lines has declined over the past decade. The total number of intra- and interstate bus lines serving Missouri declined from 52 in 1967 to 39 in 1975. In 1950 the Public Service Commission reported 117 bus lines operating in the state. Recent data indicate that the trend toward reduction in intercity bus operations may have stabilized. The size of the bus operating companies, measured in revenues and route mileage, is indeed variable. The largest company is Greyhound Lines Inc., with $9,410,649 in passenger revenue and operating over 10,278,864 miles in 1974. Several small companies receive less than $50,000 in revenues annually and have an aggregate distance traveled of less than 50,000 miles.

While costs per mile may be lower for the smaller companies serving rural areas, these companies have problems attracting sufficient passengers to pay costs and realize a profit. Routing and scheduling of buses in rural areas may be such that service to urban centers involve long waits and poor connections.

Regulation of motor carrier transportation is in the hands of the Interstate Commerce Commission and the Missouri Public Service Commission. Those companies that operate only within the state (intrastate) need obtain authority only from the Missouri commission. Charter coach operation likewise may be both interstate and intrastate and, if interstate, requires authority from both commissions.

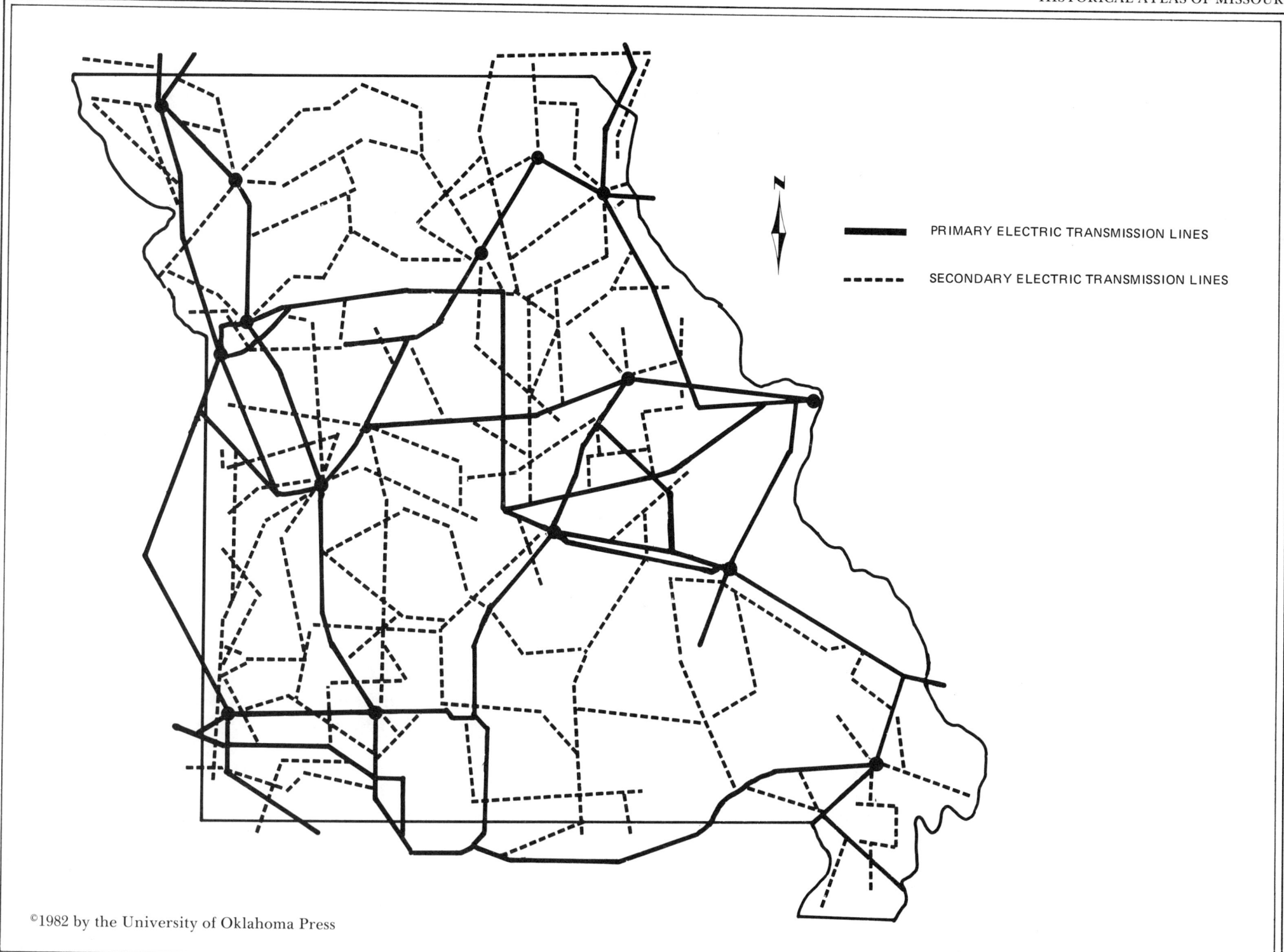

PRIMARY ELECTRIC TRANSMISSION LINES

SECONDARY ELECTRIC TRANSMISSION LINES

71. ELECTRIC POWER LINES

The automobile and electric service, more than any other technological advances, have changed the material level of living and life-style in Missouri over the past half-century. Electricity and electronic controls are revolutionizing all phases and varieties of agriculture and industry with new technological progress, new techniques, and new tools. In the farm shop, with electrical tools, the farmer performs countless improvement projects and maintenance chores easily, quickly, and efficiently. Electrical machinery has worked to eliminate much of the heavy labor in hundreds of industries. It has transformed the Missouri farm home from one of primitive drudgery and inconvenience to a home of modern comfort and ease equal to the most modern suburban home.

The interconnected, individual electric power systems of the rural electric cooperatives and the investor-owned electric power companies connect the sources of electric power in Missouri, the steam electric generating plants and the hydroelectric generating facilities, to the consumers in farms and in the cities. The first thermal electric generating plants were built in Missouri's larger cities in the 1880s, often for the purpose of supplying power for electric trolley lines. Other uses for electric power were soon discovered, and the expansion of electric generating power capacity has progressed rapidly since the turn of the century. Major hydroelectric plants were built by private industry at Powersite Dam in Taney County on the White River in 1914 and at Bagnell on the Osage River in 1937. These two projects resulted from rapidly expanding markets for electrical power in the mining districts and nearby urban centers. Subsequently, beginning in the 1950s, other hydroelectric dams were constructed by the U.S. Army Corps of Engineers. The most unusual hydroelectric station and reservoir is Union Electric Company's Taum Sauk Power Plant on Proffit Mountain in Reynolds County. The forty-acre reservoir, built on top of the mountain, furnishes water for turbines at the base of the mountain. During periods of low electrical consumption, the water is pumped back up the mountain to refill the reservoir.

Today there are some twelve thousand miles of high-voltage transmission lines which form an electrical grid throughout Missouri. Included in the network are primary high-voltage transmission lines, secondary high-voltage transmission lines, interchange points and control stations, and the generating plants, both thermal electric and hydroelectric.

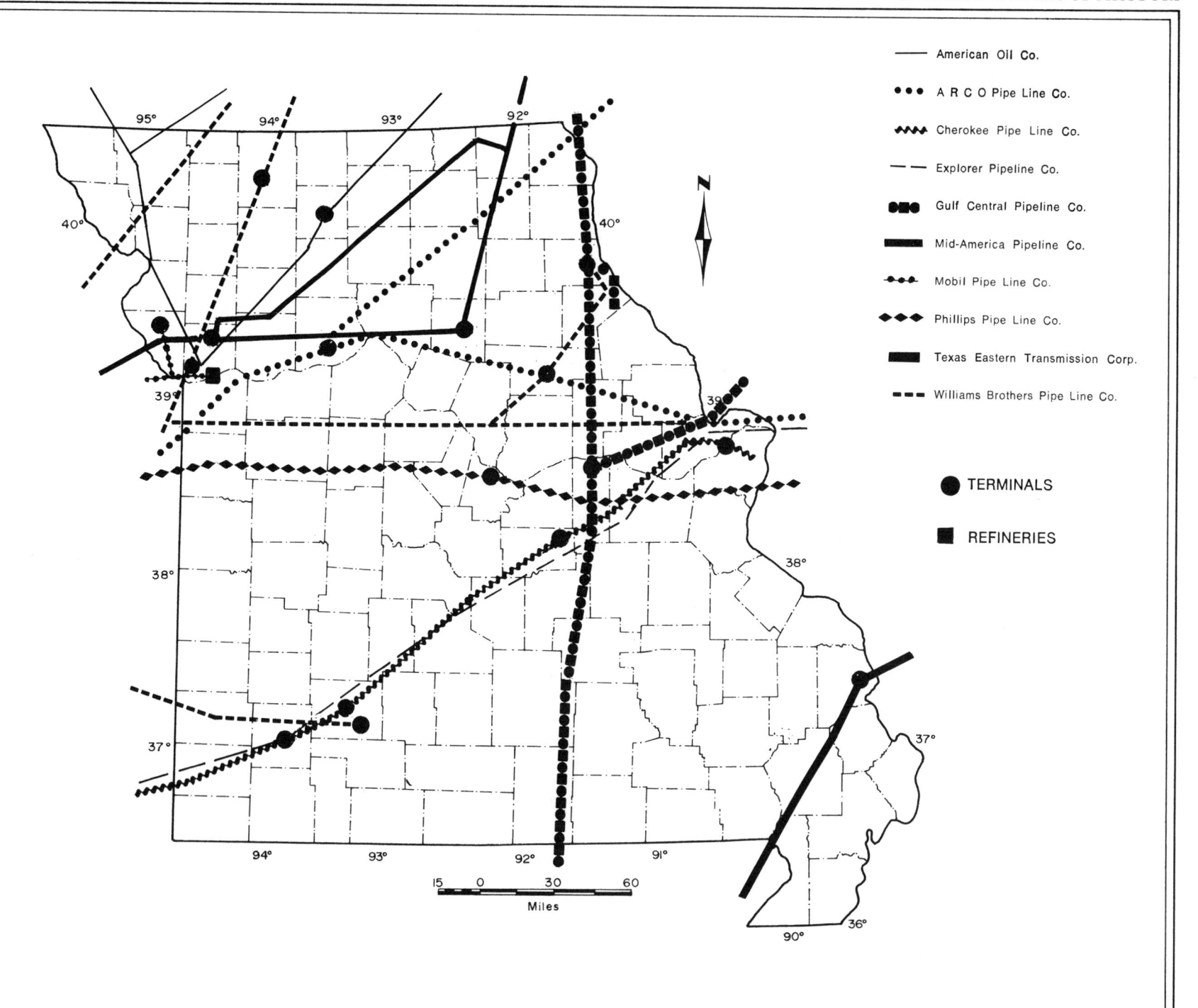

American Oil Co.

A R C O Pipe Line Co.

Cherokee Pipe Line Co.

Explorer Pipeline Co.

Gulf Central Pipeline Co.

Mid-America Pipeline Co.

Mobil Pipe Line Co.

Phillips Pipe Line Co.

Texas Eastern Transmission Corp.

Williams Brothers Pipe Line Co.

● TERMINALS

■ REFINERIES

72. CRUDE OIL PIPELINES

While precise information on individual pipeline company operations in specific states is largely unavailable, some aggregate national figures are released which provide insight into the importance of the industry. Pipelines move the preponderance of petroleum and petroleum products in the United States and, historically, since 1931, pipeline shipment of petroleum products has been increasing relative to other modes of transportation. In 1974, pipelines accounted for 47 per cent of the volume and 60 per cent of the ton-per-mile transportation of petroleum and petroleum products in the United States.

Missouri's geographic location between the petroleum basins of the Midcontinent and Gulf regions and the industrial Midwest insures that several major pipelines pass within the state's boundaries. In 1974 there were seven crude oil pipelines, six of which pass through the state to refineries in the manufacturing belt. One crude oil pipeline terminates at a refinery located at Sugar Creek, on the eastern outskirts of Kansas City, Missouri. In all, there are 2,130 miles of crude oil pipeline in Missouri.

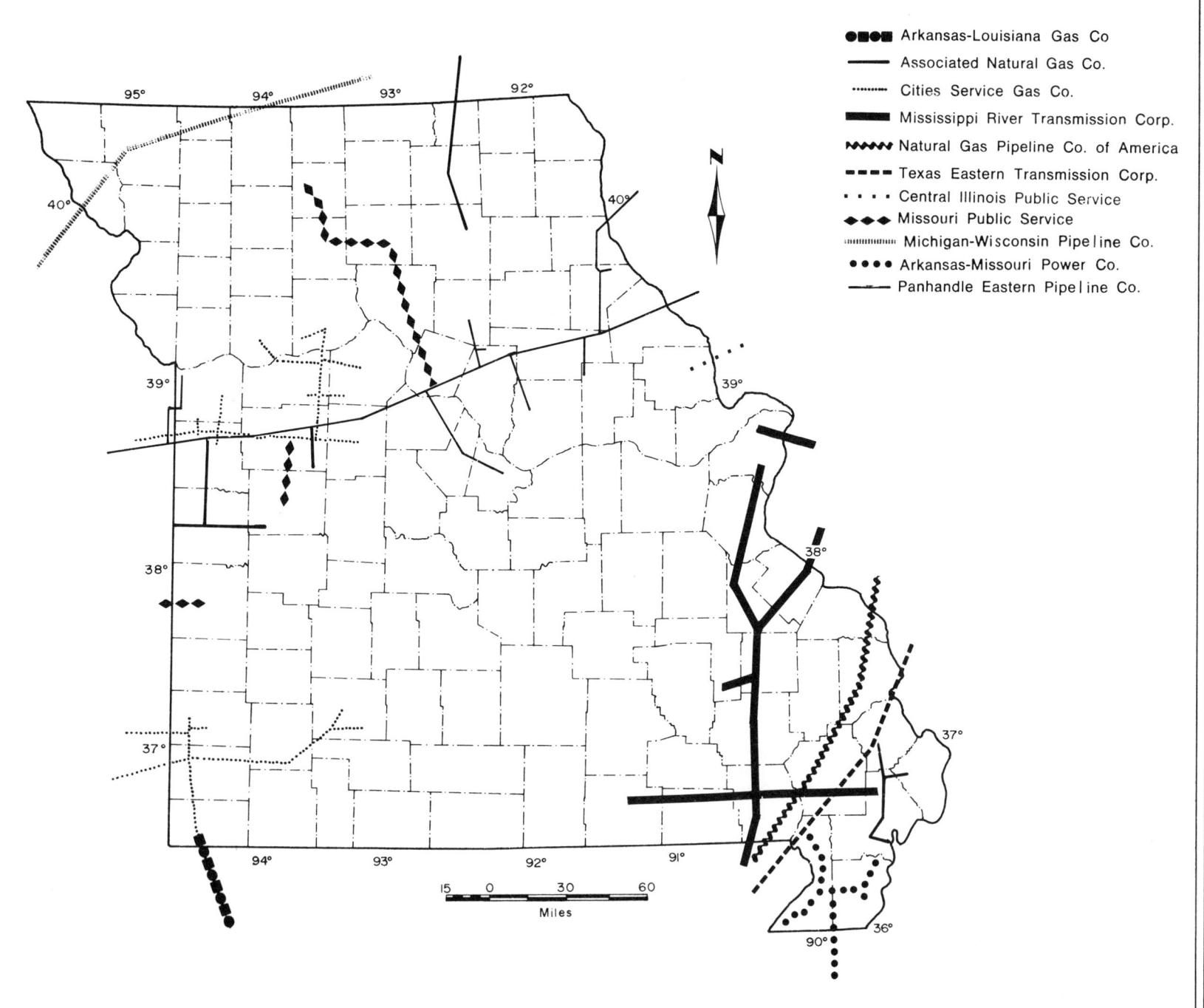

Arkansas-Louisiana Gas Co
Associated Natural Gas Co.
Cities Service Gas Co.
Mississippi River Transmission Corp.
Natural Gas Pipeline Co. of America
Texas Eastern Transmission Corp.
Central Illinois Public Service
Missouri Public Service
Michigan-Wisconsin Pipeline Co.
Arkansas-Missouri Power Co.
Panhandle Eastern Pipeline Co.

N

15 0 30 60
Miles

73. NATURAL GAS PIPELINES

The 2,005 miles of natural gas pipelines within the boundaries of Missouri are of two types: trunk lines used to transport natural gas to the heavily populated states north and east of Missouri, and feeder lines that distribute natural gas to communities in Missouri. Half of Missouri's counties are without natural gas pipeline service. The majority of these counties are in sparsely settled areas—the Ozarks and the northern rural counties.

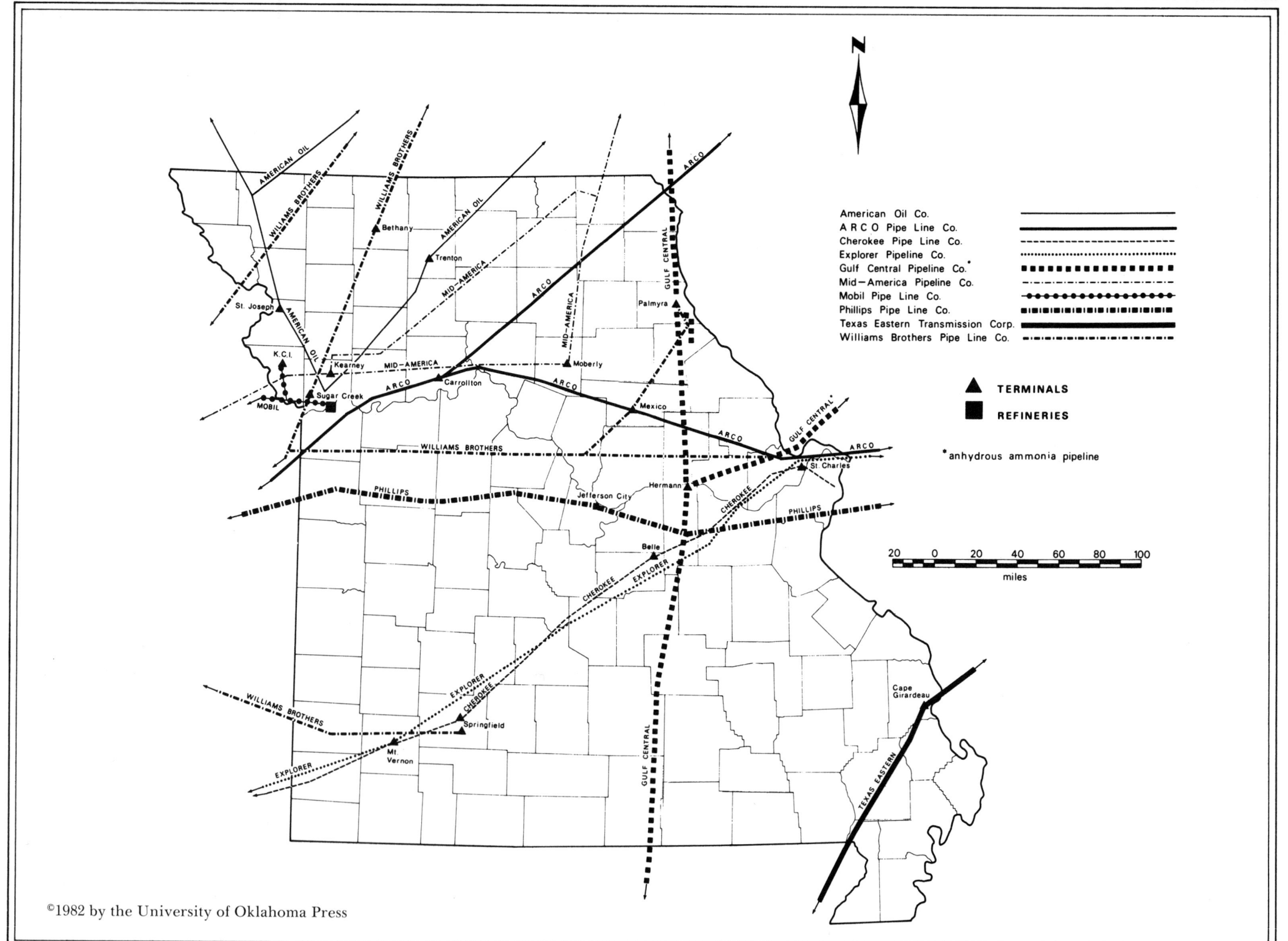

American Oil Co.
A R C O Pipe Line Co.
Cherokee Pipe Line Co.
Explorer Pipeline Co.
Gulf Central Pipeline Co.*
Mid—America Pipeline Co.
Mobil Pipe Line Co.
Phillips Pipe Line Co.
Texas Eastern Transmission Corp.
Williams Brothers Pipe Line Co.

▲ TERMINALS

■ REFINERIES

*anhydrous ammonia pipeline

20 0 20 40 60 80 100
miles

74. PRODUCTS PIPELINES

Ten products pipelines were in operation in 1974. Most of these lines entered and exited the state, performing a transit function en route. Eighteen terminals throughout the state received products from these pipelines. The refinery at Sugar Creek is served by the Mobil pipeline entering the state from Kansas. The Gulf Central Pipeline Co. anhydrous ammonia pipeline enters the state from the south, carrying chemicals from the Gulf Coast to the agricultural heartland of the United States.

Missouri's location between the petroleum- and chemical-producing areas of the South and Southwest and the agricultural and industrial heartlands of the country insures that the state will have an important role in pipeline transportation of fluid products.

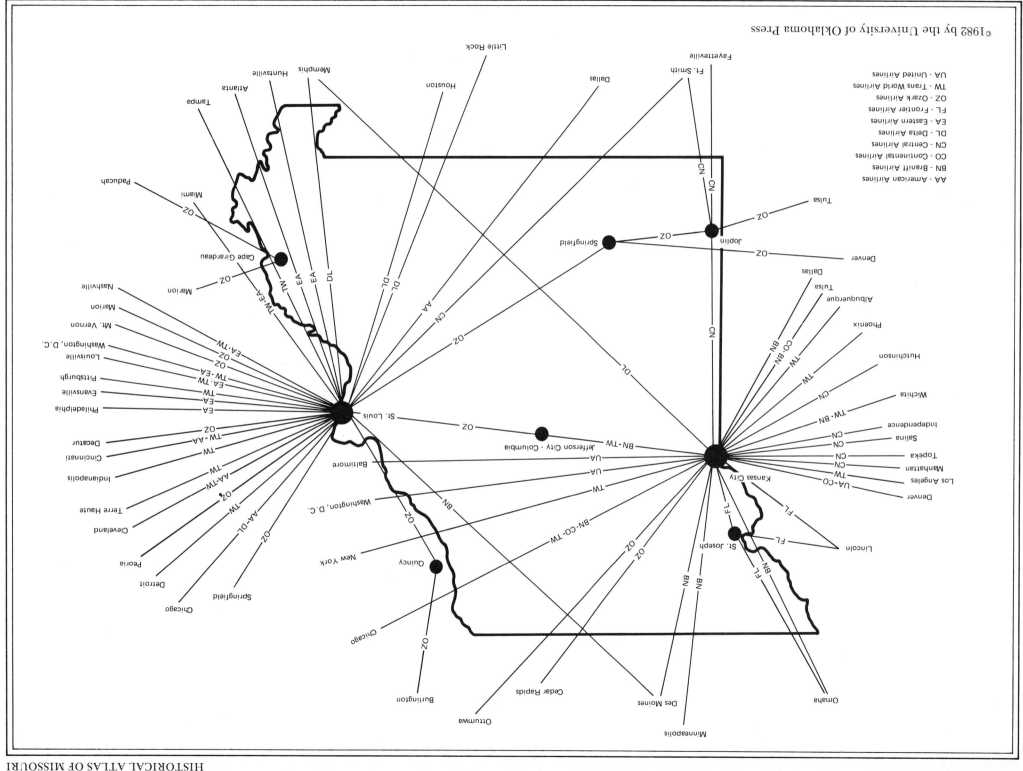

AA - American Airlines
BN - Braniff Airlines
CO - Continental Airlines
CN - Central Airlines
DL - Delta Airlines
EA - Eastern Airlines
FL - Frontier Airlines
OZ - Ozark Airlines
TW - Trans World Airlines
UA - United Airlines

Missouri contributed many pioneers in the development of aviation in the United States. In 1859, John Wise, from Pike County, flew in a balloon from St. Louis to New York. Major Albert B. Lambert, a balloonist and enthusiastic supporter of air flight, helped found the St. Louis Aero Club, which did much to interest Missourians in the new frontier of the skies. In 1907 the first "Great American Air Meet" was held in St. Louis under sponsorship of the club. Dirigibles were first raced in America at the Aero Club meet in St. Louis in 1908. In 1910 the first international aviation meet was held at Kinlock Park between Ferguson and Florissant. When regular air mail was instituted in the 1920s among the first companies to provide this service was the Robertson Aircraft Corporation of St. Louis, which secured the franchise to carry mail between St. Louis and Chicago in 1925. Charles A. Lindbergh, a young first lieutenant in the 110th Observation Squadron of the Missouri National Guard, was one of the first pilots hired by them.

As Missouri's location and physical attributes once encouraged its early settlement, so in the twentieth century its central location and freedom from mountain hazards and dangerous climate conditions have been influential in the encouragement of air travel within the state and the establishment of St. Louis and Kansas City as busy centers for continental air traffic.

Today Missouri is served by twenty-three scheduled airline carriers. Eight of these are trunk-line carriers, five are local service or second-level carriers, and ten are commuter or third-level carriers.

During 1975, nearly six million airline passengers enplaned in Missouri. St. Louis accounted for 60 per cent of the traffic, Kansas City another 36 per cent, Springfield 2 per cent, and all other cities another 2 per cent. Trans World Airlines had the largest share of the passenger market, 37 per cent.

The most active passenger route in Missouri is between St. Louis and Kansas City. One first-level carrier, Trans World Airlines, and two second-level carriers, Ozark and Frontier, provide forty-five direct flights daily between these two cities. These three carriers generate 5,585 seats per day in this one traffic lane. The Joplin-Springfield and Columbia–St. Louis city pairs are tied for the next most intensively developed route, each generating 810 seats per day. The Springfield–St. Louis route is third with 772 seats per day.

While the volume of cargo carried by air is not large when measured in tonnage, it is a rapidly expanding source of revenues for airlines. By 1974 almost ninety thousand tons of cargo and mail were being flown annually to destinations outside the state. This total represented a 62 per cent increase in air freight between 1972 and 1974.

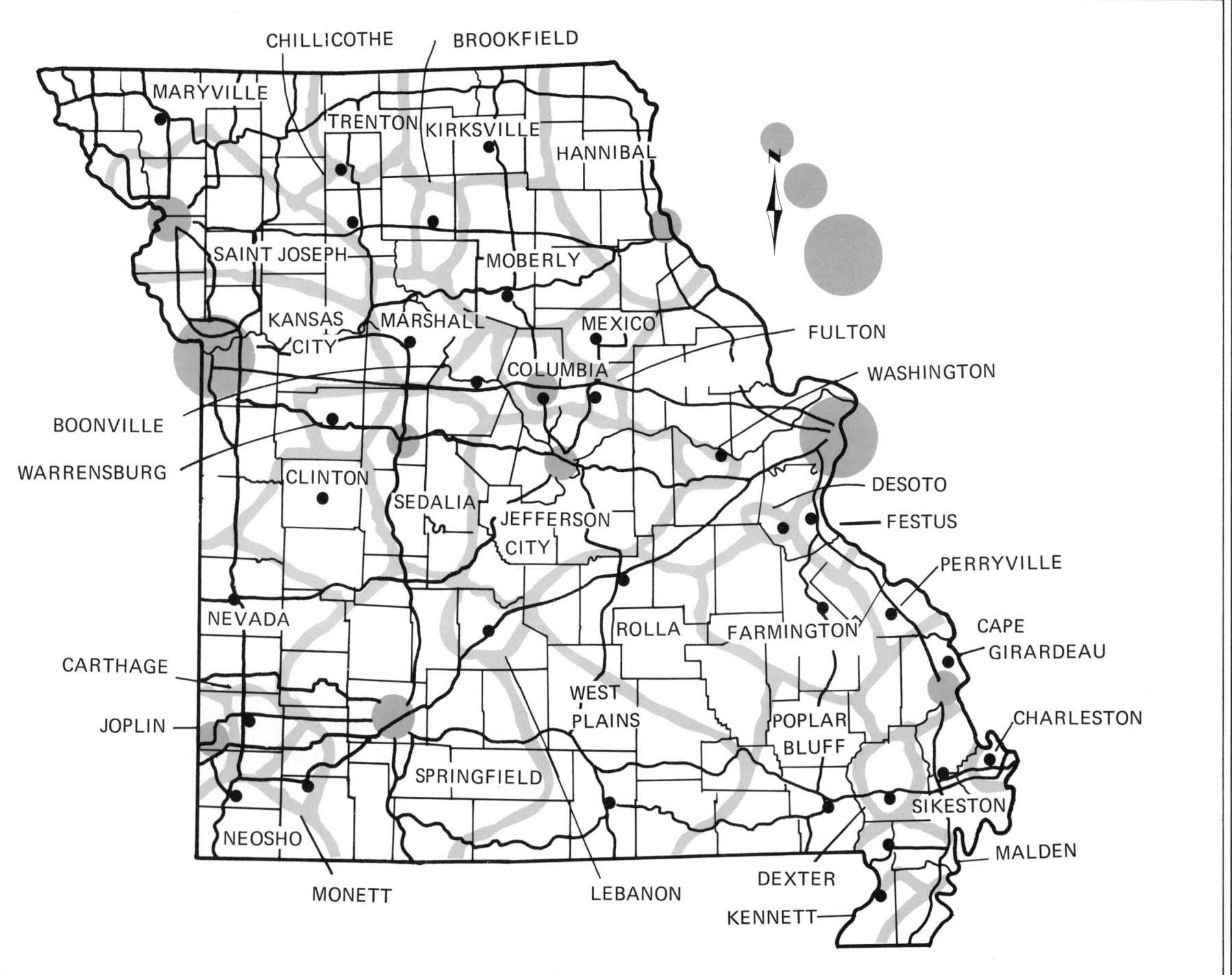

CHILLICOTHE   BROOKFIELD
MARYVILLE
TRENTON   KIRKSVILLE
HANNIBAL
SAINT JOSEPH
MOBERLY
KANSAS   MARSHALL
CITY   MEXICO   FULTON
COLUMBIA   WASHINGTON
BOONVILLE
DESOTO
WARRENSBURG   FESTUS
CLINTON
PERRYVILLE
SEDALIA
JEFFERSON   CAPE
CITY   GIRARDEAU
NEVADA
ROLLA   CHARLESTON
CARTHAGE   FARMINGTON
JOPLIN   WEST   POPLAR
PLAINS   BLUFF   SIKESTON
SPRINGFIELD
MALDEN
NEOSHO
DEXTER
MONETT   LEBANON
KENNETT

Transportation routes have always played an important part in the establishment of towns in Missouri. The earliest towns were along the navigable streams, the Mississippi and Missouri rivers. St. Louis, Ste. Genevieve, Cape Girardeau, New Madrid, and Hannibal on the Mississippi River and St. Charles, Washington, Hermann, Jefferson City, Boonville, Glasgow, Lexington, Independence, Kansas City, and St. Joseph on the Missouri River are all old towns.

Because the number of navigable streams was limited, the majority of towns were on railroads. These towns were located about six to ten miles apart. Many of the early railroad towns were "paper towns"; that is, they were planned but never built, for any one of a number of reasons. In some cases the railroad was never completed, or there was commercial competition from adjacent towns, or perhaps the proposed towns were purely fraudulent or ambitious real estate promotions. These early villages had two purposes: to serve as trade and service centers for surrounding farms and to serve as watering and fueling stations for the railroads. Few towns have been founded since the railroad construction era, which lasted from the 1850s to about 1900.

For nearly seventy-five years the percentage of the population engaged in agriculture has declined continuously. At the same time there has been a revolution in transportation. Time distance is a convenient term used as a measure of the distance a person travels in one hour. On foot men can travel four or five miles an hour, and on horseback ten or twenty miles an hour, but with today's system of highways and with improved motor vehicles it is easy to travel fifty miles an hour.

Improved transportation has worked to the advantage of the larger places. Towns under five hundred tend to decline in population. Even in the vicinity of the larger cities such as St. Louis, Kansas City, Springfield, and St. Joseph, the village or hamlet located on easily traveled and well-located roads has the best chance for growth.

Improvements in transportation have facilitated the centralization of various kinds of services. As time and cost of transportation are reduced, it becomes possible for people to travel greater distances to obtain goods and services. As a result, some centers have become the locations for various kinds of medical, legal, financial, retail, wholesale, and other specialized services.

In Missouri, traffic flow data have been used to delineate traffic sheds of various kinds of cities. The method used to identify areas of influence consists of identifying points on a highway which represent a minimum number of vehicles per day between two centers. Thus, traffic flow increases each way from the identified point. The points are then connected to show the traffic sheds or trade hinterlands.

The sizes of the resulting traffic sheds roughly correspond to the sizes of the central places. As expected, the major metropolitan centers have large traffic sheds. However, the shapes of the traffic sheds are modified by proximity of competing centers, quality of roads, and the productivity of the hinterland. For example, the St. Louis traffic shed extends out to a greater distance along Interstates 44 and 70, and Springfield's trade territory is more limited to the west, where there are larger competing centers. West Plains and Rolla serve large areas because they are the only towns of size in the central Ozarks.

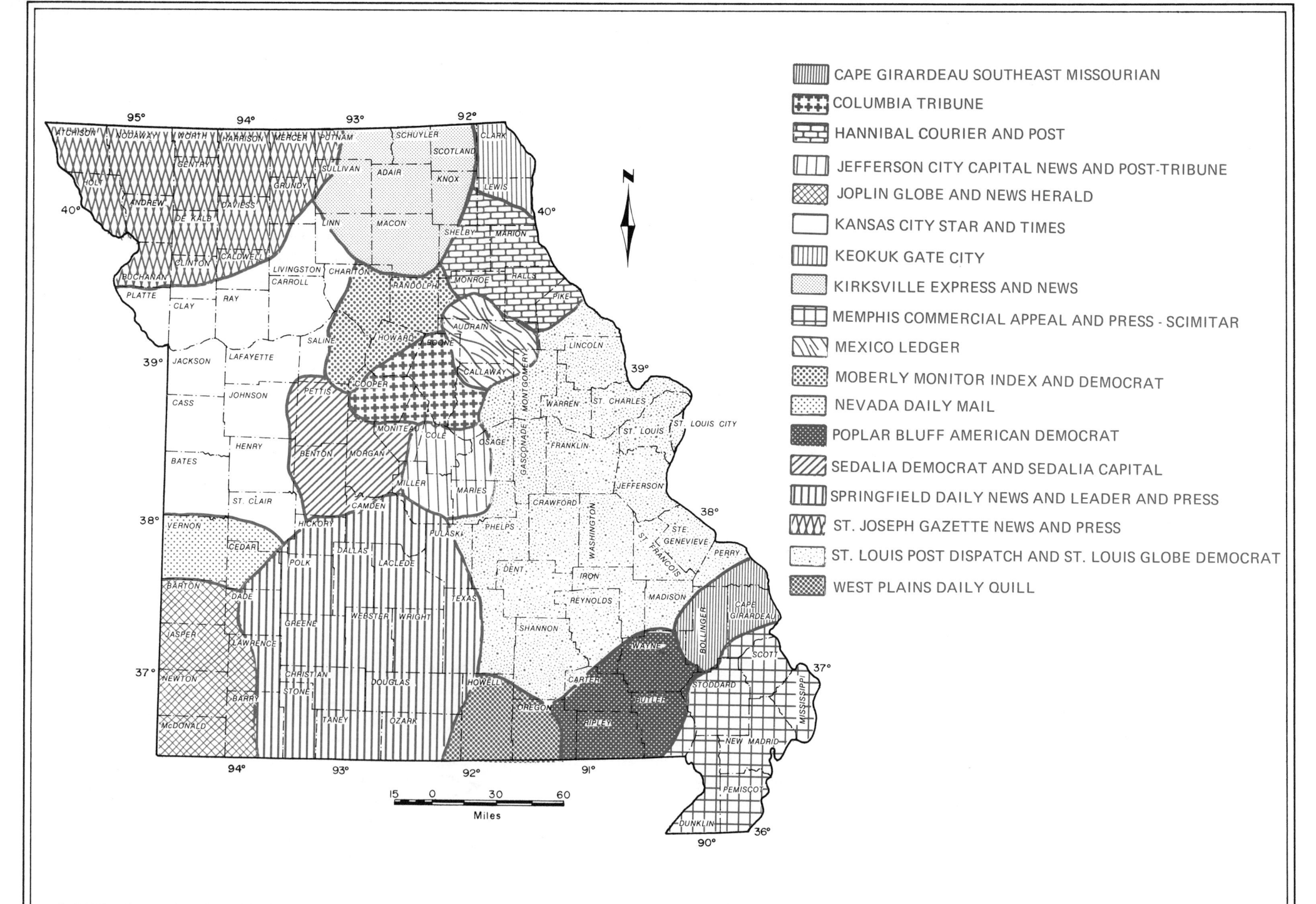

CAPE GIRARDEAU SOUTHEAST MISSOURIAN

COLUMBIA TRIBUNE

HANNIBAL COURIER AND POST

JEFFERSON CITY CAPITAL NEWS AND POST-TRIBUNE

JOPLIN GLOBE AND NEWS HERALD

KANSAS CITY STAR AND TIMES

KEOKUK GATE CITY

KIRKSVILLE EXPRESS AND NEWS

MEMPHIS COMMERCIAL APPEAL AND PRESS - SCIMITAR

MEXICO LEDGER

MOBERLY MONITOR INDEX AND DEMOCRAT

NEVADA DAILY MAIL

POPLAR BLUFF AMERICAN DEMOCRAT

SEDALIA DEMOCRAT AND SEDALIA CAPITAL

SPRINGFIELD DAILY NEWS AND LEADER AND PRESS

ST. JOSEPH GAZETTE NEWS AND PRESS

ST. LOUIS POST DISPATCH AND ST. LOUIS GLOBE DEMOCRAT

WEST PLAINS DAILY QUILL

Miles

77. CIRCULATION OF DAILY NEWSPAPERS

Daily newspaper circulation service areas reflect the retail trade areas and limits of political and cultural influence of cities. Data for this map were obtained for the newspapers of Missouri which have daily circulations of more than seventy-five hundred. The data are from the 1968 Audit Reports of the Audit Bureau of Circulations. Each county was assigned wholly to one region if one newspaper accounted for two-thirds or more of total newspaper circulation. In other cases the counties were divided in proportion to the circulation areas much as one would expect, varying mainly according to the size of the city and the distance from the nearest competition. Central Missouri has several medium-sized cities which share the daily newspaper market. The Kansas City and St. Louis dailies, in addition to dominating the largest service areas, circulate to a considerable extent throughout the state.

In many of the border counties which are close to large towns in adjacent states, out-of-state newspapers are dominant. For example, the daily newspaper printed in Keokuk, Iowa, has a large circulation in northeastern Missouri, while many people in the Bootheel area read the Tennessee newspapers.

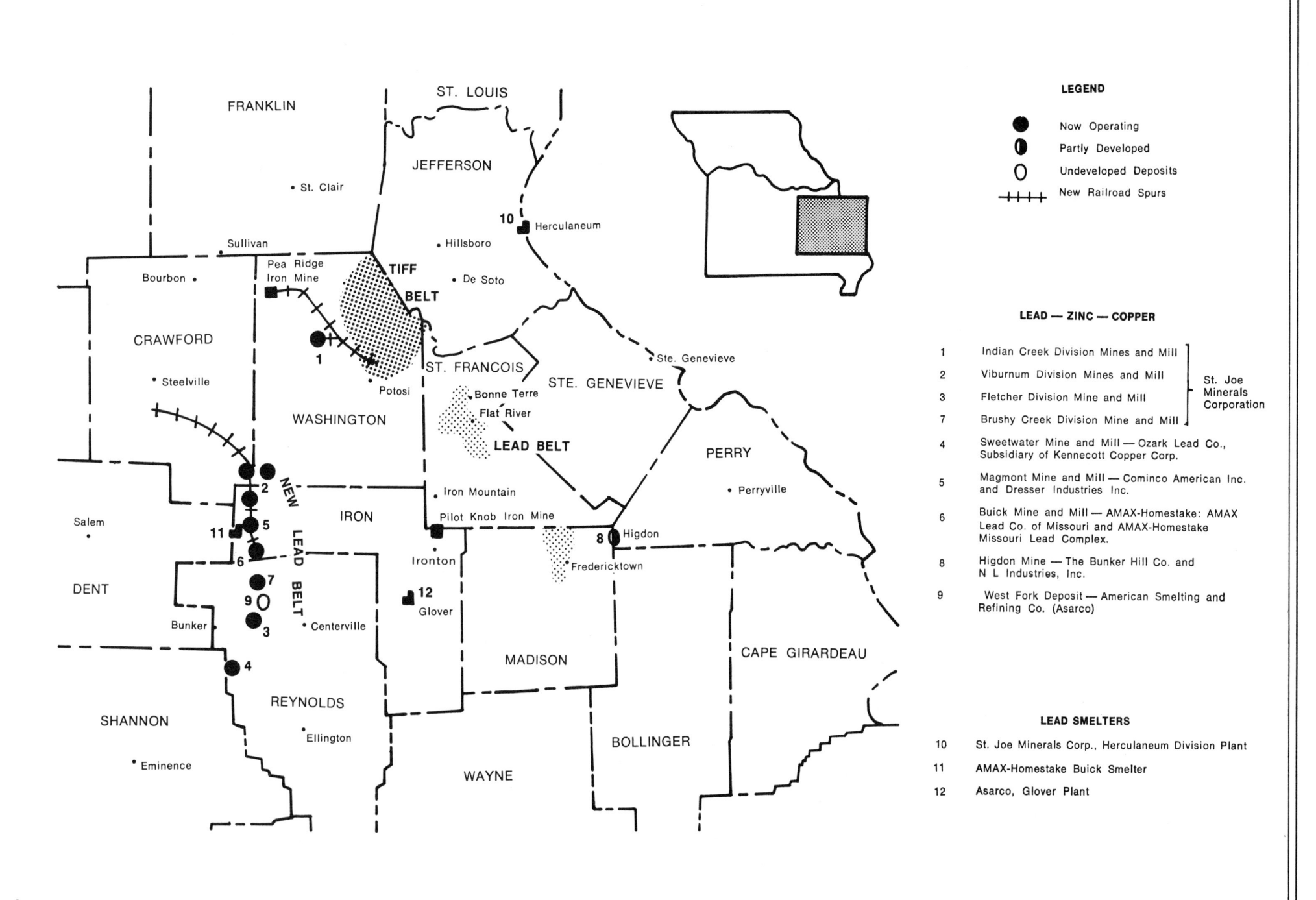

LEGEND

● Now Operating
◐ Partly Developed
○ Undeveloped Deposits
┼┼┼┼ New Railroad Spurs

LEAD — ZINC — COPPER

1 Indian Creek Division Mines and Mill ⎫
2 Viburnum Division Mines and Mill ⎬ St. Joe Minerals Corporation
3 Fletcher Division Mine and Mill ⎪
7 Brushy Creek Division Mine and Mill ⎭

4 Sweetwater Mine and Mill — Ozark Lead Co., Subsidiary of Kennecott Copper Corp.

5 Magmont Mine and Mill — Cominco American Inc. and Dresser Industries Inc.

6 Buick Mine and Mill — AMAX-Homestake: AMAX Lead Co. of Missouri and AMAX-Homestake Missouri Lead Complex.

8 Higdon Mine — The Bunker Hill Co. and N L Industries, Inc.

9 West Fork Deposit — American Smelting and Refining Co. (Asarco)

LEAD SMELTERS

10 St. Joe Minerals Corp., Herculaneum Division Plant

11 AMAX-Homestake Buick Smelter

12 Asarco, Glover Plant

©1982 by the University of Oklahoma Press

78. HISTORICAL GEOGRAPHY OF THE MINERAL AREA

The Mineral Area includes the lead-zinc ores of Washington, St. Francois, and Madison counties; the barite ore of Washington County; and the iron deposits of Iron County. The lead mining area was known as the Lead Belt, the Flat River District, and later, after the lead discoveries of the 1960s in western Iron and Reynolds counties, the Old Lead Belt. The name Tiff Belt is applied to the Washington County barite mines, while the iron mines of northeast Iron County were once known as the Iron Mountain District.

There are reports that the French had discovered lead on the eastern flank of the St. Francis Mountains by 1700. The area soon became known as a mining region, and in 1817 the ill-fated Company of the West sent an expedition to explore the Ozarks and work the mines. Several important mines were opened by Sieur Renault in the 1720s, and temporary settlement grew up around the mines in Washington, St. Francois, and Madison counties. Near the end of the nineteenth century, Americans began to settle in the area and to work the mines. Moses Austin (father of Stephen F. Austin of Texas fame), an experienced metallurgist, acquired mining property in the vicinity of Potosi and constructed improved furnaces for smelting at Potosi (Mine á Breton) and at Herculaneum.

The modern era of mining in the Lead Belt came about as outside capital was attracted to the area. The diamond drill, first used by the St. Joseph Lead Company in 1869, enabled mining companies to discover and exploit deep lead deposits.

As deep mines and large mills were developed, the imprint of mining on the landscape was substantial. Shaft houses, concentrators, furnaces, sediment basins, rail lines, and huge chat piles were visible everywhere. The core of the Lead Belt, centering around Bonne Terre, Flat River, Leadville, Elvins, and Desloge, grew to be an urbanized district of some ten small towns with an aggregate population of over thirty thousand. In 1961 the huge Bonne Terre mine was closed, and in 1973 the last of the producing operations in the Lead Belt, the Federal Lead Company mine and mill at Flat River, was closed.

The region of the Tiff Belt covers about seventy-five square miles in northeast Washington County. Until the 1850s the main product of the area was lead. The first records of the buying and selling of tiff (barite) are dated 1857. Shortly after 1900, when it was discovered that barite could be used as a drilling mud to maintain pressure in the drilling of oil and gas wells, mining companies began buying up more land.

Several iron works were established in the Iron Mountain District at an early date. Ashebran's Furnace and Springfield Furnace were the first to be established, and in the 1840s and 1850s large charcoal furnaces were constructed at Iron Mountain and Pilot Knob to exploit the ores taken from the adjacent mountains. With improved railroad transportation and the depletion of timber stands required for charcoal, the smelting of the ores shifted to St. Louis.

Since the mid-1950s there has been extensive development of a New Lead Belt in western Iron County and Reynolds County. The ore, primarily lead with some zinc, copper, and silver, lies in flat beds some nine to eleven hundred feet beneath the surface. In 1976 the New Lead Belt, or Viburnum Trend, produced 504,095 tons of lead worth $252,892,000, making it the largest producing district in the world.

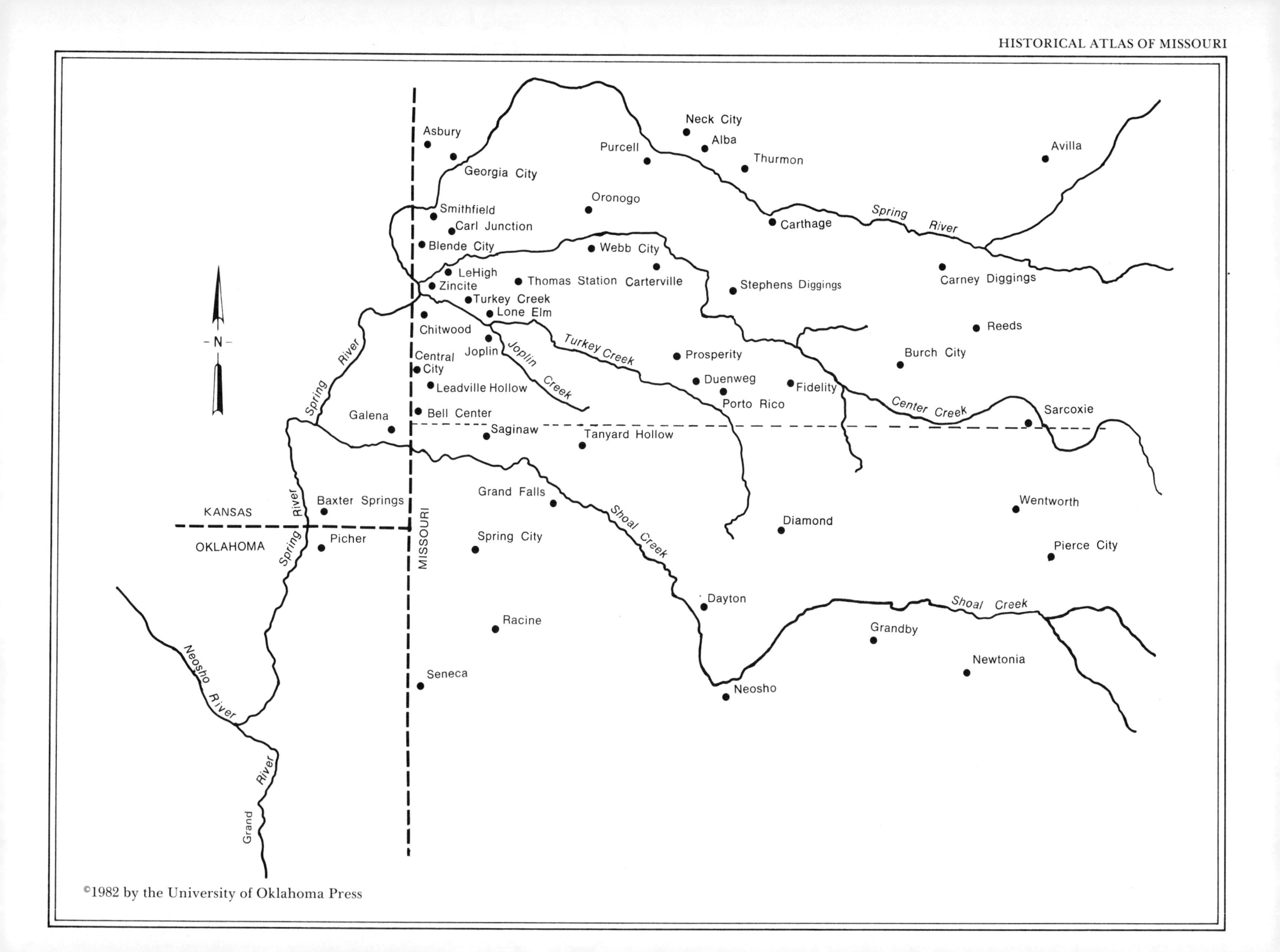

Asbury

Neck City

Alba

Purcell

Avilla

Georgia City

Thurmon

Oronogo

Spring River

Smithfield

Carthage

Carl Junction

Blende City

Webb City

LeHigh

Thomas Station Carterville

Stephens Diggings

Carney Diggings

Zincite

Turkey Creek

Reeds

Lone Elm

Chitwood

Turkey Creek

Burch City

Central City

Joplin

Joplin Creek

Prosperity

Duenweg

Galena

Leadville Hollow

Fidelity

Center Creek

Sarcoxie

Bell Center

Porto Rico

Saginaw

Tanyard Hollow

Spring River

Grand Falls

Wentworth

KANSAS

Baxter Springs

Spring River

Diamond

OKLAHOMA

Picher

Spring City

MISSOURI

Pierce City

Shoal Creek

Dayton

Shoal Creek

Racine

Grandby

Neosho River

Newtonia

Seneca

Neosho

Grand River

©1982 by the University of Oklahoma Press

Although eastern and central Missouri were fairly well populated by 1820, the southwestern section of the state remained largely uninhabited. Henry Rowe Schoolcraft, who visited the region in 1818–19, called it a "howling wilderness" but predicted that it would become famous the world over as a lead producing district. Schoolcraft's prediction proved to be correct when southwestern Missouri, southeastern Kansas, and northeastern Oklahoma developed as the Tri-State Mining District.

While the first settlers were agriculturalists, there were several reports of lead discoveries in the 1840s. By the time of outbreak of the Civil War, mining operations were well established at several locations in Newton and Jasper counties, including Granby and Neosho in the drainage basin of Shoal Creek, Turkey Creek Camp, Leadville Hollow, and Blytheville in the drainage basin of Turkey Creek, and French Point and Minersville (Oronogo) on Center Creek.

Although lead was mined and shipped from the Granby area before the Civil War, the discovery of large deposits in 1870 within what are now the Joplin city limits is generally considered to be the starting point of the district's growth. The tempo of mining increased tremendously between 1880 and 1900, and the peak value of zinc production in southwestern Missouri came in 1916. By that time larger deposits had been discovered near Picher, Oklahoma, which soon became the chief center of mining.

After World War I, production declined rapidly as a result of depletion of ores, flooding of mines, and competition from areas with lower-cost production. By 1957 all mining in the Missouri portion of the Tri-State Mining District had ceased.

Ore minerals of the district are primarily galena and sphalerite, occurring as circular sink-fill deposits or as tabular "sheet ground" or linear "runs." In the early years, mining here was carried out with practices established in the Mineral Area. Miners from the Lead Belt are known to have immigrated to the mines of southwestern Missouri by 1849. These professional miners were joined by local farmers. Most of the districts were regarded as "poor man's camps" because the ores were shallow and could be dug with little besides a pick, a shovel, and a bucket and windlass for hoisting the ore.

Zinc ore was frequently encountered in conjunction with lead, often at deeper levels, but little was known of this associate mineral's value. Huge piles of sphalerite (zinc ore) were thrown onto debris piles. The accumulated zinc at Granby reportedly was used to construct a stockade for protection during Civil War raids. Following the war, this mineral was removed from the walls and marketed at three dollars a ton.

In the early days, each camp had its smelter, but with the arrival of the railroad in 1870 and discovery of the large deep deposits mining expanded and smelters were concentrated in Joplin. Later much of the smelting was done near natural gas and coal supplies in Kansas and Oklahoma.

The geology of the Tri-State Mining District was a great influence in the founding, growth, and longevity of mining camps and towns. Limited means of transportation required the miners to live adjacent to the mine workings, and this necessity in turn gave rise to a large number of mining camps. If the ore bodies were large, the mining camp became a town, but if the deposits exhausted quickly, the camp folded.

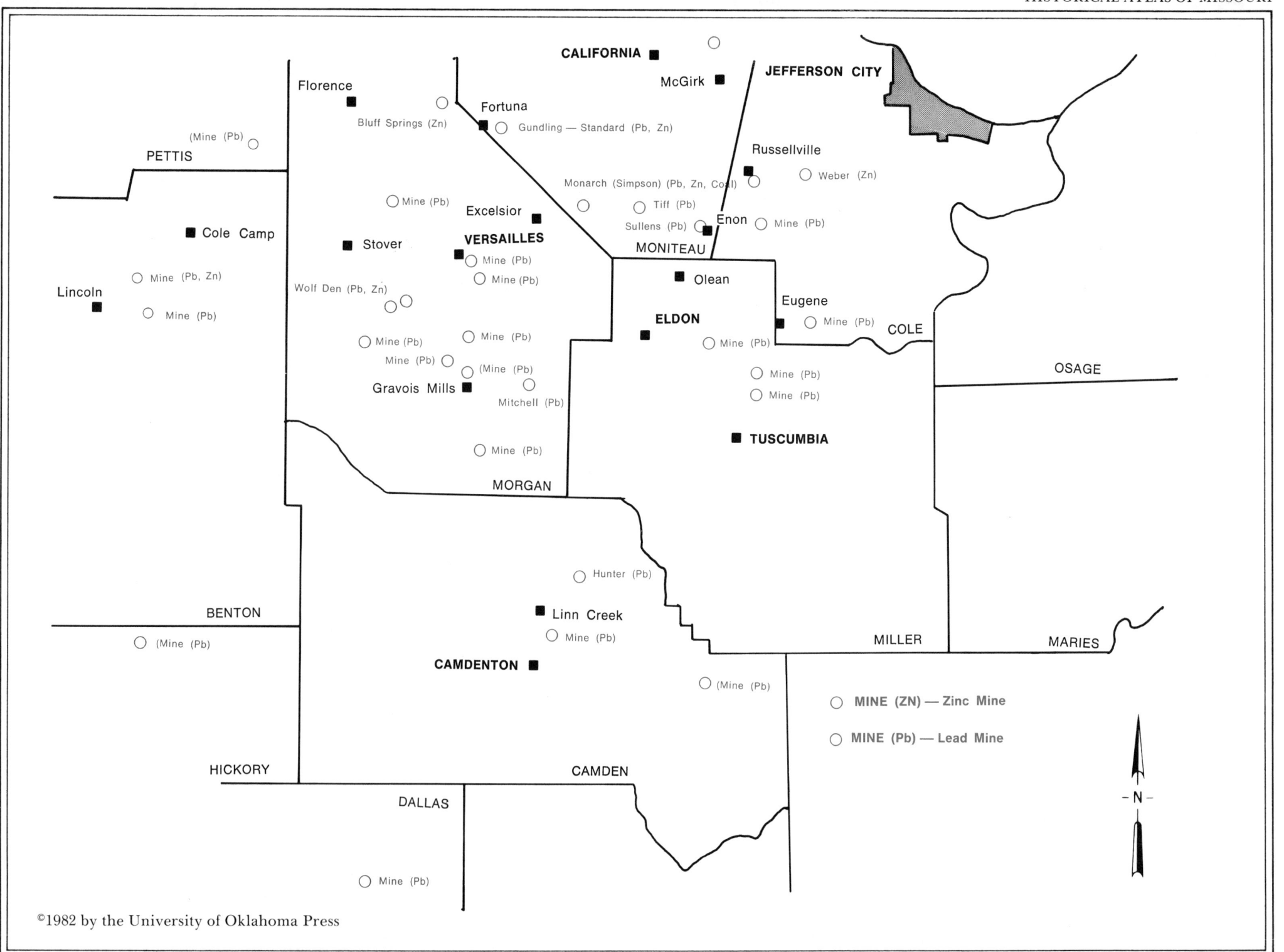

CALIFORNIA ■

○

JEFFERSON CITY

McGirk ■

Florence ■

○

Fortuna

PETTIS

(Mine (Pb) ○

Bluff Springs (Zn)

○ Gundling — Standard (Pb, Zn)

Russellville

■

○ Weber (Zn)

○ Mine (Pb)

Monarch (Simpson) (Pb, Zn, Coal)

Excelsior

■ Cole Camp

○

○ Mine (Pb)

○

○ Tiff (Pb)

■

Enon

■ Stover

VERSAILLES ■

Sullens (Pb) ■

○ Mine (Pb)

MONITEAU

○ Mine (Pb, Zn)

○ Mine (Pb)

○ Mine (Pb)

Lincoln

■

○ Mine (Pb)

Wolf Den (Pb, Zn)

○ ○

■ Olean

○ Mine (Pb)

ELDON

Eugene

■

COLE

○ Mine (Pb)

○ Mine (Pb)

○ Mine (Pb)

○ Mine (Pb)

○ Mine (Pb)

■

Gravois Mills ■

○ (Mine (Pb)

○ Mine (Pb)

OSAGE

Mitchell (Pb)

○ Mine (Pb)

○ Mine (Pb)

TUSCUMBIA ■

○ Mine (Pb)

MORGAN

BENTON

○ Hunter (Pb)

■ Linn Creek

○ (Mine (Pb)

○ Mine (Pb)

MILLER

MARIES

CAMDENTON ■

○ (Mine (Pb)

○ **MINE (ZN)** — Zinc Mine

○ **MINE (Pb)** — Lead Mine

HICKORY

CAMDEN

- N -

DALLAS

○ Mine (Pb)

The Central Mineral District is on the northern flank of the Ozark uplift in a gently dipping series of rocks that range in age from Late Cambrian through Pennsylvanian. Although all of the rock formations in the district are mineralized, deposits are mainly in the Jefferson City dolomite.

Initial lead discoveries in the district were made in southern Cole County in 1810, mining began about 1820, and the first lead smelter was erected in 1827. Lead mining and smelting reached a peak in the 1870s. There were fifty-one mines and seven furnaces in Morgan County, twenty mines and two furnaces in Cole County, and thirteen mines and two furnaces in Miller County. By 1900 the cumulative output was over 10,500 tons of lead and 600 tons of zinc. Mining was revived between 1900 and 1913, with most of the output coming from the Fortuna area in Moniteau County. Metal mining was terminated in 1950 when the district totals had reached about 16,000 tons of lead and 3,500 tons of zinc. Moniteau, Cole, and Morgan counties were the production leaders. The total tonnages are minor by today's standards, but they represent a tremendous amount of time and effort because of early hand mining and sorting methods.

Barite mines and a grinding plant were in operation on the Osage River at Herley in Cole County as early as 1866 or 1869. Output, which has been continuous since then, peaked between 1937 and 1941, when over 30,000 tons of concentrates were shipped during three of the five years. The deposits, numbering in the hundreds but usually small, are widely scattered. About thirty mines and washers have been operated, at one time or another, in eight counties in the northern Ozarks. Production increases in the early 1970s resulted from operations of Circle Mines, Inc., in Miller and Cole counties. The total district output of over 330,000 tons of barite is about 3 per cent of the state's total barite output to date.

81. BARITE DEPOSITS AND MINING

Barite is a relatively soft, white to gray, heavy mineral. The properties of softness, chemical inertness, and weight make it valuable for a number of purposes. About 90 per cent is used in oil drilling operations to hold gas pressure; the remaining 10 per cent is used as filler in paint, ink, paper, textiles, rubber goods, and asbestos products.

More barite is produced in Missouri than in any other state. The deposits are exploited in two areas: the Washington County Tiff Belt, seventy-five miles southwest of St. Louis, and the Central District in Cole, Miller, Moniteau, and Morgan counties. The Washington County District is one of the leading barite districts of the United States. The deposits of the Central District are scattered and can support only small operations. There is no active mining in the Lupus District.

The region of the Tiff Belt covers about seventy-five square miles in northeast Washington County. This region early on became a French pocket and remains so today. The French in the region around Old Mines, Fertile, Cannon Mines, Belle Fontaine, Shibboleth, Mineral Point, and Potosi have both exploited the area and retained their old ways of living.

Almost immediately after the Louisiana Purchase, progressive Americans began to accumulate land in the region around Old Mines. Moses Austin and John Smith T. acquired large properties. John Smith T. was a colorful and well-educated individual who legally affixed the letter *T* to his name to distinguish himself from other John Smiths and to show that he was from Tennessee. By various deceptions and by a persistence in locating "floating Spanish claims," he gained control of a large amount of land which was being lived on and worked by Creole families. Thus, he became wealthy but gained the ill will of many persons in the area.

The French Creoles, living by their old traditions and with their old language and religion, mined lead and barite and sold it to the landowners, who kept out royalties for themselves. The Creoles earned barely enough to purchase their necessities from the stores, which often were owned by these same landowners. This mode of life closely resembled the feudal system, the Creoles living rent-free on the land but impoverished and working for the landowners.

Until the 1850s, the main mining product was lead. The first records of the buying and selling of barite are dated 1857. As the mining of barite replaced lead mining as the major industry of the area, the established relationship between landowner and tenant miner persisted.

Since 1925, when the use for drilling mud was developed, annual production of barite in Missouri has only rarely dipped below one hundred thousand tons, and has exceeded three hundred thousand tons fairly often since 1950. Nearly all of the production comes from the Washington County Tiff Belt.

In 1969 there were ten companies with sizable operations in the Tiff Belt. These companies operate between twenty-five and thirty washing plants in Washington County. Total employment in all facets of the barite industry is estimated at about six hundred. Since the best deposits have been worked out, the mining companies are becoming interested in reworking the huge tailings ponds with improved techniques for recovering the ore.

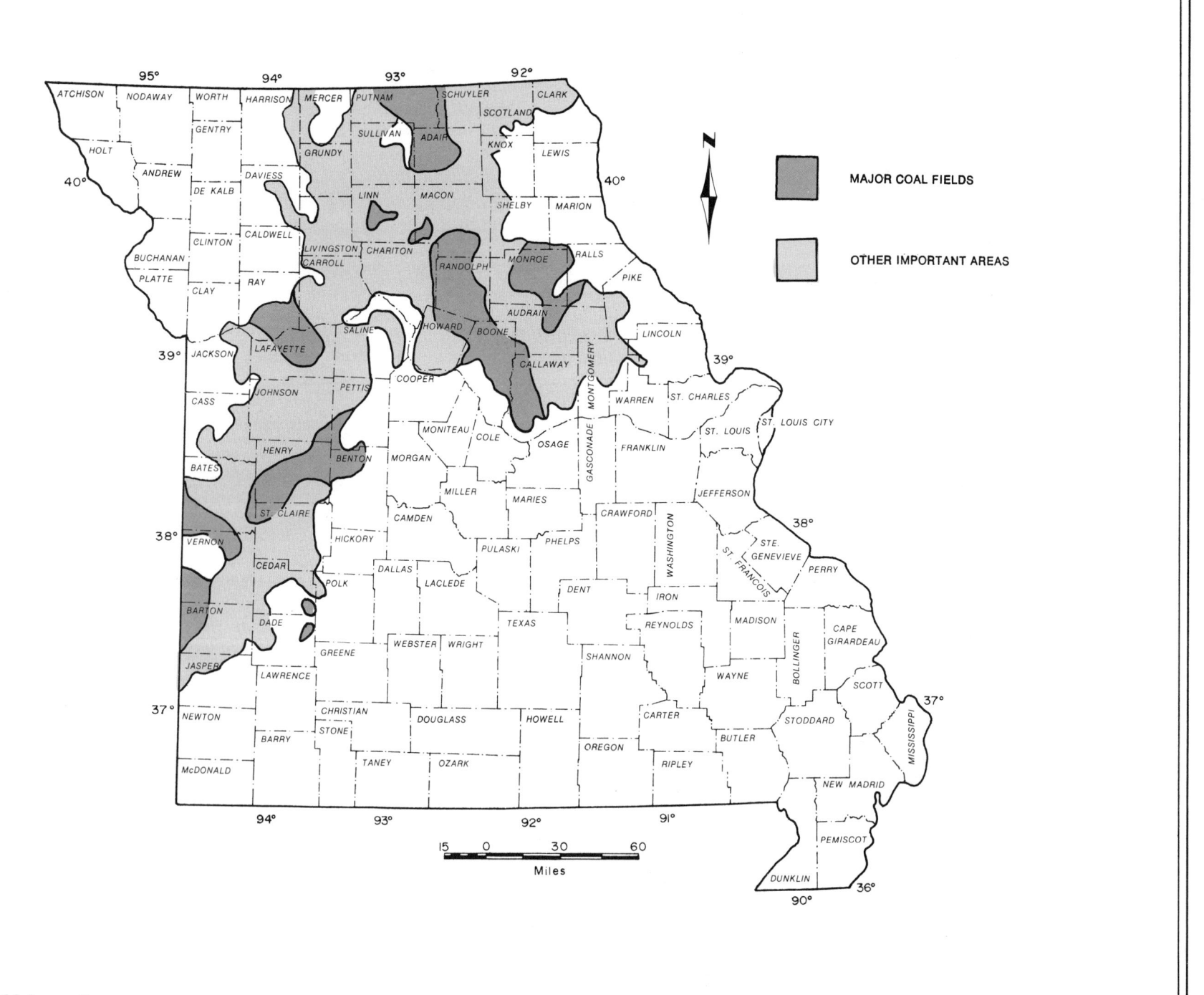

MAJOR COAL FIELDS

OTHER IMPORTANT AREAS

Miles

82. COAL DEPOSITS AND MINING

About one-third of Missouri is underlain by bituminous coal-bearing strata, and coal has been mined in fifty-five of the sixty-three counties in which it occurs. The deposits extend northeastward across the state from Jasper County to Clark County. Coal occurs in more than forty different beds, all associated with the Pennsylvanian period.

About four-fifths of Missouri's electrical power is produced by coal. The demand for coal is expected to triple by 1990. However, of the more than 9 million tons of coal consumed in Missouri in 1967, only about 3.5 million tons were mined within the state's boundaries. Almost all of the non-Missouri coal is shipped in from Illinois, with small amounts supplied by Kentucky, Virginia, West Virginia, and Pennsylvania.

Some of the first mines in Missouri were opened in Ray and Lafayette counties from strip mines and shallow shaft mines. Shaft and tunnel mines, in which vertical shafts were sunk and tunnels made following the seams of coal, were operated by Stealy and Fowler Company in the Lafayette Coal Field near Higginsville as early as 1847. Getting into the mines, getting the coal to the surface, and hauling it to a market was all done with teams of horses and by hand labor.

Most of Missouri's coal has been mined from five fields: (1) the Southwest Coal Field in southern Bates County and Vernon and Barton counties adjacent to Amoret, Foster, Sprague, and Hume; (2) the Tebo Coal Field, mainly in Henry County but including parts of Johnson, St. Clair, and Bates counties; (3) the Lexington Coal Field, mainly in Lafayette County, now mostly abandoned; (4) the Bevier Coal Field in Macon, Chariton, Randolph, Howard, Boone, and Callaway counties, the largest field in the state with a length of over seventy-five miles; and (5) the Mendota-Novington Coal Field in Putnam County.

The reserves of coal in Missouri are estimated at 23,400 million tons.

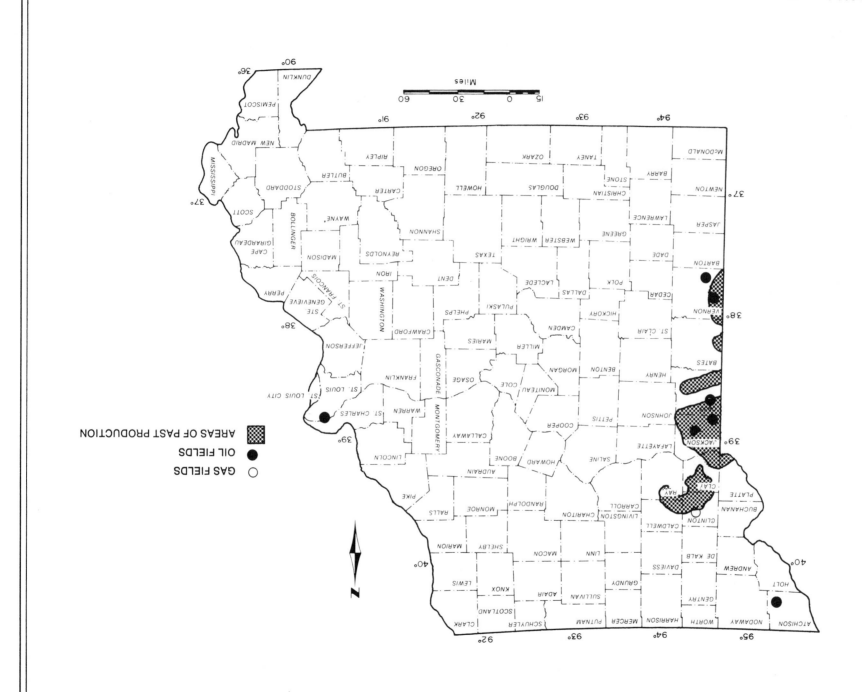

GAS FIELDS ○

OIL FIELDS ●

AREAS OF PAST PRODUCTION

Miles

15 0 30 60

83. OIL AND GAS FIELDS

Oil and gas have been produced in Missouri since the earliest drilling in the Kansas City area shortly after the Civil War. The oil is mainly of the low-gravity, high-viscosity type and is at relatively shallow depth. Some of the early wells were drilled to supply individual homes and communities with natural gas.

Many of the fields in western Missouri, opened in the late 1800s and early 1900s, are now depleted. Among the more recent strikes are the Tarkio Pool (1942) in Atchison County, the Florissant Pool (1953) in St. Louis County, and the Turney Gas Pool (1952) in Clinton County.

The Florissant Pool, because of its location in the St. Louis urbanized area and its unusually porous reservoir rocks, is used as a subsurface storage reservoir for gas piped in from other sources. Gas is pumped into the subsurface rock strata during times of low rates of consumption, and during periods of heavy use, the gas is pumped out and distributed to customers.

Essentially all of the shallow wells in western Missouri are classed as stripper wells and have averaged less than ten barrels per day. The oil and gas are produced from strata mainly of Pennsylvanian age, mostly in association with small domes of anticlinal structures.

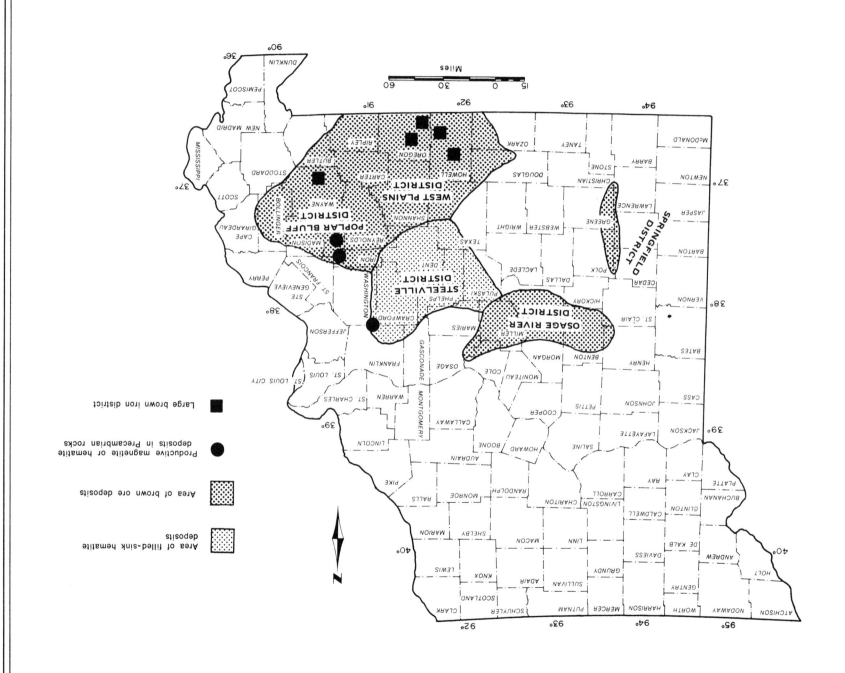

Miles

Large brown iron district

Productive magnetite or hematite deposits in Precambrian rocks

Area of brown ore deposits

Area of filled-sink hematite deposits

Missouri had the distinction of being the site of the first iron furnace to be built and operated west of the Mississippi River when Ashebran's Furnace was erected in 1815 near Ironton in Iron County. Several additional charcoal furnaces were built in Missouri in the 1850s.

Three types of iron ore deposits have been important in Missouri: filled-sink hematite deposits, brown iron ore (limonite) deposits, and Precambrian hematite and magnetite deposits. Outstanding mines in the filled-sink deposits were the Cherry Valley, Moselle No. 10, Meramec, Ruppele, and Scotia mines, all located in the Steelville district. Brown iron ores were mined in the vicinity of West Plains and in the southeastern Ozarks.

The Precambrian ores have been by far the most important in the state in the past. Their present role is even more impressive. Near-surface mines at Iron Mountain and Pilot Knob accounted for the bulk of the production of these iron ores, practically all of it hematite. Magnetic anomolies have led to the discovery of several buried magnetic-rich Precambrian ore deposits. Among the deposits discovered largely through the agency of magnetic surveys are those at Pea Ridge and Pilot Knob. Undeveloped deposits of this type are found at Bourbon, Boss, Kratz Spring, and Camel's Hump.

The only integrated steel plant near Missouri is the Granite City Steel Company plant across the Mississippi River in Illinois. That company's blast furnaces have been charged with Missouri iron ores for many years, much of it supplied from the Hanna Mining Company's Iron Mountain Mine in St. Francois County. The Armco Steel Corporation works in the Kansas City metropolitan area has three electric furnaces for steelmaking. It is the only major steelmaking facility in Missouri but does not include blast furnaces and therefore is not a consumer of iron ore.

In December, 1977, the Pea Ridge Iron Mine near Sullivan was shut down. Reasons for the closure included the low prices paid for iron concentrates resulting from foreign competition in the United States iron market and the high cost of pumping water from the thousand-foot-deep mine.

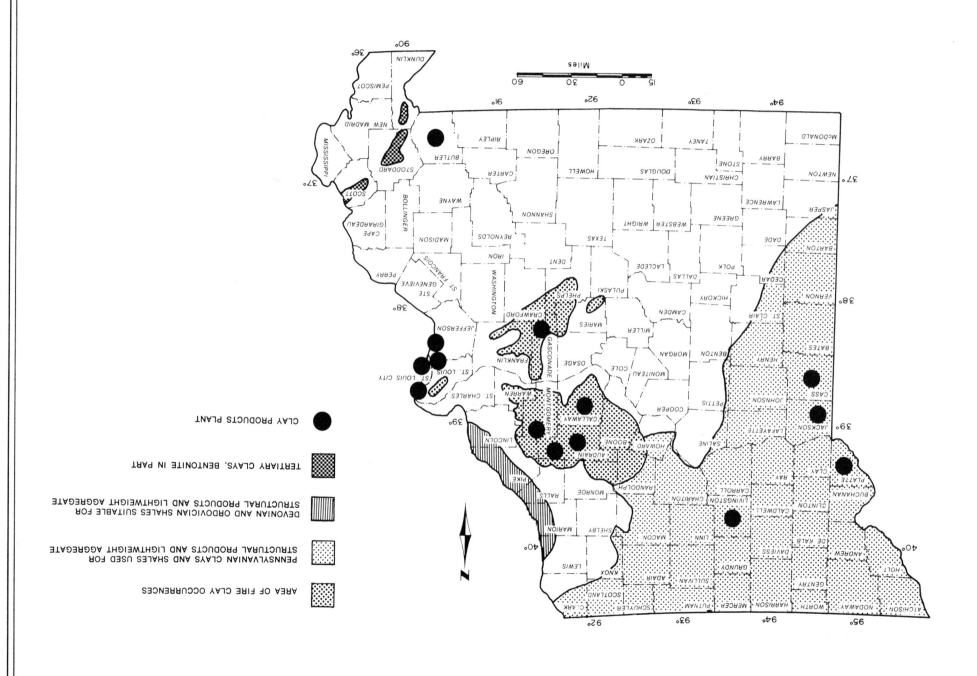

CLAY PRODUCTS PLANT

TERTIARY CLAYS, BENTONITE IN PART

DEVONIAN AND ORDOVICIAN SHALES SUITABLE FOR STRUCTURAL PRODUCTS AND LIGHTWEIGHT AGGREGATE

PENNSYLVANIAN CLAYS AND SHALES USED FOR STRUCTURAL PRODUCTS AND LIGHTWEIGHT AGGREGATE

AREA OF FIRE CLAY OCCURRENCES

Miles

60 30 0 15

Clay was mined and fashioned into pottery in Missouri by the Indians long before the arrival of the first Europeans. The manufacture of common brick for chimneys and more pretentious buildings began with the settlement of the first French communities along the Mississippi River. There are many old buildings that are still in use in the river border region of Missouri that are constructed of hand-made bricks.

Clay and shale can be divided into two principal groups — refractory and nonrefractory — by type of product produced. Refractory clays (commonly called fire clays) are those that are resistant to high temperature (above 2,770° F) without change other than dehydration. Refractory clays are used widely in the manufacture of firebrick, fire-resistant mortars, clay crucibles, retorts, and miscellaneous materials for foundries and steelworks. They are the most valuable clays produced in Missouri, accounting for somewhat less than 50 per cent of the tonnage but more than 75 per cent of the value of all clays. Missouri ranks third after Ohio and Pennsylvania in the production of refractory clays and their products.

Refractory clay deposits occur in three areas: the Northern Fire Clay District (Audrain, Boone, Monroe, Callaway, and Montgomery counties), the St. Louis Fire Clay District, and the Southern Fire Clay District (Gasconade, Franklin, and Crawford counties).

The first firebrick plant in Missouri was built in 1845. The industry continued to expand and is now well established. Seven companies with ten plants are operating in the state. The A. P. Green Refractories Company plant at Mexico in Audrain County is one of the largest facilities of its type in the United States. Refractory plants are also located in Callaway, Montgomery, and St. Louis counties.

Nonrefractory clays and shales, for the most part, are those that fire at lower temperatures and exhibit plasticity. This characteristic enables them to be formed into desired shapes that are retained during drying and firing. Thus, they find wide use in the arts and in the building and construction trades. Common products include building brick, drain tile, roofing tile, terra-cotta, pottery, and stoneware.

Clays and shales suitable for most of nonrefractory purposes are present mainly in the western and northern parts of the state. A nonswelling bentonitic clay in the Bootheel of southeastern Missouri has been found to be suitable for uses as an absorbent and carrier and as a binder for ore pellets.

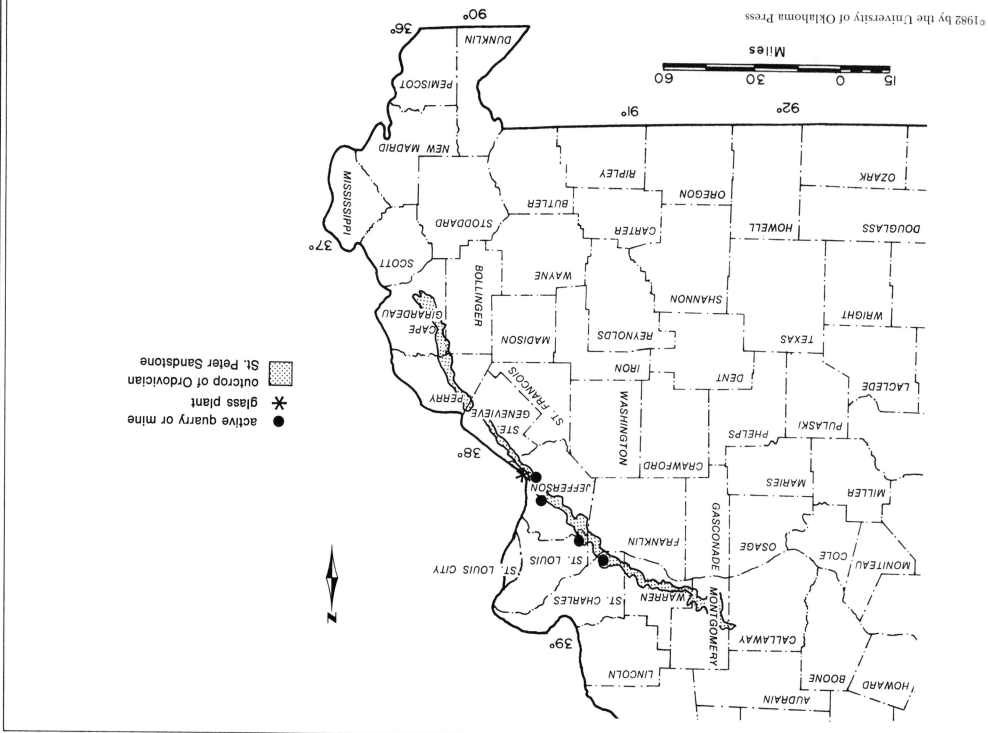

Miles

15   0   30   60

90°
36°

DUNKLIN

PEMISCOT

91°

92°

NEW MADRID

RIPLEY

OZARK

OREGON

BUTLER

STODDARD

37°

HOWELL

DOUGLASS

CARTER

SCOTT

MISSISSIPPI

WAYNE

SHANNON

WRIGHT

BOLLINGER

MADISON

REYNOLDS

TEXAS

CAPE GIRARDEAU

LACLEDE

IRON

DENT

St. Peter Sandstone

outcrop of Ordovician

PERRY

WASHINGTON

PHELPS

PULASKI

glass plant

MARIES

MILLER

active quarry or mine

STE. GENEVIEVE

ST. FRANCOIS

38°

CRAWFORD

GASCONADE

OSAGE

COLE

MONITEAU

JEFFERSON

FRANKLIN

MONTGOMERY

CALLAWAY

ST. LOUIS

ST. LOUIS CITY

WARREN

ST. CHARLES

BOONE

HOWARD

39°

LINCOLN

AUDRAIN

N

86. SILICA SAND

The term *silica sand* or *industrial sand* is applied to sand and sandstone of chemical and physical specifications that can be used for a number of industrial purposes. The prime requisite is that the sand be essentially pure silicon dioxide. The bulk of silica sand production is consumed by the glass industry. Another use is in abrasives, and metallurgical silica is used in preparing silicon alloys and as refractory material.

Practically all of the silica sand production in Missouri comes from the St. Peter sandstone. This formation crops out in a belt, ranging from less than one-fourth mile to 10 miles in width, roughly parallel to the Mississippi and Missouri rivers. The outcrop belt extends eastward from western Montgomery County through Warren County into western St. Charles County, where it turns southward passing through Franklin, St. Louis, Jefferson, Ste. Genevieve, Perry, and Cape Girardeau counties, a distance of about 150 miles.

The St. Peter sandstone is mined by both open pit and underground methods. Glass production at the Pittsburgh Plate Glass Company plant at Crystal City in Jefferson County began in 1874. Other localities where the St. Peter sandstone is quarried included Festus, Pevely, Pacific, and Augusta. The localities where the St. Peter sandstone can be easily quarried are listed on the map by number.

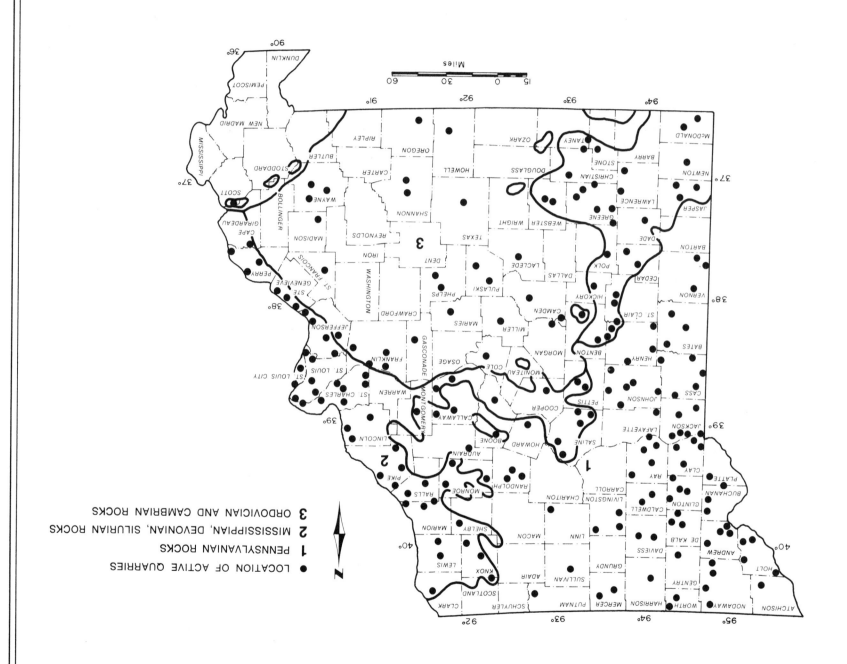

• LOCATION OF ACTIVE QUARRIES

1 PENNSYLVANIAN ROCKS

2 MISSISSIPPIAN, DEVONIAN, SILURIAN ROCKS

3 ORDOVICIAN AND CAMBRIAN ROCKS

N

Miles

60 30 0 15

Possibly no other type of rock plays as important a role in the modern economy as do the carbonate rocks. They are outstanding in the diversified uses to which they are put and with their interrelations with other commodities. Limestone and dolomite, the principal carbonate rocks, are the major mineral commodity in both tonnage and value, presently produced in Missouri. They form the predominant bedrock type over nearly 60 per cent of the state. The main areas of outcrop are the Ozarks, the Osage Cuestas, and the eastern third of the Dissected Till Plains.

One of the early industries in Missouri was the manufacture of lime from locally quarried stone. This lime was manufactured in the rudest manner. Log heaps were built, and blocks of limestone were thrown on them and burned. Later, rough stone walls were built to support the limestone blocks, and the lime was burned in these temporary kilns. In the 1880s, modern methods of lime manufacture were introduced.

Several quarries were opened in the vicinity of St. Louis at a very early date to provide building stone for churches, public buildings, and numerous private homes. Likewise, dimension stone was quarried at an early time in the vicinity of Kansas City, St. Joseph, Jefferson City, Hannibal, Springfield, Carthage, and Cape Girardeau. Two high-quality limestones, the Kimmswick in eastern Missouri and the Carthage in the west, have been marketed as marbles.

By far the most important market for crushed limestone and dolomite in Missouri is highway base and aggregate for Portland cement concrete, asphaltic concrete, and bituminous surfaces. Substantial quantities of agricultural lime ("aglime") are used for treatment of acid soils. Large tonnages of broken stone are produced annually in the counties bordering the Missouri and Mississippi rivers for revetment, dike, and wing-dam projects of the Corps of Engineers. Miscellaneous uses of limestone and dolomite—asphalt filler, railroad ballast, flux, poultry grit, chemical manufactures—amount to slightly over one million tons.

The carbonate rock resources of Missouri are in the three major areas shown on the map. Area 1, consisting of Pennsylvanian rocks, is underlain by beds of sandstone, shale, limestone, and coal. Nearly all of the area 1 limestone units have been quarried, and a few units, such as the Bethany Falls limestone which outcrops in Kansas City, have been quarried extensively. A profitable business has been developed in Kansas City by using the underground space left by the quarrying for commercial and industrial purposes.

Area 2 produces the largest tonnages in the state. High-calcium limestone is present in several formations, including St. Louis, Burlington, Callaway, Kimmswick, and Platte formations in eastern and central Missouri and the Warsaw, Keokuk, and Burlington formations in the southwest. The Burlington limestone is by far the most widely quarried unit in the state.

The carbonate rocks of area 3 are predominantly dolomite. The principal stone resources are in the Cotter, Jefferson City, Potosi, Derby-Doe Run, and Bonneterre formations.

IMPROVED LAND, 1850-1860

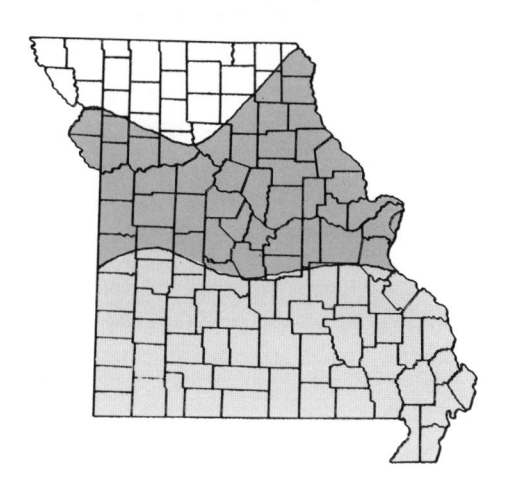

IMPROVED LAND, 1860-1870

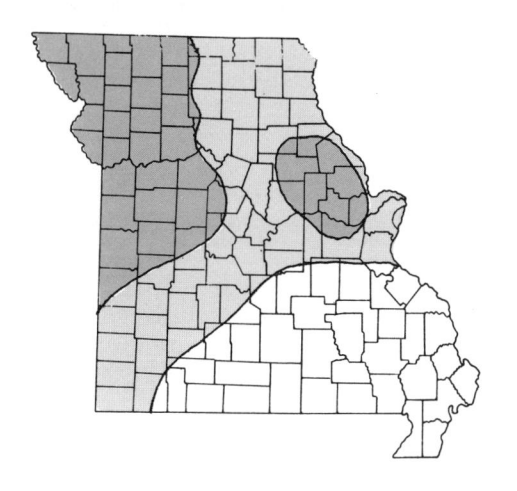

IMPROVED LAND, 1870-1880

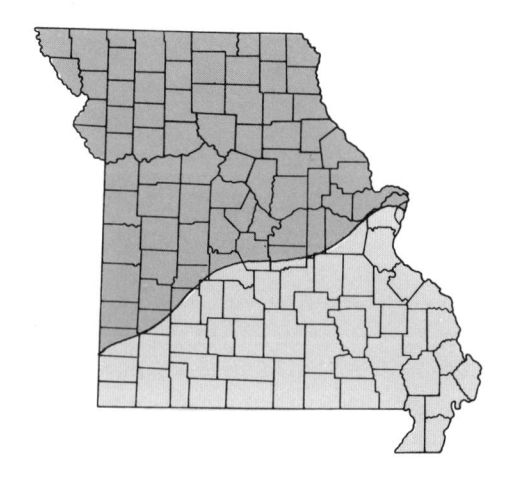

IMPROVED LAND, 1880-1890

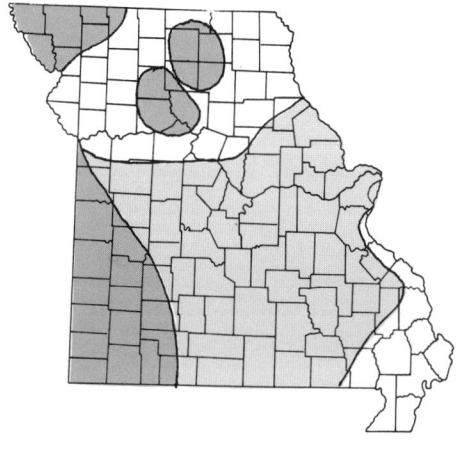

PRIMARY AREA OF INCREASE

SECONDARY AREA OF INCREASE

88. IMPROVED LAND, 1850–90

This series of maps, based on the U.S. census reports, illustrates trends in land use since 1850. Improved land includes land under cultivation, fenced pasture, managed woodlots and idle or fallow farmland, including acreages of failed crops. The Morrill (Homestead) Act required that land claimants improve their lands through cultivation of buildings and fences. Improvement of land was an important activity during the frontier period and a generation or so thereafter. Thus, the acreage of improved land for each census period provides evidence of the passing of the settlement frontier and the transition to systems of more organized agriculture.

For purposes of mapping, the areas where land improvement was most rapid are designated as primary areas, and areas where there was substantial acreage of improved land are designated as secondary areas. Because the largest number of immigrants to Missouri were primarily interested in agriculture, it is not surprising that there is a strong correlation between increase in population and increase in improved land. Improvement of land for agriculture during the 1850s progressed most rapidly in counties bordering the Missouri River between St. Joseph and St. Louis and along the Mississippi River border. During the 1860s and 1870s there was rapid improvement of land in the plains sections of northern and western Missouri. The decade of the 1880s saw the agricultural frontier pass into the prairie states. The primary areas of land improvement in Missouri were in the western part of the state.

IMPROVED LAND, 1890-1900

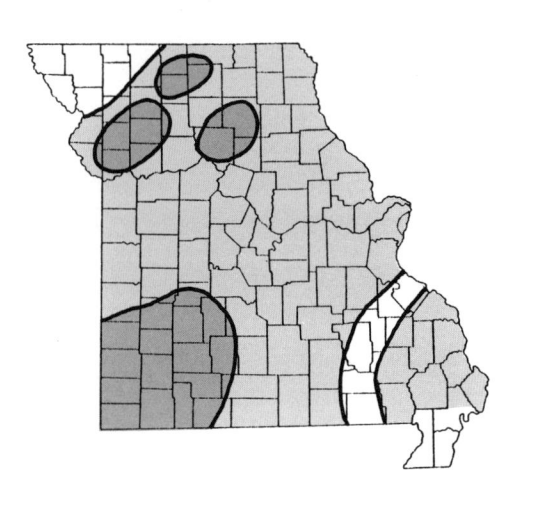

IMPROVED LAND, 1900-1910

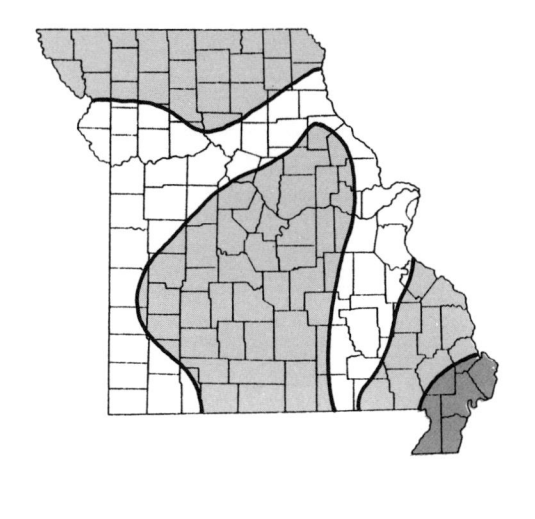

IMPROVED LAND, 1910-1920

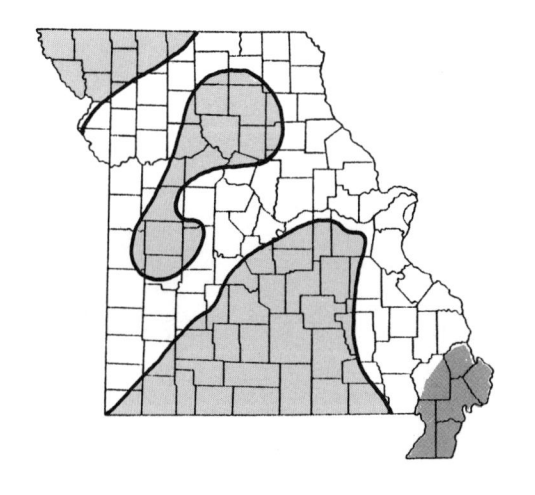

PRIMARY AREA OF INCREASE

SECONDARY AREA OF INCREASE

89. IMPROVED LAND, 1890–1920

The period 1880 to 1890 was a time when specialized agriculture was beginning to develop. This trend was most pronounced in the southwestern part of the state, where dairying and fruit growing gained in importance. As a result, the largest area of intensive improvement of land was in the southwestern counties.

By the 1890s the agricultural frontier had passed well into the plains states, and land improvement in Missouri was confined largely to the development of farms in the cutover Ozark timberlands and the reclamation of poorly drained land in the Southeast Lowlands. Certainly the most significant development during the 1920s was the large amount of ditching, drainage, and reclamation of swamplands in the Southeast Lowlands. Drainage and reclamation had begun before the turn of the century, but following the successful organization of the Little River Drainage Project in 1905, drainage and improvement of land for agriculture reached their peak during the 1920s.

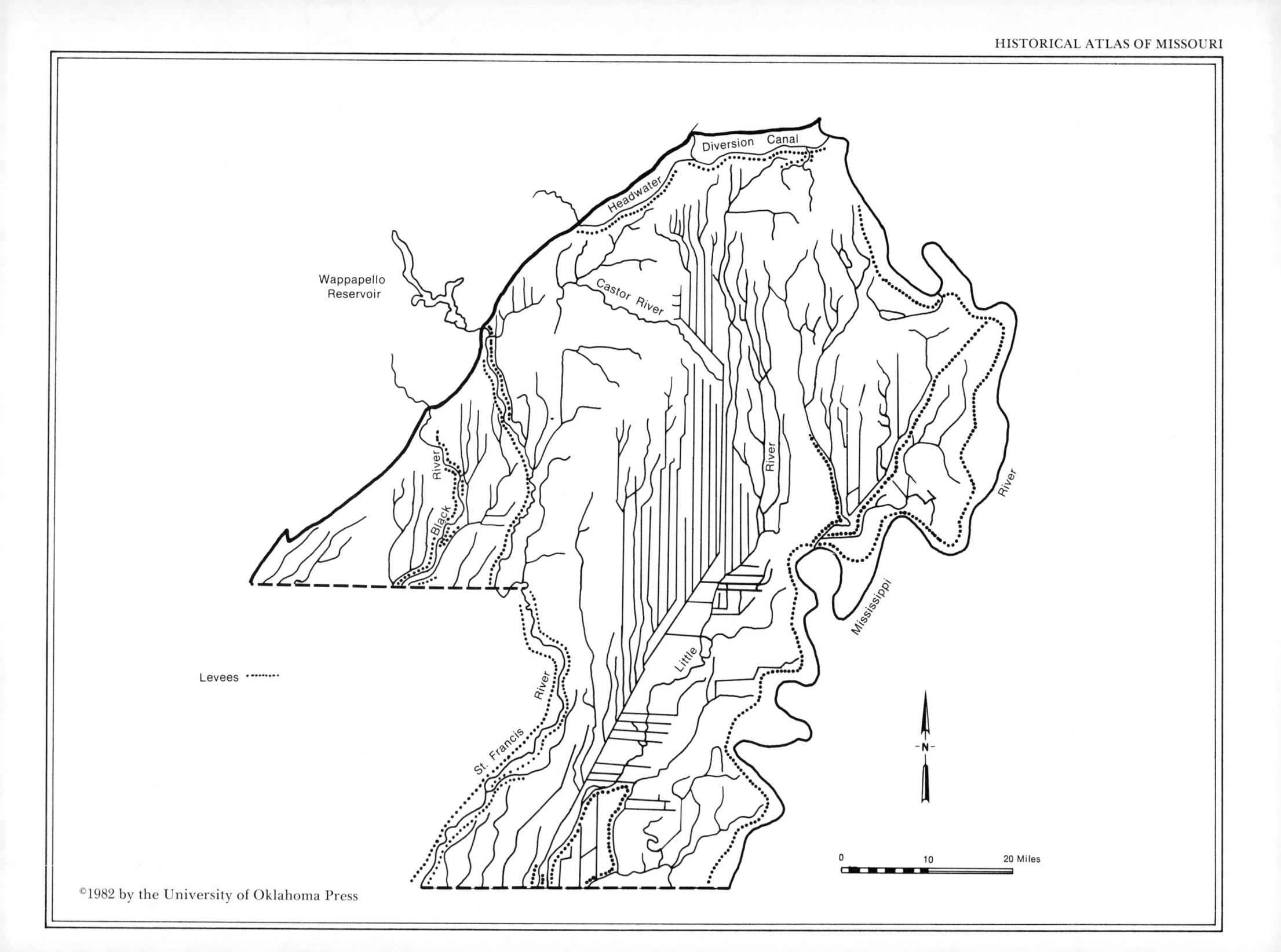

Diversion Canal

Headwater

Wappapello
Reservoir

Castor River

Black River

River

River

Mississippi River

Little River

Levees ·········

St. Francis River

N

0   10   20 Miles

90. LAND RECLAMATION IN THE SOUTHEAST LOWLANDS

The Southeast Lowlands area of Missouri, nearly all of which was originally heavily forested, is nearly level, but in all parts of it there are irregular, north–south-trending sloughs, low swells, and ill-defined terraces. The swells and terraces, along with the major upland, Crowley's Ridge, are the sites of the first settlements, many of which were owned and operated by large lumber companies such as the Himmelberger-Harrison Lumber Company and the Chicago Mill and Lumber Company, each of which owned large tracts of land. As the timber was removed and more and more land cleared, many of the mill-site settlements developed into farming communities. Gideon, Bernie, and Dudley are typical examples. As all the relatively high land was brought under cultivation, there arose a lively interest in drainage of the adjacent swamplands.

About 1900 the dragline dredge was developed. These huge floating dredges could tear out the shallow-rooted trees and dig ditches for drainage of the swamps. Several thousand acres of wet lands were drained under the County District Law, but the drainage movement culminated in the Little River Drainage District in 1905.

The location of the drainage district in relation to adjacent areas which drain into it complicated the engineering problem. The plan finally adopted, and carried out, provided for diver-sion of waters discharged into the district by streams from the Ozark Highlands and for a series of ditches and canals within the district to carry off local water. The runoff which entered the district from the highlands was diverted into the Mississippi River at the northern end of the district by means of a diversion canal, a floodway, and levees. These works begin where the Castor River flows onto the plain and extend eastward to the Mississippi just below Cape Girardeau. Within the district the general scheme is a system of small north-south ditches about one mile apart leading to main canals which conduct the waters southwest out of Missouri and ultimately to the St. Francis River.

The costs of reclamation and maintenance are assessed against the lands benefitted, and the amount to be paid each year is fixed by a board of supervisors. Land that could be purchased for a few dollars per acre before drainage were selling at prices ranging from $50 to $150 per acre in 1925. These lands were selling for $600 to $1,000 per acre or more in 1977.

The Little River Drainage Project stands out as one of the larger and more important reclamation projects of modern times. Although of considerable interest as an engineering feat, it is of greater interest geographically and is a striking example of adjustment to a difficult and complex environment.

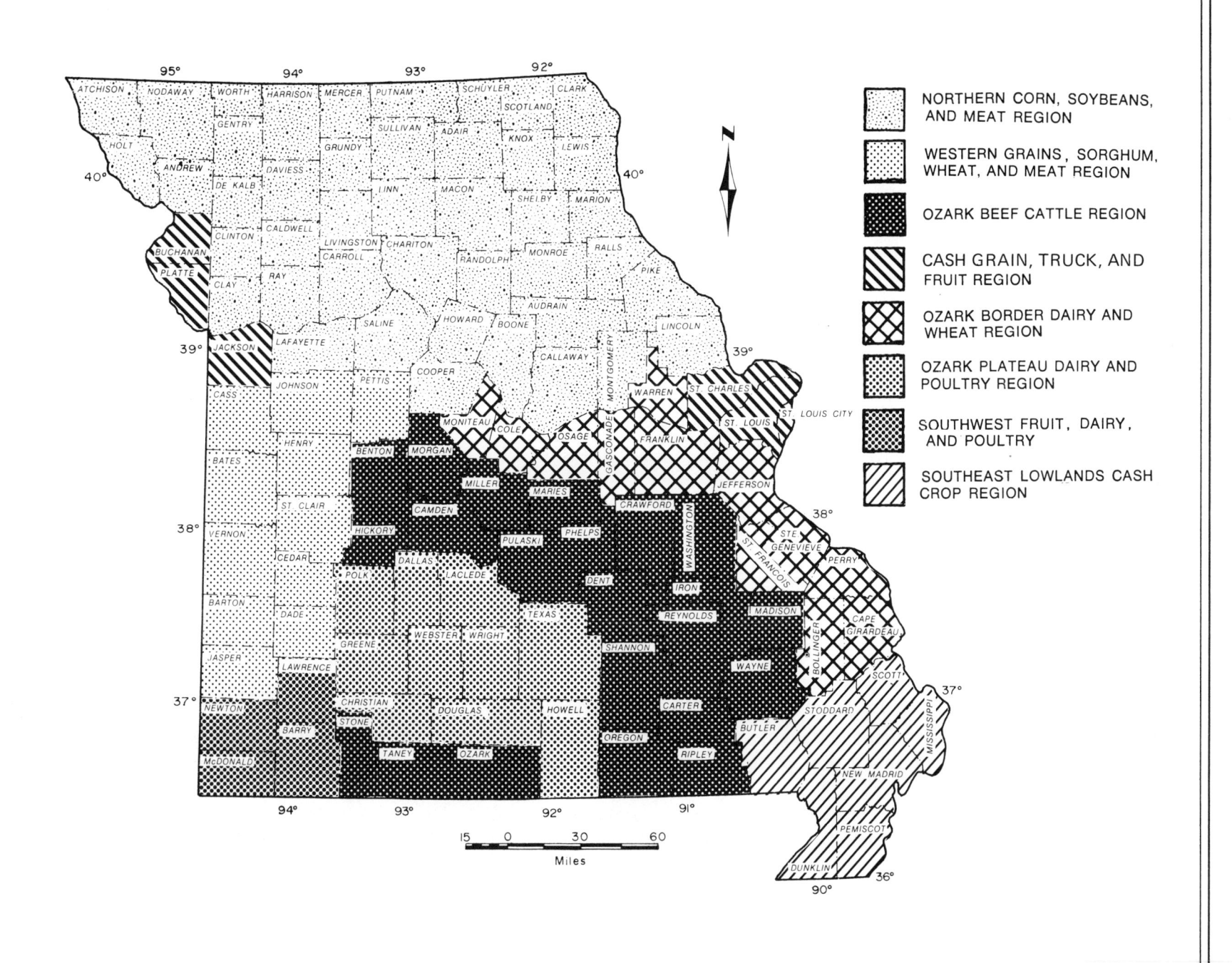

NORTHERN CORN, SOYBEANS, AND MEAT REGION

WESTERN GRAINS, SORGHUM, WHEAT, AND MEAT REGION

OZARK BEEF CATTLE REGION

CASH GRAIN, TRUCK, AND FRUIT REGION

OZARK BORDER DAIRY AND WHEAT REGION

OZARK PLATEAU DAIRY AND POULTRY REGION

SOUTHWEST FRUIT, DAIRY, AND POULTRY

SOUTHEAST LOWLANDS CASH CROP REGION

15 0 30 60
Miles

91. AGRICULTURAL REGIONS

Cash receipts from farming in Missouri during 1976 totaled $2.65 billion, up 72 per cent from 1968. Missouri ranked ninth among the states in the nation in cash receipts in 1976. A wide range of crops is grown commercially in the state, including such disparate commodities as small grains, corn, cotton, and tobacco. However, Missouri agriculture is definitely oriented toward the production of livestock and its products. Approximately two-thirds of the state's total farm income derives from the sale of livestock and livestock products.

Intensity of agricultural production varies significantly from region to region within the state. However, all of Missouri's 114 counties report over four hundred thousand dollars in agricultural receipts annually. The areas of most intensive production are those associated with the state's two great river systems: the highly productive loess areas of west central and northwestern Missouri associated with the Missouri River and the black, fertile alluvium of the Mississippi River floodplain in the Southeast Alluvial Lowland (delta region) of southeastern Missouri. Twelve of Missouri's top thirteen agricultural counties lie in these two regions.

The west central and northwestern areas specialize in livestock and livestock products. Cash grains, although well represented in these areas, are deemphasized in favor of animal feed crops such as corn. By contrast, the delta region of southeastern Missouri produces primarily field crops. The most important crop in this region is soybeans. However, corn, wheat, and cotton are also widely grown.

The remainder of Missouri, consisting primarily of the Ozarks and bordering areas, is characterized by less intensive agriculture as measured by the value of all farm products sold. Soils are generally of lower quality, and slope becomes more of a factor. As a result, much of the land in this region is not used agriculturally, and much of the remainder is used only as pasture land. Beef production, dairying, and poultry are emphasized, although small but significant areas are devoted to fruits and vegetables.

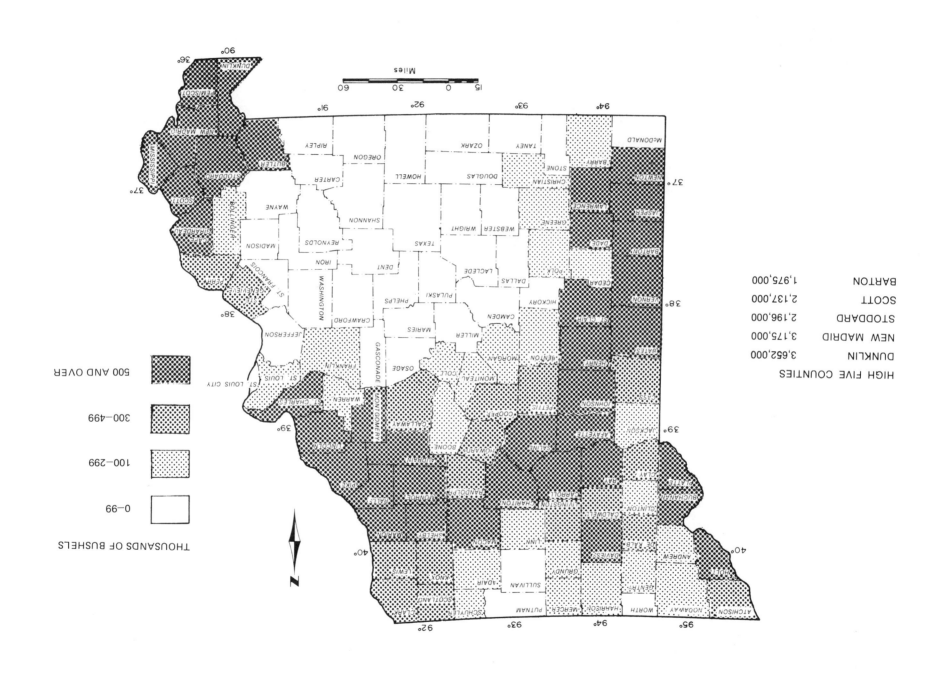

HIGH FIVE COUNTIES

DUNKLIN	3,652,000
NEW MADRID	3,175,000
STODDARD	2,196,000
SCOTT	2,137,000
BARTON	1,975,000

THOUSANDS OF BUSHELS

500 AND OVER

300—499

100—299

0—99

Miles

60   30   15   0

N

92. WHEAT

Although corn was the chief crop grown by pioneers in Missouri, wheat has been grown from the time of the first agricultural settlements. Wheat was the chief agricultural product shipped from the French settlements at Kaskaskia and Ste. Genevieve to the city of New Orleans. Wheat was grown on most pioneer farms to make white bread and biscuits.

Missouri has ranked as high as eighth in the nation in winter wheat production (1964). However, acreage reductions resulting from government supply control programs and competition from soybeans and grain sorghums reduced the acres in the state planted to wheat to less than the acreage during the depression years. Missouri wheat production totaled 33,100,000 bushels in 1969, 21 per cent below the 42,200,000 bushels produced in 1968. High prices resulting from large sales of wheat in foreign markets, coupled with drought and crop failure in some of the world's great grain growing regions, encouraged Missouri farmers to expand the acreage planted to wheat. Acreage and production of wheat expanded in the 1970s, reaching 1.9 million acres and 54,340,000 bushels in 1976.

The leading wheat region in the state is the Southeast Lowlands. The four leading counties in wheat production (Dunklin, New Madrid, Pemiscot, and Stoddard) are all located here. A second area of concentrated wheat production is in the southwestern part of the state, including Jasper, Barton, and Vernon counties. Wheat is grown to some extent as a rotation crop. The Ozarks stand out conspicuously as an area with little wheat production.

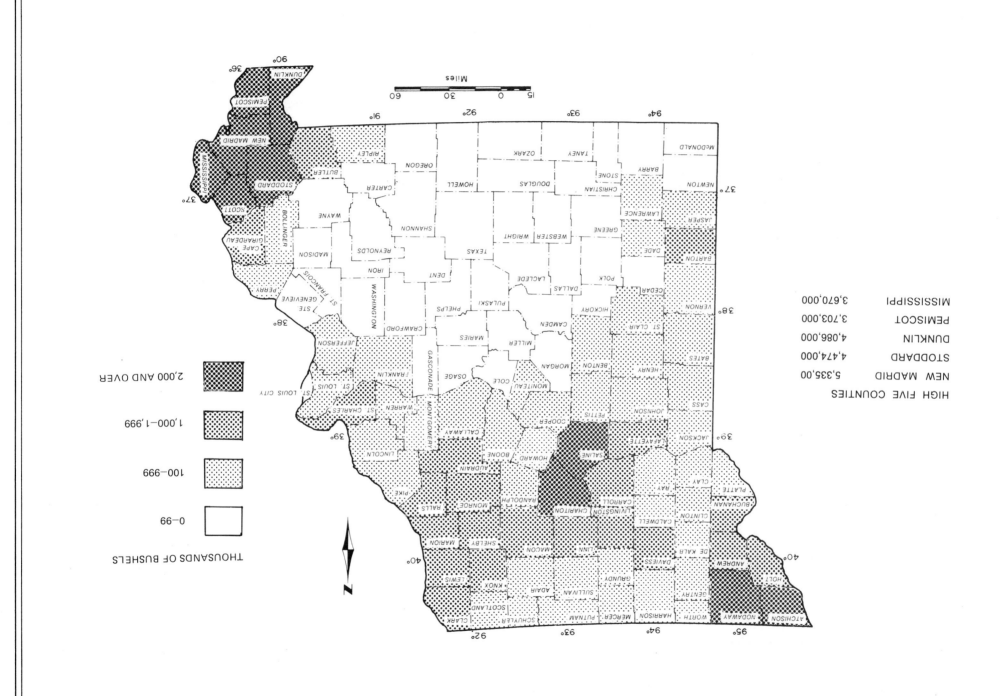

THOUSANDS OF BUSHELS

2,000 AND OVER

1,000–1,999

100–999

0–99

HIGH FIVE COUNTIES

NEW MADRID   5,335,00
STODDARD   4,474,000
DUNKLIN   4,086,000
PEMISCOT   3,703,000
MISSISSIPPI   3,670,000

Miles

93. SOYBEANS

Soybeans (soya beans) are largely consumed in the Far East. The plant is indigenous to eastern Asia, and it is widely cultivated there; before the Second World War, China and Manchuria were credited respectively with one-half and one-third of the world production of 12 million tons at that time. Cultivation of the bean has increased rapidly in North America, and now the giants in production are the United States and China. The United States production increased from 15.5 million tons in 1958 to 31.8 million in 1971—more than half the world total of 48.2 million tons and more than double China's production.

Soybeans have a high oil content—about 17 per cent. The oil has long been used for cooking in China, and with the discovery early in this century of methods to rid it of a rancid flavor, it began to be used in the West in the manufacture of compound lard and margarine. Apart from direct human consumption, the soybean is useful for cattle food and for its oil content. It is widely used in industry for the manufacture of soap, paints, and plastics.

Missouri shares in both of the great soybean districts of the United States—the Corn Belt and the Mississippi Alluvial Valley. The largest soybean production lies north of the Missouri River in the Missouri portion of the famed Corn Belt. The largest block of highly productive counties, however, is situated in the delta areas of southeastern Missouri. New Madrid, Stoddard, Dunklin, Mississippi, and Pemiscot counties are normally the leading producing counties.

Soybean acreage in 1976 totaled 4.2 million acres, or 1.35 million acres more than corn in the same year. Cash receipts from the sale of soybeans accounted for 24 per cent of the total cash receipts from the sale of all crops and livestock.

THOUSANDS OF BUSHELS

2,000 AND OVER

1,000–1,999

250–999

0–249

HIGH FIVE COUNTIES

ATCHISON	9,765,000
SALINE	8,329,000
NODAWAY	7,571,000
HOLT	7,266,000
LAFAYETTE	5,972,000

Miles
0 15 30 60

N

94. CORN

Corn, or maize, as it is known in Europe, is the only grain crop grown in Missouri that is native to North America. The climate of Missouri is nearly ideal for corn; a growing season four and one-half to seven months long, without frost, the middle portion of which is hot both day and night; sunny skies; and sufficient rains to supply the demands of a rapidly growing and luxuriant crop, falling at such intervals as best to provide sufficient moisture without making the soil over-saturated. Corn is thus a summer crop, and one that requires summer rains (or irrigation), though not very heavy and frequent rains.

World production of corn has more than doubled over the past quarter-century, and the United States grows nearly 46 per cent of the present crop of some 308 million metric tons; China is the second-largest producer, with a crop estimated to exceed 40 million metric tons. For many years corn was king of Missouri's field crops, but in recent years soybeans have become the leader in both acreage planted and value. Nevertheless, corn is grown on one-half of the farms, and the three

million acres reported in corn in 1976 occupied one-fourth of the harvested cropland. In the same year, Missouri ranked eighth in total corn production.

Corn production has declined from record levels in the early 1970s, when prices reached the highest ever. Likewise, yields per acre have declined somewhat in response to adverse weather conditions and more restricted use of fertilizers on marginal lands. The average yield of corn in 1976 was sixty-one bushels per acre. Generally, corn yields in the southwestern quarter of Missouri run 25 per cent lower than those in other parts of the state. Most of the harvested corn is fed to livestock where it is raised, and relatively little finds its way into commercial marketing channels. For this reason cash corn sales accounted for only 8 per cent of the state's cash farm receipts in 1976. The leading corn-producing counties in the state are Saline, Atchison, and Nodaway, all in the northern part of the state. The Ozarks stand out as a region where corn is noticeably absent.

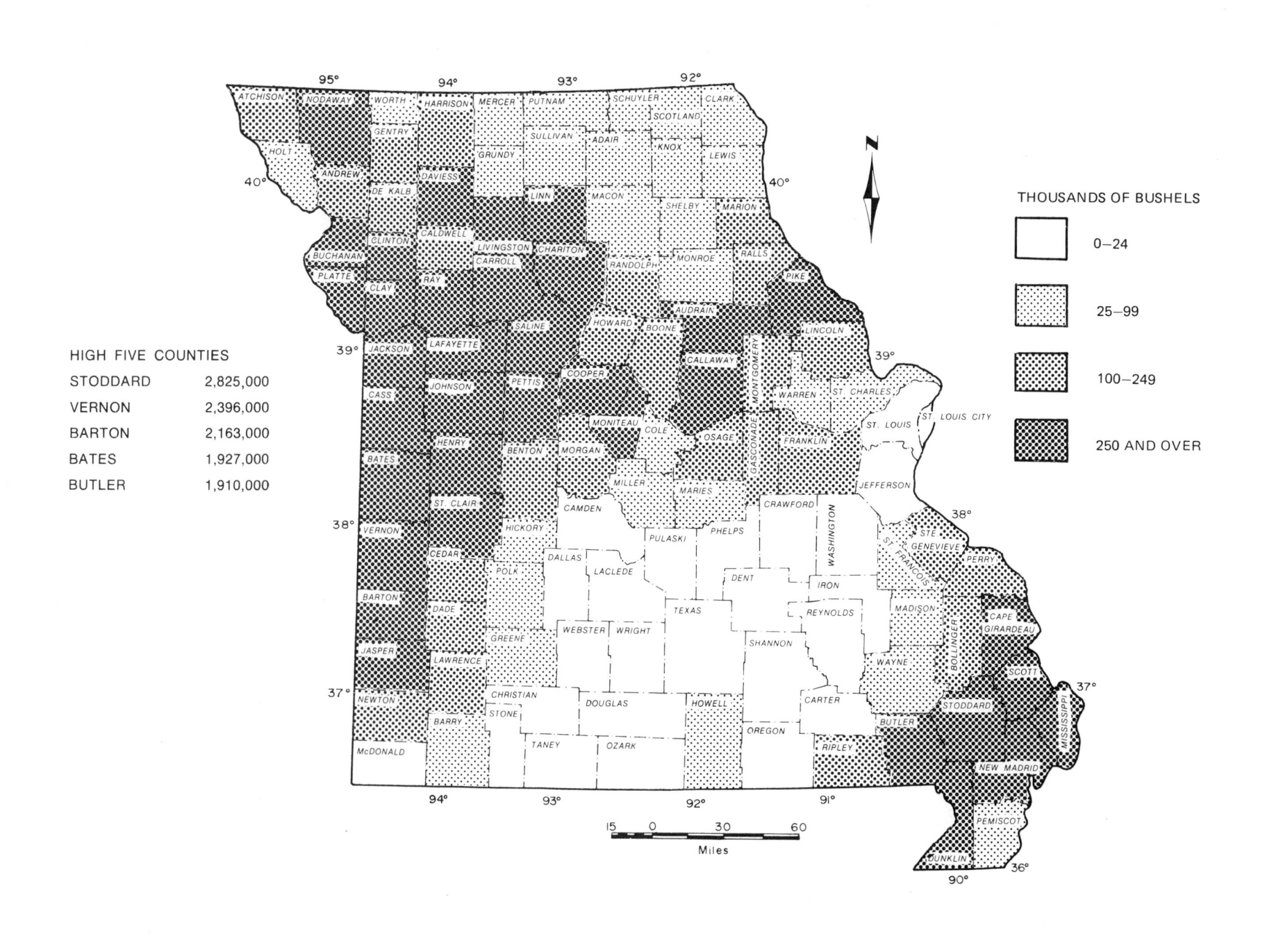

THOUSANDS OF BUSHELS

0–24

25–99

100–249

250 AND OVER

HIGH FIVE COUNTIES

STODDARD	2,825,000
VERNON	2,396,000
BARTON	2,163,000
BATES	1,927,000
BUTLER	1,910,000

95. GRAIN SORGHUM

Sorghums are tropical grasses from Africa and Asia. All the kinds of sorghum fall into four main groups: grain sorghums, sweet sorghums, grassy sorghums, and broomcorn.

More than 20 million acres of grain sorghum are planted on farms in the United States each year, especially in the Great Plains region. They are grown especially for their round, starchy seeds. The grain serves as a substitute for corn in feeding animals. While some grain sorghums grow as much as fifteen feet tall, plant breeders have produced "dwarf" varieties two to four feet tall that can be harvested with a grain combine. In the United States sorghum grain is fed to livestock, or the entire plant may be made into silage. In India, Africa, and China the grain is ground into a flour and made into pancakes or mush as food for man. Common types of grain sorghum include durra, milo, and kafir. Nearly all of the grain sorghums grown in the United States are milos. Because grain sorghums are more drought-resistant than corn, and may be planted later, farmers rely on grain sorghum as an alternative crop in dry years.

Missouri's grain sorghum production has been highly variable, being largely dependent on the weather cycle. During the dry years from 1954 to 1959 sorghum production increased sharply. But as the drought broke, acreage declined, and by 1964 sorghum occupied only half its 1959 acreage. Since 1965, sorghum acreage has stabilized at approximately two hundred thousand acres. While dry weather in the late fifties was the dominant influence in stimulating sorghum production, the development of hybrid varieties which out-yielded by one-third the older standard strains was also important. The newer varieties have the added advantages of being suited to combine harvesting.

Drying the crop in the field without spoilage is a major problem sorghum producers face in Missouri. Autumns are too humid to facilitate natural drying, and artificial drying is often required before storage.

Missouri's production is concentrated in the western half of the state south of the Missouri River and, particularly, on the Osage Plain. The leading counties in sorghum production are Vernon, Audrain, and Bates.

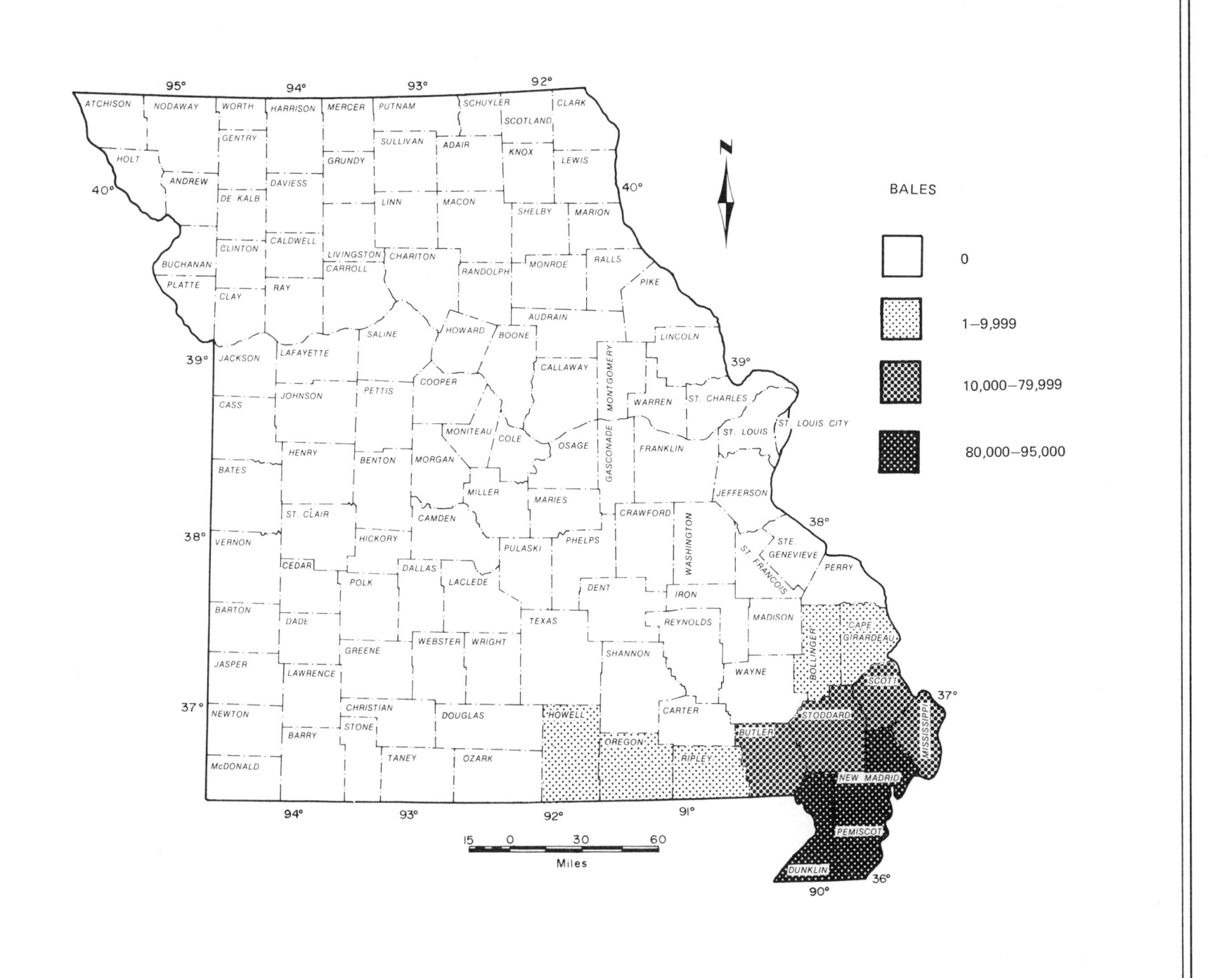

BALES

0

1—9,999

10,000—79,999

80,000—95,000

The first settlers in Missouri planted cotton for the fiber to manufacture cloth for clothing and for household use. Not being familiar with the climate, they planted cotton in the counties north of the Missouri River. Some of the accounts by early settlers, such as that of Gottfried Duden, claimed that Missouri's climate was altogether well suited for growing cotton. While in a given year the growing season might have been long enough (two hundred frost-free days) to grow cotton, very soon the planting of cotton was restricted to the extreme southern counties. Only relatively small acreages were planted in Missouri until the great drainage projects opened the Southeast Lowlands for agriculture around the turn of the century. The early 1920s were a time of phenomenal increase in cotton acreage as a result of the combined circumstances of relatively cheap reclaimed lands and high prices for cotton.

Cotton ranked as Missouri's fourth most important cash crop in 1976, which was an average year for cotton production. Cotton is grown in significant amounts in only seven counties. Cotton production in the state for 1976 was larger than the production of the previous year, but smaller than that of 1974. Except for 1973 and 1975, the acreage planted in cotton has remained over 300,000 acres since 1970, reaching the highest point in recent years, 435,000 acres, in 1972. Cotton acreage is primarily dependent on market prices, the cost of production, and the relationship of these factors to those of alternative crops.

Per-acre yields have been increasing in recent years, and that increase will likely permit the state to retain or possibly improve its relative position in U.S. cotton production.

The advent of the mechanical picker has accelerated the trend toward larger farms in the cotton-producing region. Since 1959 the number of cotton farms in Missouri has declined by more than one-fourth, and a continuing decline is probable.

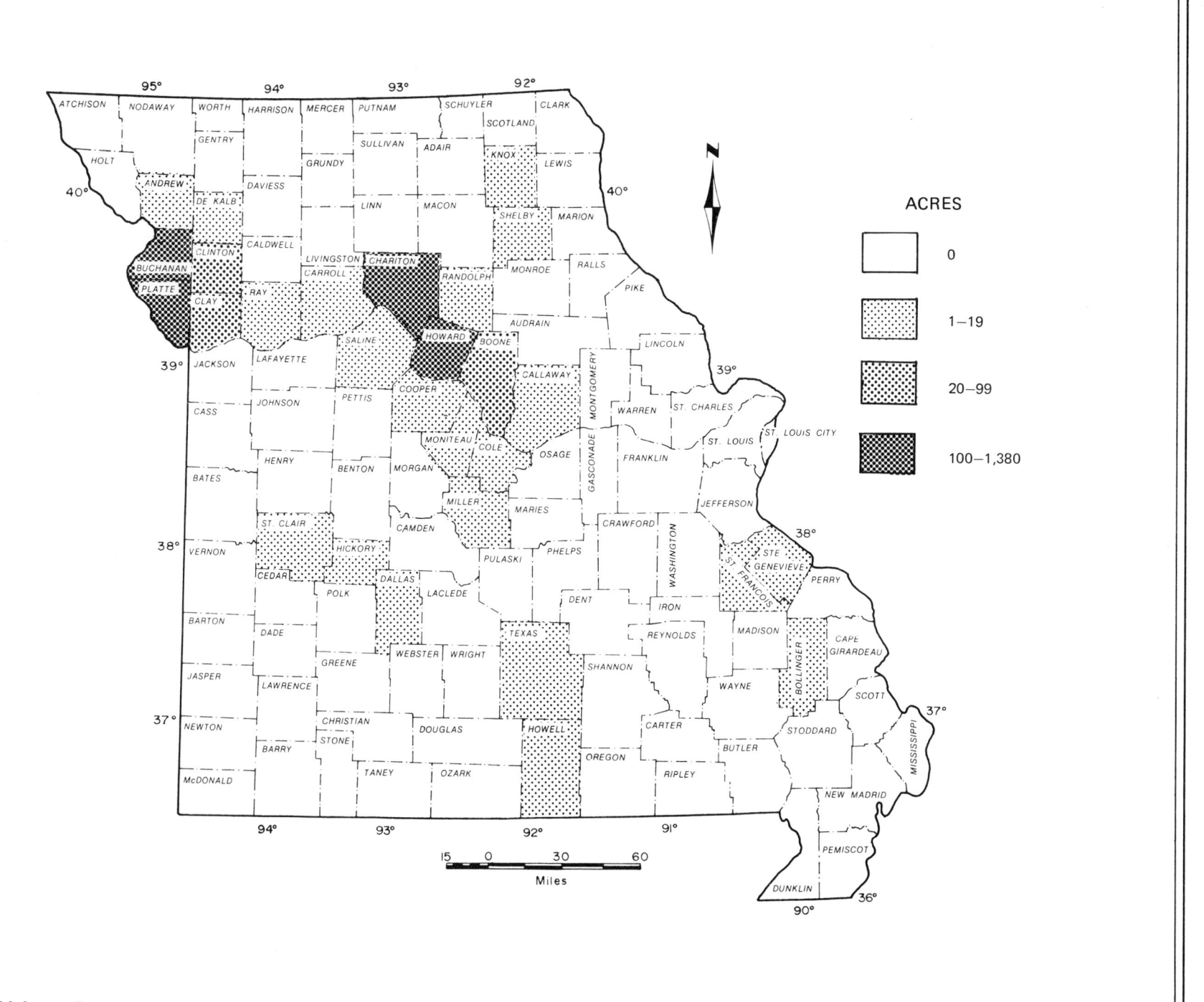

ACRES

0

1–19

20–99

100–1,380

97. TOBACCO

Tobacco, along with hemp, was an important commercial crop grown in the central part of Missouri, particularly in the counties bordering the Missouri River. In the early years the largest tobacco acreage was planted in the Boonslick country in central Missouri, but gradually the most important growing area came to be centered in western Missouri between Kansas City and St. Joseph.

Culture of burley tobacco in the vicinity of Weston in Platte County was encouraged in the 1890s by the excellent prices a local firm, Berry and Hawkins, obtained in Kentucky. About 1910, J. B. Doran built the first Weston warehouse where sales were made to independent buyers and speculators. Weston, the market for all Missouri tobacco, claims to be the largest tobacco market west of the Mississippi River.

In 1976 the value of all tobacco grown in the state was $6.3 million. Platte County accounted for almost two-thirds of this total. Most of the remainder was grown in only three additional counties: Buchanan, Howard, and Chariton.

Tobacco production is rigidly controlled by government marketing quotas, and reductions in acreage in recent years are almost exclusively due to lower allotments.

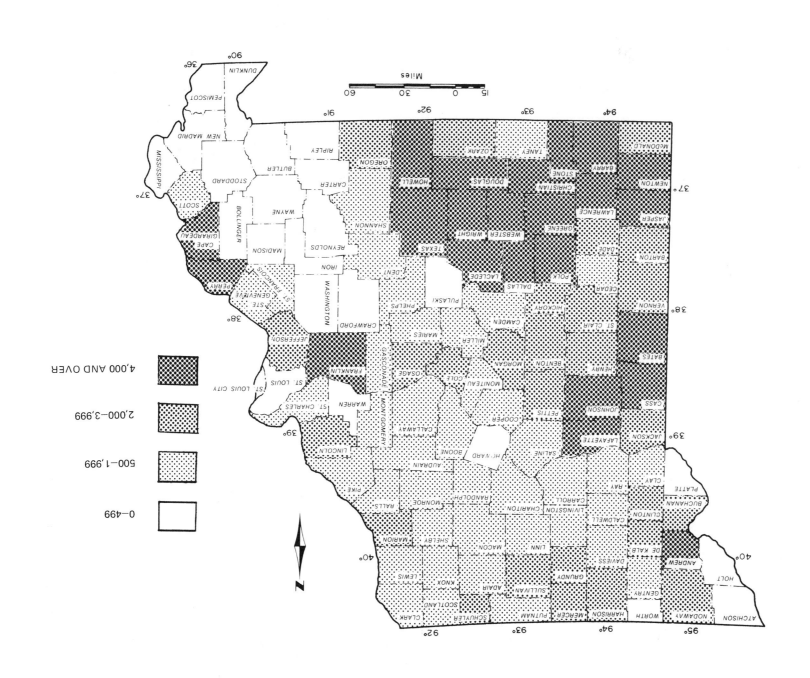

Miles

60 30 15 0

4,000 AND OVER

2,000–3,999

500–1,999

0–499

N

The pioneers who settled Missouri usually led one or more cows as they migrated. Most of them were nondescript and of the beef type, but a few were crossed with dairy breeds. These cattle supplied both milk and meat; some were used as oxen. Good-quality livestock, of the various dairy breeds, did not reach Missouri in great numbers until after 1900.

Commercial dairying began shortly after 1900. At first, very few farms made a specialty of dairying, but a number of farms had as many as ten to fifteen milk cows. Gradually, farmers began to specialize. Because dairying developed before there were large numbers of automobiles and trucks, most of these dairy farms were located close to the railroads. Springfield, with a substantial local market and several railroad lines, formed a nucleus around which dairy farms were established.

The demand for dairy products from markets outside the area became more discriminating and competitive, requiring herd improvement, better management, and better feeding. Many herds were developed from purebred Holsteins and Jerseys, but other popular dairy breeds included Brown Swiss, Guernsey, and the Milking Shorthorn.

Remarkable growth of commercial dairy farming occurred from its inauguration until 1940. In 1910, dairy cattle in the eight-county area surrounding Springfield totaled 64,361, but by 1940 the number had increased to 113,200. The growth during the 1920s was especially rapid. Lawrence County rose from twenty-ninth place to third place among Missouri counties in the number of dairy cattle in only three years. Between 1921 and 1924, the number of dairy cattle in the county increased from 9,640 to 14,530. By 1924, Springfield ranked fourth in the nation in churned butter, and eleven large creameries in that city employed more than 650 workers. Nearly every town of fifteen hundred or more had creameries, and the larger trade centers began to develop more elaborate milk processing plants. A second smaller dairy farming area became established in the Chariton River Hills of northern Missouri, and large dairies were established near St. Louis and Kansas City.

The shift to larger and more efficient dairy manufacturing plants, along with improvements in farm technology, management, and cooperative marketing, contributed to fewer but larger dairy farms with improved methods of production. In the early days milk was separated on the farm, the skimmed milk was fed to calves and hogs, and the cream was traded for household and farm supplies. Modern dairying is geared to fast, efficient transportation. Today, most of the cows are milked in inspected milking sheds using modern equipment. The cream can has disappeared from the roadside, having been replaced by bulk milk tanks serviced by tank trucks.

Dairy cattle numbers and production in Missouri reflect national trends. In the past two decades, Missouri's milking herd declined by one-third, yet during that same period milk sales increased by more than 40 per cent. Fewer farms now keep milk cows. On the other hand, many of the remaining dairy farmers are expanding their herds. From 1960 to 1970 the number of farms selling whole milk declined by 40 per cent, but more milk was being sold. Four out of every ten farms in Missouri maintain milk cows, and one out of five sells milk. Missouri ranks ninth in the nation in the number of milk cows and tenth in milk production.

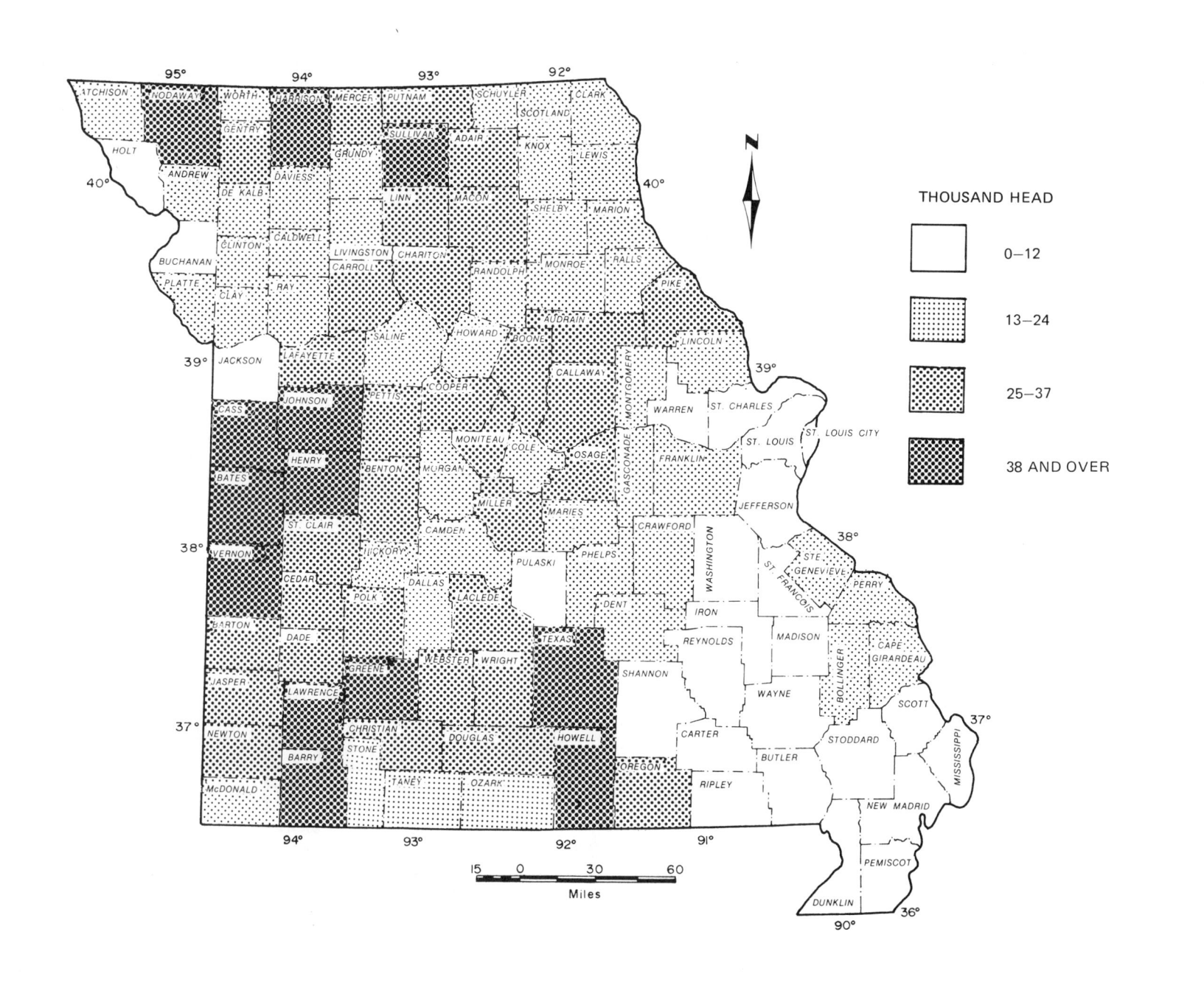

THOUSAND HEAD

0—12

13—24

25—37

38 AND OVER

15 0   30   60
Miles

Before the coming of the railroads, livestock husbandry was the only possible system of commercial agriculture. The cost of shipping grain or other bulky products over rough terrain to distant markets outside the Ozarks was prohibitive except in the eastern and northern border areas. Cattle could be driven from Missouri farms to St. Louis and even to New Orleans. Many cattle went to market on flatboats and steamboats that could navigate the Missouri, the Mississippi, and a few of the larger tributary streams. Salt meats, cured hides, tallow, and lard were major exports via the river route.

In addition to the cattle and half-wild hogs that ran at large on unfenced commons, early stock farmers also raised horses and mules. Horses were in strong demand both locally and in northern cities, and most of the mules were sold in the Southern states, where they were used in the cotton fields.

As open range livestock farming gave way to general farming, cultivated crops, particularly corn, received more emphasis, and farmers gave greater attention to raising hogs and poultry. Also, stall feeding of cattle, to produce finished animals, became more common. From about 1900 to 1940, when general farming reached its height, a livestock economy like that of the Corn Belt became popular. Corn was used for production of finished hogs and beef. Production of beef cattle attained its greatest importance in the loess and glacial soils regions in northern Missouri, where the natural conditions were better suited to the production of corn and other feeds.

In the Ozarks, in the years since World War II, there has been a marked shift back to a livestock economy based on the production of unfinished feeder cattle. In the last few years this shift in emphasis has reached major proportions and constitutes one of the most significant economic changes in the Ozarks. As a result, land use and landscape patterns have been greatly altered, and the changes promise to continue for some time to come. High cattle prices made conversion of timberland to pasture profitable. Between 1966 and 1969 more than seventy-three thousand acres were defoliated and aerially seeded to pasture by one southwestern Missouri farmers' cooperative.

The trend to beef cattle is nationwide, but the growth rate in beef cattle in the Ozarks is substantially above the national average. Numbers of beef cattle in Missouri increased 75 per cent from 1958 to 1967, considerably more than the 43 per cent increase in the United States. In the Springfield vicinity of southwestern Missouri, the increase in beef cattle amounted to 136 per cent.

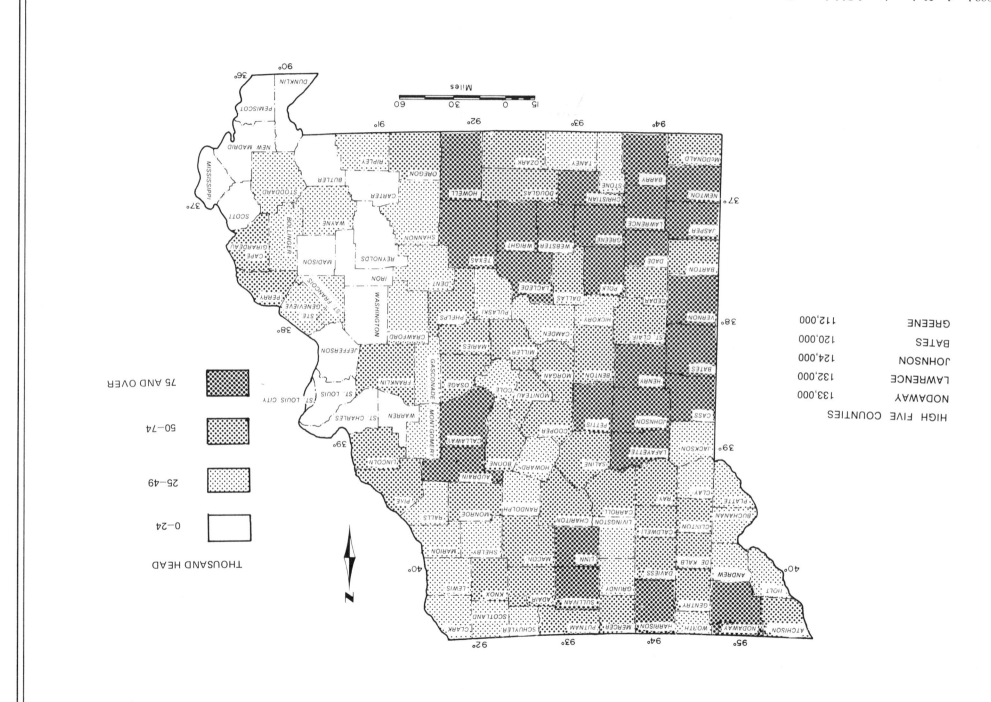

Miles

15   0   30   60

THOUSAND HEAD

75 AND OVER

50–74

25–49

0–24

HIGH FIVE COUNTIES

NODAWAY	133,000
LAWRENCE	132,000
JOHNSON	124,000
BATES	120,000
GREENE	112,000

In 1975, of every dollar of cash farm income in Missouri, 33 per cent came from the sale of cattle and cattle products. The sale of cattle and calves accounted for 24 per cent, and dairy products accounted for 9 per cent. The inventory of all cattle in Missouri on January 1, 1977, was 6.4 million, or 30 per cent above January 1, 1970. Numbers of beef cattle, unlike other types of livestock in Missouri, have been increasing steadily in the past two decades. In addition to the popular Hereford and black Angus breeds, several other breeds, including Simentals and Charolais, are increasing in numbers.

The areas of most intensive beef production in Missouri are in the central and western portions of the state. Cow-calf herds provide a profitable outlet for much of the state's extensive permanent pasture and open timberlands. Cattle feeding operations tend to concentrate near the areas of intensive corn and small grain production. Nodaway and Saline are the state's leading counties in beef cattle production. In the Ozark counties, production of feeder cattle has increased greatly over the past twenty years. Increased acreages of hay and pasture have been planted for cow-calf operations. Major concentrations of dairy cattle are in southwestern Missouri and in the Chariton River Hills region in northern Missouri.

Marketing facilities for beef cattle are well developed in and near Missouri. Terminal public markets are located at Kansas City, St. Joseph, Springfield, Joplin, and East St. Louis, Illinois.

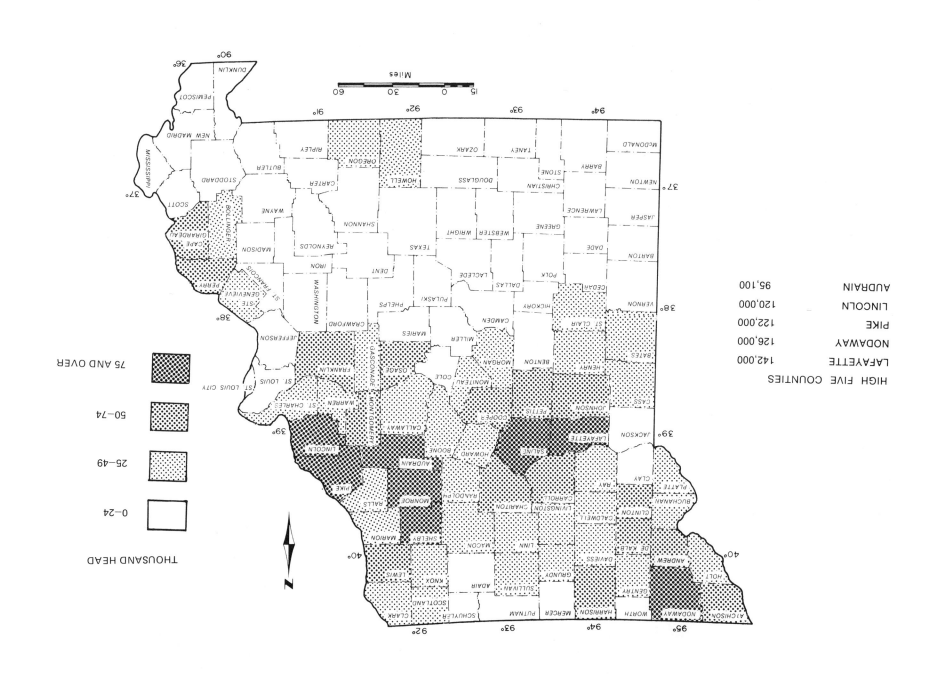

THOUSAND HEAD

75 AND OVER

50–74

25–49

0–24

HIGH FIVE COUNTIES

LAFAYETTE	142,000
NODAWAY	126,000
PIKE	122,000
LINCOLN	120,000
AUDRAIN	95,100

Miles

15   0   30   60

N

The sale of animals brings in most of the revenue of farms in the Corn Belt. Although many animals could be raised for meat, the people of the United States prefer beef, bacon, and ham. Of the total of digestible plants harvested (not including graze forage) and used within the United States, 87 per cent is fed to livestock. This may seem like an inefficient way to use arable land, but it is pleasant for those who like meat, milk, and eggs.

There is a very close correlation between the locational pattern of hog raising and the mixed-farming region from eastern Nebraska to Ohio. Few other areas in the United States have many swine at all. In 1976 Missouri ranked fourth nationally in numbers of hogs and pigs marketed. Swine are produced in every county in the state, but by far the largest numbers are produced north of the Missouri River. Hogs and pigs account for 21 per cent of gross farm receipts.

Missouri's hog industry has been slowly expanding in recent years, and the number of hogs slaughtered in 1976 was 16 per cent larger than in 1975. The hog industry is becoming concentrated on fewer and fewer farms. The number of farms marketing hogs has declined by nearly one-half since 1960.

Two distinct types of hog-raising enterprises are found in Missouri. On the one hand is the production of market hogs for slaughter. This system dominates in the feed grain–producing areas of northwestern and west central Missouri. On the other hand, Missouri has become an important producer of quality feeder pigs, particularly in the southern Ozarks.

COOPER

CALLAWAY

MONTGOMERY

LINCOLN

WARREN

ST. CHARLES

MONITEAU

COLE

OSAGE

GASCONADE

FRANKLIN

ST. LOUIS

ST. LOUIS CITY

MORGAN

MILLER

MARIES

CAMDEN ● 1

PULASKI

PHELPS

CRAWFORD

WASHINGTON

JEFFERSON

DALLAS

LACLEDE

DENT

IRON

ST. FRANCOIS

STE. GENEVIEVE

PERRY

WEBSTER

WRIGHT

TEXAS

REYNOLDS

MADISON

BOLLINGER

CAPE GIRARDEAU

SHANNON

WAYNE

SCOTT

DOUGLASS

HOWELL

CARTER

● 25

STODDARD

MISSISSIPPI

OZARK

OREGON

RIPLEY

BUTLER

NEW MADRID

26 ●

PEMISCOT

DUNKLIN

8
9
7
10
4 6
2 3
5
23
24
16
17
18
19
20
21
22
11
12 13
14 ● 15

N

1. OSAGE IRON WORKS
2. OZARK FURNACE
3. MARAMEC FURNACE
4. MIDLAND FURNACE
5. SCOTIA IRON FURNACE
6. THICKETY CREEK BLOOMERY
7. REEDSVILLE FURNACE
8. IRON MILL FURNACE
9. MOSELLE FURNACE
10. HAMILTON FURNACE
11. KIMMSWICK FORGE
12. PIONEER IRONWORKS
13. JUPITER FURNACE
14. VULCAN IRONWORKS
15. MISSOURI FURNACE CO.
16. SPRINGFIELD FURNACE
17. IRONDALE FURNACE
18. CALEDONIA CHAFFERY
19. AMERICAN IRON MOUNTAIN CO.
20. VALLÉ FORGE
21. PILOT KNOB IRONWORKS
22. ASHEBRAN'S FURNACE
23. SLIGO FURNACE
24. NOVA SCOTIA FURNACE
25. MIDCO FURNACE
26. BRANDSVILLE

15   0   30   60
Miles

The first ironworks in Missouri was Ashebran's Furnace, which was built about 1815 or 1816 by Corbin Ashebran and James Tong. The furnace, located two miles east of Ironton on Stout's Creek, was closed in 1819 because of poor business conditions. In 1819 or 1820 the Harrison-Reeves Bloomery was built in Crawford County about four miles southwest of Sullivan. The bloomery ceased operations sometime between 1825 and 1840.

The Springfield Furnace, was established in 1823 on what is now called Furnace Creek about six miles south of Potosi in Washington County. The forge was located five miles south of the furnace at the town of Caledonia.

The Meramec Ironworks (Furnace) or Massey's, as it was frequently called, was founded in 1829 by Thomas James and Samuel Massey of Ohio. The ironworks was built at Meramec Spring about six miles southeast of St. James in Phelps County. It operated for forty-seven years, closing in 1876.

In 1846 a furnace was built by the American Iron Mountain Company in St. Francois County to develop the supposedly inexhaustible ore deposit at Iron Mountain. Smelting continued at Iron Mountain until 1876, when the supply of timber for fuel approached exhaustion. The Moselle Furnace, in Franklin County, also was built in 1846. Next to be established was the Madison Iron Company plant at Pilot Knob. The Iron Hill Furnace, reportedly built in the late 1840s was built near Moselle and used local sink-fill hematite ores. Vallé Forge, constructed about twenty-five miles east of Farmington in 1853, was built primarily to convert Iron Mountain pig iron into blooms. The Irondale Furnace, built in 1859 in Washington County, operated until 1879 or 1880.

From 1863 to 1875, ten hot-blast furnaces which could burn Illinois coke or coal were built in or near St. Louis. The charcoal furnaces built after 1870 suffered severely from competition with the low-cost coke and coal furnaces in St. Louis. Nevertheless, several furnaces were constructed and operated with varying success in the Ozark iron fields.

Scotia Furnace, in Crawford County, was built in 1870 and operated until 1879. Reedsville Furnace, located about five miles west of Sullivan, was built in 1871 but apparently was in production only briefly. Hamilton Furnace, built in 1873 on Hamilton Creek in Washington County closed in 1876. The Osage Ironworks, established near the Osage River in Camden County in 1873 or 1874, produced iron from nearby limonite deposits. Ozark Furnace, located two miles west of Newburg in Phelps County, was built in 1873 by William James and James Dunn. It operated only three or four years. Midland Furnace, built in 1874 one mile north of Steelville, operated until 1894. Sligo Furnace, the most successful of the later charcoal furnaces, was built at Sligo in Dent County in 1880 and operated until 1920.

Two hot-blast charcoal furnaces were built in Missouri to meet war needs for iron and for wood alcohol. The first, Midco, located near Fremont in Van Buren County, built by the Mid-Continent Iron Company about 1916, operated only three or four years. The second plant, the Missouri Iron and Steel Company furnace at Brandsville in Howell County, was abandoned before completion because of the termination of the war.

The last charcoal furnace to be built was at Houston in Texas County. Using a mixture of ore and scrap iron, the furnace produced for only a few years.

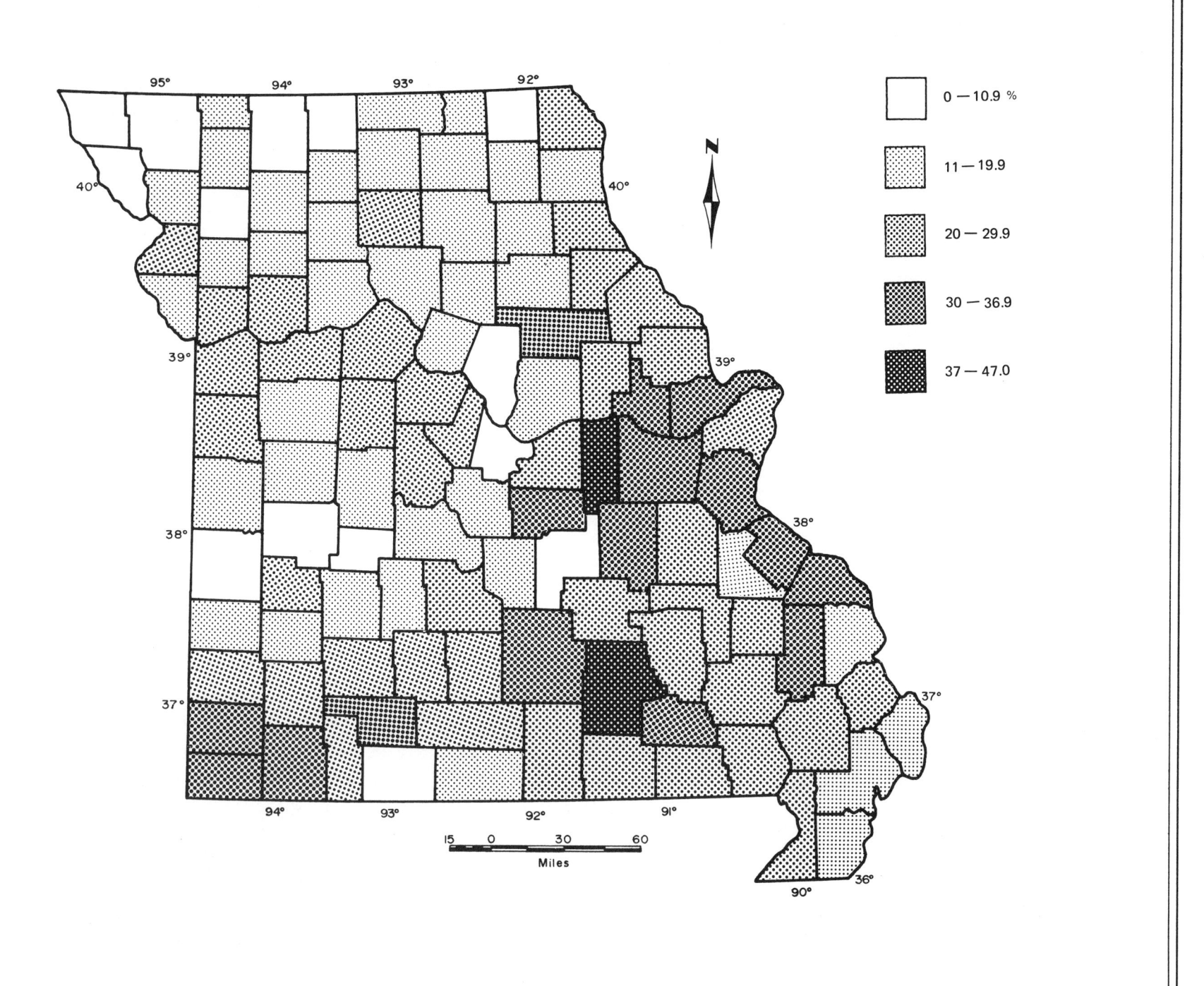

0 — 10.9 %

11 — 19.9

20 — 29.9

30 — 36.9

37 — 47.0

103. PERCENTAGE OF LABOR FORCE EMPLOYED IN MANUFACTURING

Missouri manufacturing produces the following subgroups: lumber and wood products except furniture; furniture and fixtures; stone, clay, and glass products; metal manufactures; machinery, except electrical; electrical machinery, equipment, and supplies; transportation equipment; professional and photographic equipment and watches; ordinance; other durable goods; food and kindred products; tobacco products; textile mill products; apparel and other fabricated textile products; paper and allied products; printing, publishing, and allied manufactures; chemicals and allied products; petroleum and coal products; rubber and miscellaneous plastic products; leather and leather products; and other nondurable goods.

Although most manufacturing plants are located in the urban centers, the highest percentages of total employment in manufacturing are found in less heavily populated counties. The highest percentage of total employment that was engaged in manufacturing in 1970 was in Shannon County, where a relatively small number of manufacturing plants play a major role in the economy of the county. Cities offer varied employment so that manufacturing employment, though high, does not make up extremely high percentages of the total.

The lowest rates are found in northern Missouri and in the agricultural counties in the Osage Plains of western Missouri. The state's lowest percentage, 5.4 per cent, is in Holt County. Many Ozark counties have rather moderate levels of manufacturing employment.

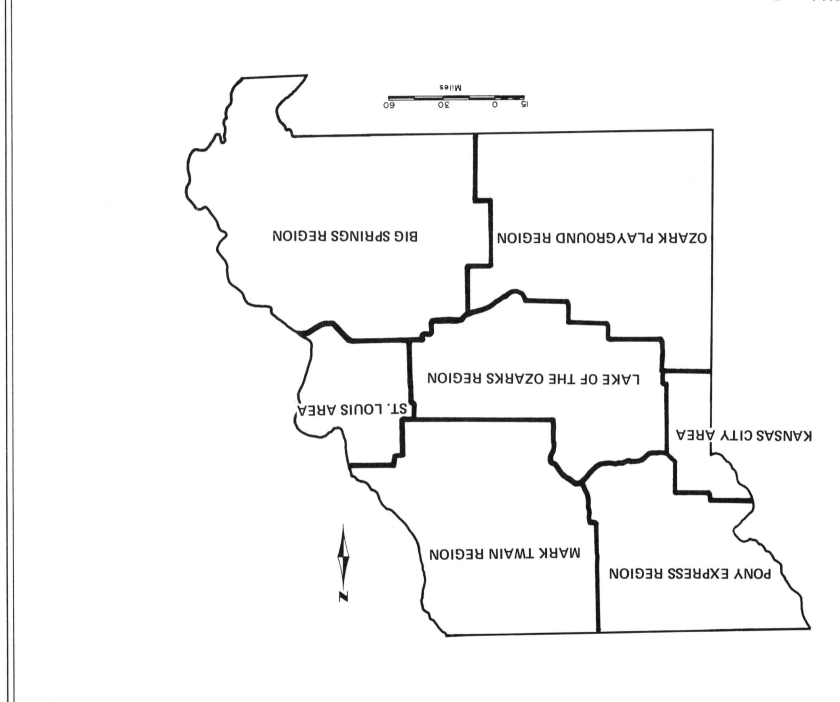

BIG SPRINGS REGION

OZARK PLAYGROUND REGION

LAKE OF THE OZARKS REGION

ST. LOUIS AREA

KANSAS CITY AREA

MARK TWAIN REGION

PONY EXPRESS REGION

Miles

15 0 30 60

N

The Pony Express region is in northwestern Missouri. In St. Joseph, the region's largest city, the old Pony Express stables are preserved as a museum of the city's history. Other points of interest in St. Joseph include the Patee House, first headquarters of the Pony Express; the house where the outlaw Jesse James was killed; and the historic Robidoux home.

In the Mark Twain region Hannibal is famous for its river lore, and for two famous citizens: Samuel Clemens (Mark Twain) and Margaret Tobin Brown (the Unsinkable Molly Brown). Mark Twain Lake is near the tiny town of Florida, where Mark Twain was born.

The Kansas City area holds attractions both old and new. Among the historic attractions are Fort Osage, the Mormon Visitor Center, historic Independence, the Truman Library, the Nelson Gallery of Art, the Liberty Memorial, and the River Quay. The Country Club Plaza, built in the 1920s as America's first shopping center, is famous for its stores, restaurants, and fountains. New attractions include the Harry S Truman Sports Complex; Kemper Memorial Arena; Crown Center; Worlds of Fun; and the $250 million Kansas City International Airport.

Lake of the Ozarks region is named for the Lake of the Ozarks, impounded by Bagnell Dam in 1931. It includes 1,375 miles of shoreline. Virtually every form of water-oriented recreation and other entertainment is available at year-around resorts. Lake Ozark State Park is Missouri's largest, and there are six commercial caves in the area. Recreation development is now in progress around the Harry S Truman Dam and Reservoir.

The St. Louis area has America's tallest man-made monument, the 630-foot Gateway Arch; Six Flags over Mid-America; the Jefferson Memorial, including the Old Court House and the Old Cathedral; and Busch Memorial Stadium, spanned by historic Eads Bridge. Excursion boats such as the *Admiral,* the *Huck Finn,* and the *Sam Clemens* ply the Mississippi River. Elsewhere in the city are the National Museum of Transport, the Museum of Science and Natural History, the Municipal Opera, McDonnell Planetarium, and the Art Museum.

The Ozark Playground region is famous for its rugged hills and sparkling clear streams. Man-made lakes—Table Rock, Taneycomo, Bull Shoals, Norfolk, Stockton, and Pomme de Terre—provide more outdoor activities. Silver Dollar City and the Shepherd of the Hills Farm are located near Table Rock Lake. Seven commercial caves are in the area.

Some of the key battles in the western campaigns of the Civil War were fought in the western Ozarks. The national cemetery in Springfield and Wilson's Creek National Battlefield, located southwest of the city, commemorate the bitter struggle.

The Big Springs region includes the rugged granite knobs of the St. Francis Mountains, huge springs, and the rich, flat delta lands of southeastern Missouri. Major historic attractions include Ste. Genevieve, the Old Lead Belt, the German settlements of East Perry County, Bollinger Mill, and Covered Bridge. For outdoor activities this region has the Ozark National Scenic Riverways on the Current River and Jacks Fork; the Eleven Point, Black, and St. Francis rivers; Clark and Mark Twain national forests; Johnson's Shut-ins State Park; Elephant Rocks State Park; Trail of Tears State Park; Clearwater Lake; and Lake Wappapello.

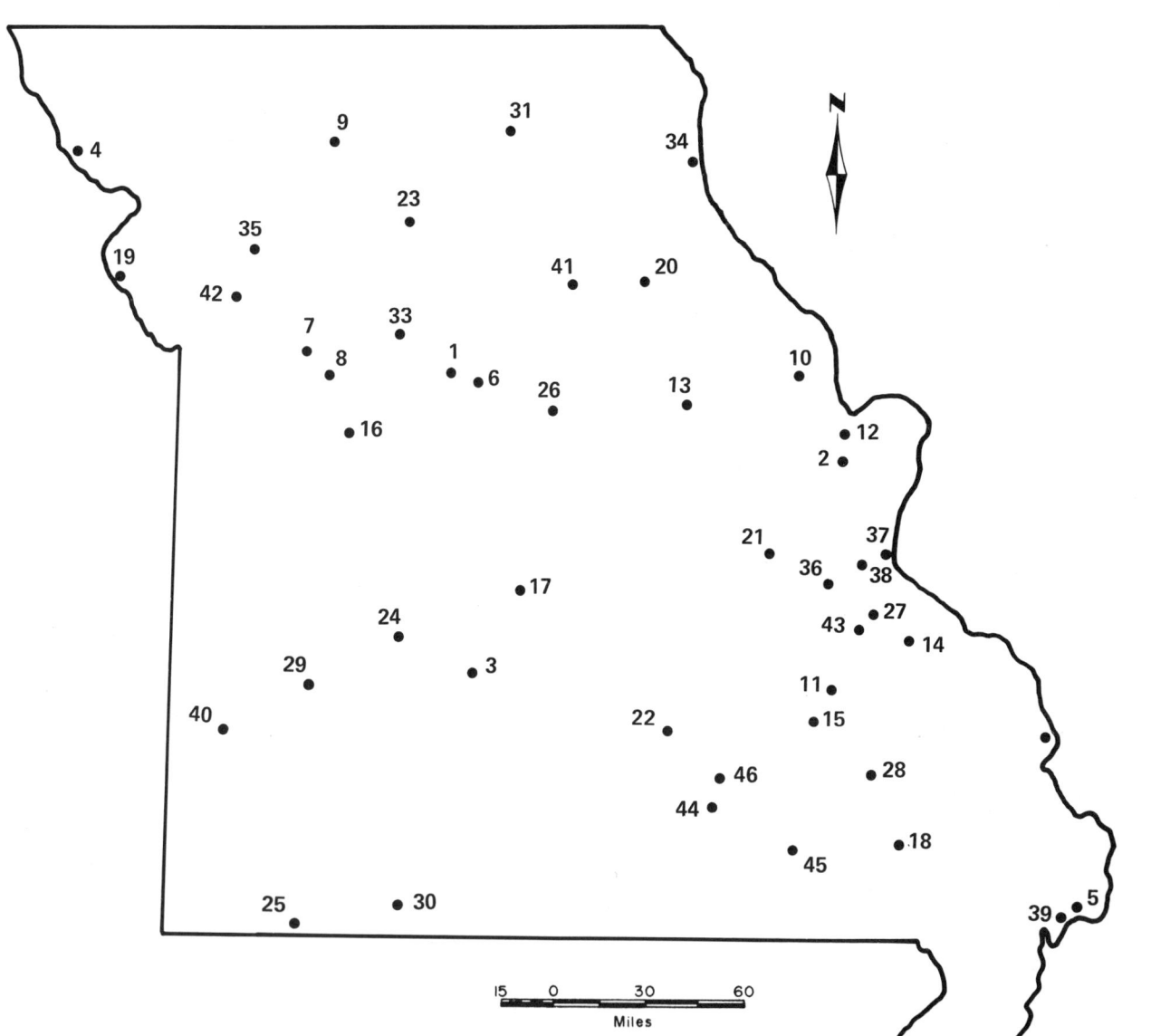

1. Arrow Rock
2. Dr. Edmund A. Babler Memorial
3. Bennett Spring
4. Big Lake
5. Big Oak Tree
6. Boonslick
7. Civil War Battle of Lexington
8. Confederate Memorial
9. Crowder
10. Cuivre River
11. Elephant Rocks
12. Fort Zumwalt
13. Graham Cave
14. Hawn
15. Johnson's Shut-ins
16. Knob Noster
17. Lake of the Ozarks
18. Lake Wappapello
19. Lewis and Clark
20. Mark Twain
21. Maramec
22. Montauk
23. Pershing
24. Pomme de Terre
25. Roaring River
26. Rock Bridge
27. St. Francois
28. Sam A. Baker
29. Stockton
30. Table Rock
31. Thousand Hills
32. Trail of Tears
33. Van Meter
34. Wakonda
35. Wallace
36. Washington
37. Governor Daniel Dunklin Grave
38. Sandy Creek Covered Bridge
39. Towosahgy
40. Harry S Truman Birthplace
    Memorial Shrine
41. Union Covered Bridge
42. Watkins Mill
43. St. Joe
Ozark National Scenic Waterways
44. Alley Spring
45. Big Spring
46. Round Spring

Miles
15 0 30 60

105. STATE PARKS

The state parks system was first authorized under the administration of Governor Frederick Gardner (1917–21), and during the 1920s the state of Missouri began to purchase and improve scenic and unusual areas of the state to be established as parks for the use of Missourians and tourists. In a single year, 1924, during the administration of Governor Arthur M. Hyde, Missouri established seven parks. The first parks were Bennett Spring in Laclede and Dallas counties, Round Spring in Shannon County, Big Spring in Carter County, Alley Spring in Shannon County, Deer Run in Reynolds County, Indian Trail in Dent County, and Mark Twain in Monroe County. In 1926 Meramec State Park in Franklin County, Sam A. Baker State Park in Wayne County, and Montauk State Park in Dent County were added to the system. In the same year, the state acquired property in Lawrence County for the Chesapeake Fish Hatchery, and the Old Tavern at Arrow Rock in Saline County was purchased. The Daughters of the American Revolution, with the assistance of the state, remodeled the Old Tavern for use as a restaurant, hotel, and museum.

Considerable improvement of the state parks was accomplished during the 1930s with the assistance of federal work programs. In 1933 the federal Civilian Conservation Corps (CCC) was established to help young unemployed and untrained men acquire job skills and earn modest wages. Men between the ages of eighteen and twenty-three years, who came from needy families, were eligible for jobs performing construction tasks or conservation work in national and state forests and parks. The men lived in CCC camps and received a minimum of thirty dollars a month in salary, twenty-two dollars of which they were required to send to their dependents. The development of Mark Twain State Park at Florida and major construction at Big Spring, Roaring River, Bennett Spring, and Washington state parks; Dr. Edmund A. Babler Memorial Park; Henry Shaw's Gardenway, and the Cuivre River Recreation Area were accomplished by the men of the CCC. Camps of the CCC were also established in state forests at Sullivan, Ellington, and Salem and at several locations in national forests where reforestation, wildlife conservation, and soil erosion projects were carried out.

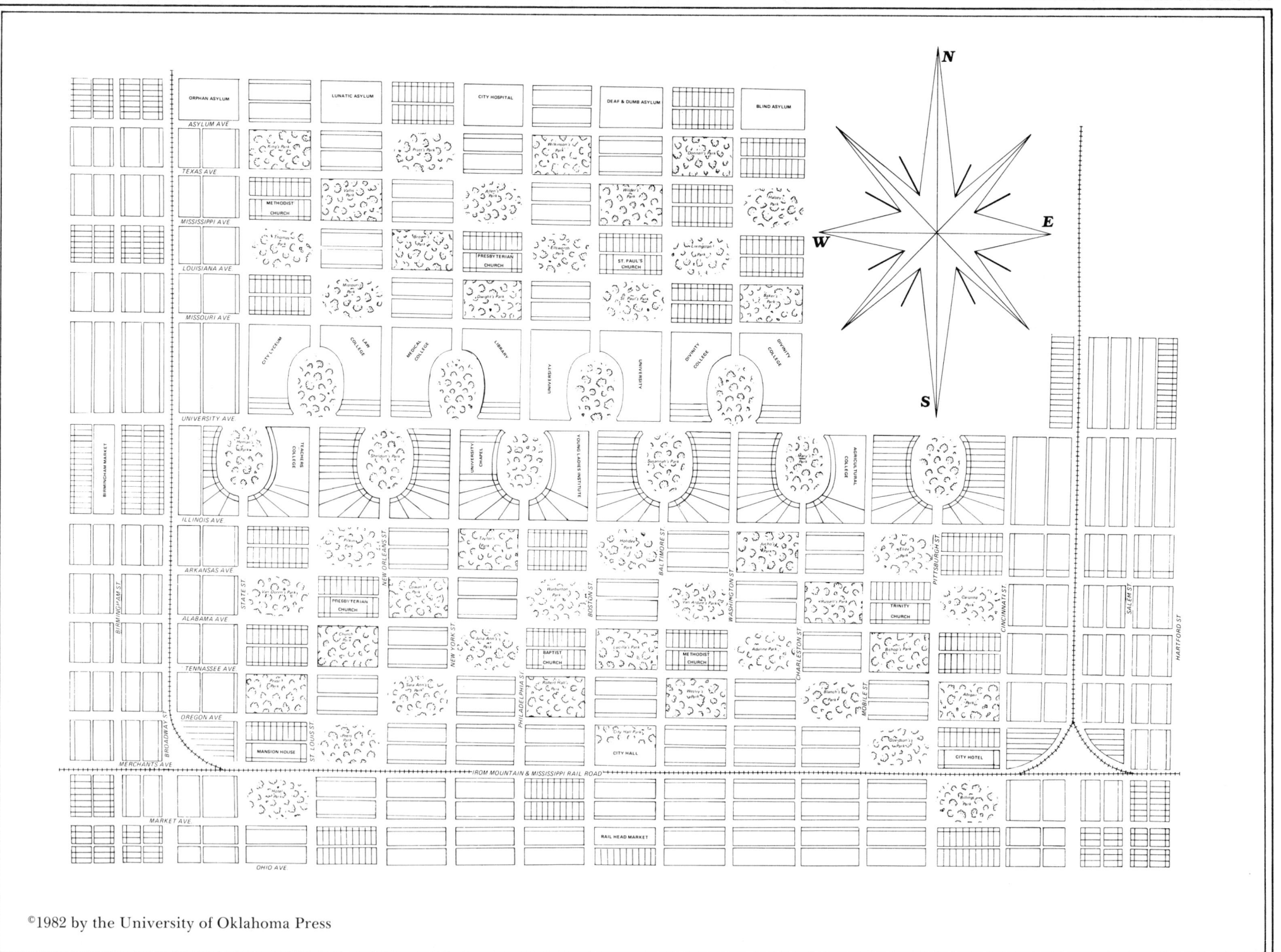

If the great promotional schemes that were started during 1835, 1836, and 1837 had been carried out in St. Francois County, it would have been a great center of culture and prosperity. On March 16, 1835, the Washington County Turnpike Company was formed, and a charter was granted them to construct a "McAdamized road" from Caledonia to the Mississippi River. This charter was later amended to allow the construction of a railroad over the same territory. The State of Missouri chartered on December 31, 1836, a company to operate under the name of the Missouri Iron Company. These projects were all part of a scheme to put the western part of St. Francois County into big business.

Iron Mountain and Pilot Knob, which were both believed to be composed of "pure" iron, were to make the stockholders of the newly formed company extremely wealthy. From their prospectus we learn that they were to confine themselves to the manufacture of railroad iron and bar iron until the National Armory was built. Congress had before them a bill to establish such an armory on the banks of the Mississippi River south of St. Louis.

"Missouri City" was to be located at the base of Iron Mountain, and near this embryonic city of perhaps eight or ten thousand people there were to be more than two thousand farms of one hundred acres each. These farmers, when they were unoccupied in the winter, were to be given jobs in the iron foundry.

A great university was designed for Missouri City in which there were to be departments of law, medicine, divinity, teaching, and agriculture. There was to be an academy and an introductory school. There was to be a Young Ladies Institute in another part of the town. One part of the town was to be restricted to literature and retirement, and it was proposed to have the manufacturing part of the town well removed so it would not disturb the other.

The by-laws of the Missouri Iron Company specified that the university was to receive seventy-five thousand dollars per year from the profits of the company. The plan was: "The income will be found sufficient to erect all the buildings of the University and the Young Ladies Institute, and so far support all the teachers and professors, that parents residing in Missouri City may have all their sons and daughters educated free of expense, from the grammar school till they receive their diplomas from the Institute, the College or for one or more of the learned professions."

The avenues of the city were to be 100 feet wide, and the cross streets were to be 80 feet wide. Provision was made for eight church lots to measure 200 by 150 feet. Lots were reserved for asylums for "Lunatic, Deaf and Dumb, Orphans and Widows, and for the blind and a City Hospital."

The panic of 1837 commenced in the East, and on October 8, 1837, the banks in Philadelphia stopped payment on paper money. It was not long until banks all over the country were in trouble. The Bank of Missouri was not so gravely hurt, but business was seriously crippled, and investors did not invest.

Another urban center, Iron Mountain City, was also planned on the present site of St. Mary's. Situated on the banks of the Mississippi River, it was to have been the eastern terminus of the railroad from Missouri City, a town similar to Missouri City but without a university.

N

• BETHEL (1844)

MULTITUDE INC. (1902)

NINEVEH (1850)

• MORMAN (1836)

• MORMAN (1833)

• MORMAN (1831)

• ICARIONS (1856)

NEW HELVETIA (1844)

ALTRUIST COMMUNITY (1907)

FRIENDSHIP COMMUNITY (1871)

• LIBERAL (1881)

BENNETT COOPERATIVE (1873)

• REUNION (1868)

MUTUAL AID COMMUNITY (1833)

15   0   30   60
Miles

Nineteenth-century America saw the establishment of utopian communities in many places, several of them in Missouri.

The first group of religious utopians, the Mormons, arrived in 1831, settling in Jackson County. Joseph Smith, prophet of the newly organized Church of Jesus Christ of Latter-Day Saints, led his group of followers to Independence to found the "New Jerusalem" organized on a form of religious communism. Anti-Mormon violence forced the Saints to move across the Missouri River into Clay County in 1833. In 1836, following continued anti-Mormon sentiment, the Missouri General Assembly designated Caldwell County as a special "Mormon county," where the Saints might live in peace, but continued harassment led the Mormons to emigrate to Nauvoo, Illinois.

Shortly after the Mormons fled Missouri, another group of religious utopians arrived in the state. They were the followers of a German mystic, Dr. William Keil. Bethel, located on 2,560 acres in the valley of the North River, was founded in 1844 shortly after Dr. Keil's conversion to communism. In 1849 a branch colony, Nineveh, was established by twenty-five colonists on a 160-acre farm in the Chariton River valley. The colonies in Missouri eventually disbanded after the Civil War.

The small communal colony near Westphalia in Osage County was established in 1844 by another German utopian, Andreas Dietsch. The settlement, called New Helvetia, was short-lived. Beset by greed, egotism, and laziness on the part of some members, the colony fell apart when Dietsch died in 1846.

Known as Icarians, some 180 French communists, followers of the French utopian Etienne Cabet, settled in St. Louis in 1856, but by 1859 the colony had already begun to disintegrate.

Reunion, a secular utopian colony founded in 1868 near Carthage in Jasper County, was the creation of Alcander Longley. After it failed, Longley established Friendship Community, near Buffalo in Dallas County. This colony was in existence from 1871 until 1877. In 1883, Longley established the Mutual Aid Community near Glen Allen in Bollinger County. Again, the community consisted of only a handful of people, and it was abandoned in 1887. Longley also attempted to establish the Altruist Colony at Sulphur Springs.

The first of Missouri's cooperative communities was established by William H. Bennett at Long Lane, a crossroads in eastern Dallas County. The Bennett Cooperative Company ceased to operate in 1877.

The most ambitious cooperative venture was Multitude Incorporated, which, when incorporated in 1902 by Walter Vrooman, already owned a great deal of property in Trenton, Missouri. By the end of 1902 the holdings included Ruskin College, the Trenton-Ruskin Factory, a hardware store, a drugstore, a dry goods store, two grocery stores, and a chemical manufacturing plant, but it was liquidated in 1904 after financial collapse.

In 1881, G. H. Walser, a religious agnostic and follower of Robert G. Ingersoll, founded the settlement of Liberal. Christians settled near the town in order to send missionaries there, and a barbed-wire fence was built to keep out the missionaries. About ten years after the founding of Liberal, the leaders of the town turned to spiritualism, and Walser himself married a medium. Christians had been moving to Liberal over the years and soon were in the majority.

The Town of Kansas

A true copy of the original plat
filed 30th day of April, A.D. 1846

Scale 250 ft to an inch

— N —

The proprietors reserve to themselves and to their heirs
and assigns forever the exclusive right of passage
on this Town Tract

The courses are set down as they appear upon the compass
without regard to declination of needle.
All lots south of Second St. are 60 ft front by 141 ft deep
with the exception of those in Blocks No. 7 and 32.
All the alleys are 18 ft wide.

DELAWARE ST.

FIFTH ST.

VINE ST.

PUBLIC SQUAIR

spring

FOURTH ST.

THIRD ST.

MAIN ST.

WALNUT ST.

MARKET ST.

SECOND ST.

WYANDOTTE ST.

ELM ST.

FRONT ST.

Missouri River

The map of the town of Kansas is adapted from a photograph in the archives in the Missouri Historical Society. The map was drawn at the time the town company was reorganized and a new sale of lots was authorized.

Kansas City had its beginning in two frontier settlements: the Missouri River town of Kansas, and the bullwhacking, wild town of Westport, four miles to the south on the Santa Fe Trail. The town of Kansas originated in the post which Francois Chouteau, an employee of the American Fur company, established in the Kaw River Bottom in the spring of 1821. Chouteau's post served as a depot from which the other posts of the company could be supplied and their furs collected. In all there were fifteen or twenty families in the Chouteau party. When a flood destroyed Chouteau's warehouse in 1830, he moved his post a few miles east to the foot of present Grand Avenue, where Peter Roy had established a ferry in 1828.

For a time in the 1830s there was a three-way struggle among Independence, Westport, and the town of Kansas (or Westport Landing, as it was called by its competitors) for the Santa Fe trade and dominance of the western trade. The opening of the Platte Purchase in northwestern Missouri for settlement in 1836 brought more trade to the town of Kansas.

When Gabriel Prudhomme, who owned the land, died in 1838, the Kansas Town Company purchased his farm of 271 acres for $4,220 and platted it into lots as the town of Kansas. The town site was bounded by the Missouri River, Broadway, Forest Avenue, and the section line that crosses Main Street at Missouri Avenue. Because of a disagreement among the investors, development was curtailed until 1846, when the town was reorganized, and another sale of lots was held. The population of the town in 1846, when the map was drawn, was seven hundred. On February 22, 1853, a charter was obtained incorporating the town as the "City of Kansas." At that time Kansas City was in an all-out race with Leavenworth and St. Joseph for supremacy as the trading city for the far West.

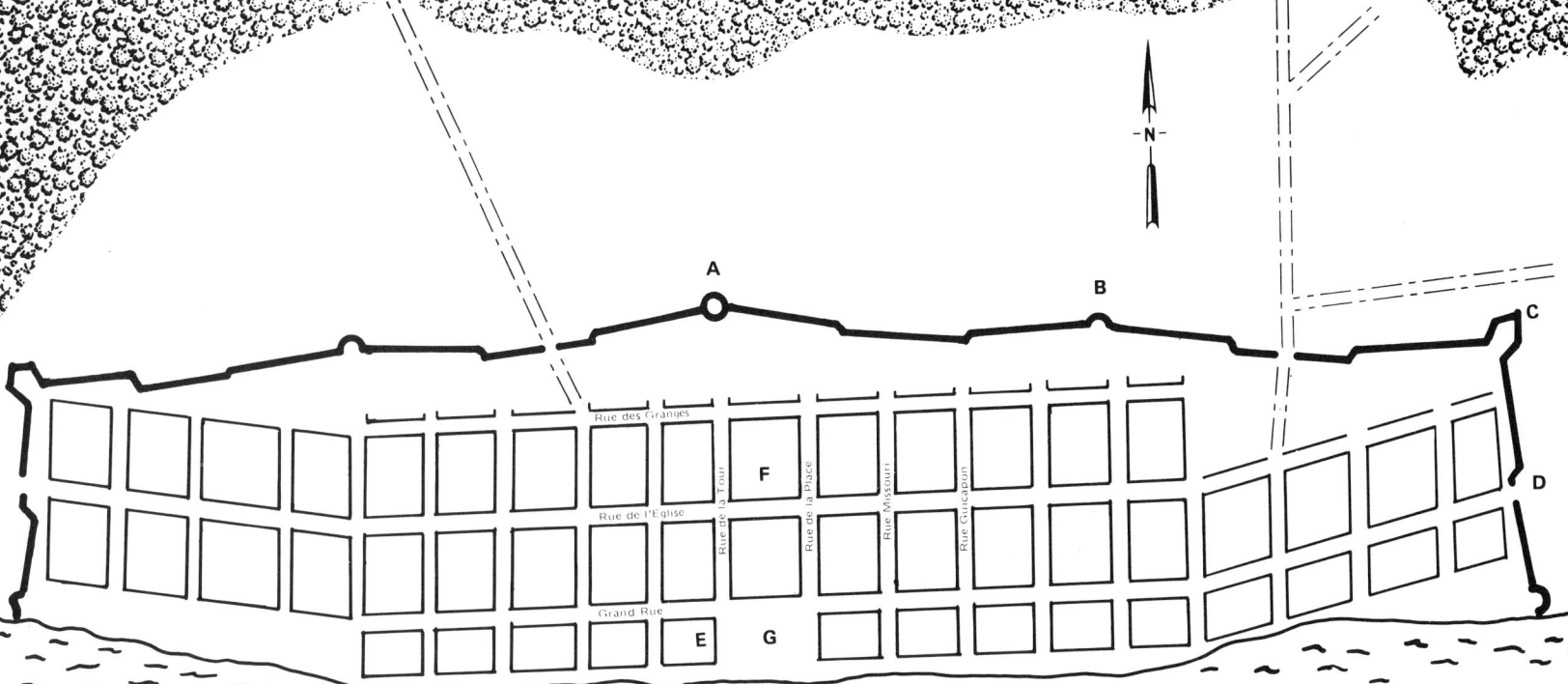

Scale ¼ of the original map

ST. LOUIS IN 1780

from the original map made by

AUGUSTE CHOUTEAU

and now on file in the U.S. Recorder's Office

St. Louis des Ilinois

fortifier par Dom Francois de Crusat
Lieutenant Colonel et Lieutenant
gouverneur de la partie occidental des Ilinois

A. TOUR
B. DEMI TOURS
C. BASTIONS
D. PORTES
E. GOUVERNMENT
F. EGLISE
G. PLACE

The map of St. Louis in 1780 is from the original map made by Auguste Chouteau. The map is adapted from the one drafted and engraved for *Campbell's Gazetteer of Missouri.*

René Auguste Chouteau accompanied Pierre Laclède Liquest in 1763 when he explored the country near the confluence of the Missouri and Mississippi rivers in order to select a suitable site for a fort and trading post for the firm of Maxent, Laclède, and Company. During the Spanish domination, Auguste Chouteau was the most prominent merchant and businessman of St. Louis, and in large measure he controlled the fur trade. He enjoyed the confidence of the Spanish officials at New Orleans. When the United States acquired Louisiana, Chouteau was appointed one of the judges of the St. Louis Court of Common Pleas and Quarter Sessions. In 1808 he was colonel of the militia, and afterward he served as a U.S. pension agent.

Situated on the first high ground touching the Mississippi south of the Illinois and the Missouri rivers, the site selected for St. Louis was gently rolling upland, alternately prairie and open woodland, covered with a high and luxuriant growth of grass, well watered by springs, and with fertile soils and a moderate climate. The village of "Paincourt," as St. Louis was commonly known, was fortified in a hurried and rude fashion before an English-Indian attack on April 26, 1780. A wooden tower was built overlooking one end of the town, and five cannons were placed in it. Two intrenchments were built and were manned by 25 veteran soldiers and 281 militia. The English-Indian attack on April 26 was successfully repulsed, but the Indians scattered over the countryside, where they killed more than fifty people. Following the attack, the fortifications were improved according to the plan shown on the map.

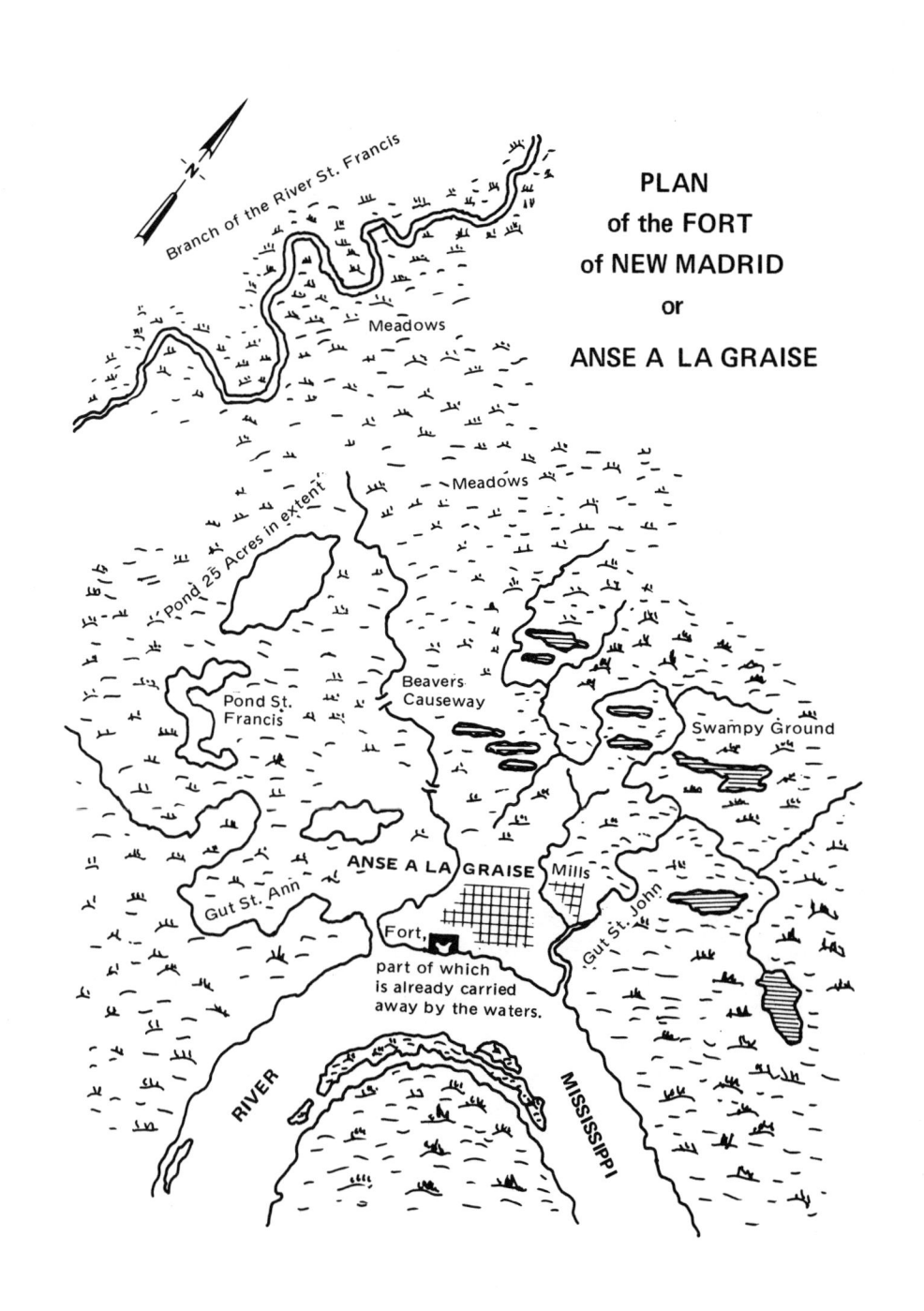

PLAN
of the FORT
of NEW MADRID
or
ANSE A LA GRAISE

Branch of the River St. Francis

Meadows

Meadows

Pond 25 Acres in extent

Pond St. Francis

Beavers Causeway

Swampy Ground

ANSE A LA GRAISE

Mills

Gut St. Ann

Gut St. John

Fort, part of which is already carried away by the waters.

RIVER

MISSISSIPPI

The exact date of the map of New Madrid and its environs is unknown, but it was probably drawn near the end of the eighteenth century. This map is adapted after a photographic copy of a map in the archives of the Missouri Historical Society. It was originally published in *A Journey in North America* by Victor Collot, Paris, 1826.

The bend of the Mississippi River where the town of New Madrid is situated was known to the French as L'Anse a la Graisse — "cove of fat or grease." Houck, in his *History of Missouri*, offers three possible origins for the name. The first explanation, attributed to the governor of Pensacola, was that the name originated from the fact that great quantities of very oleose bear meat were stored there for the use of the garrison and the French and Spanish boatmen who traveled up and down the Mississippi. A second explanation stems from the fact that the soils there were extremely black, fertile, and "greasy." Other especially fertile areas in the Mississippi Valley were said to have "greasy" soils. Two such areas were the American Bottom opposite St. Louis and the Oil Trough Bottom below Batesville on the White River. The third explanation suggests that the first traders found abundant game in the vicinity, especially bear and buffalo — hence the name, L'Anse a la Graisse.

New Madrid was situated where the great bend in the Mississippi River touched a low clay and alluvial ridge which extended north to the Scott County Hills just south of Cape Girardeau. Because the ridge provided an easy overland route through the swamp, the Indians had established a trail to New Madrid, and there is evidence that Indians occupied the site. The area around New Madrid was described as parklike, with open prairie and scattered trees, a nearby lake with sandy beaches, fertile soil, and abundant canebrakes where game such as bear, deer, otter, and beaver could be hunted.

Had not Colonel George Morgan's grandiose scheme to colonize the region with American settlers failed, New Madrid might have grown to be a large city. However, the huge grant of land Morgan hoped to acquire was never assigned by the Spanish government, and Morgan's plans to establish a great city near the confluence of the Mississippi and Ohio rivers were abandoned.

The site of New Madrid, although better than most of the land bordering the Mississippi, had distinct geographical disadvantages. Except for the route north by way of Sikeston Ridge, it was isolated by nearly impenetrable swamps, and it was frequently subject to floods which cut into the soft alluvium and eroded the town site. At the time this map was drawn, nearly half of the fort had fallen into the river. Finally, the disastrous earthquakes of 1811 and 1812 caused many of the settlers to move and discouraged prospective settlers from moving there.

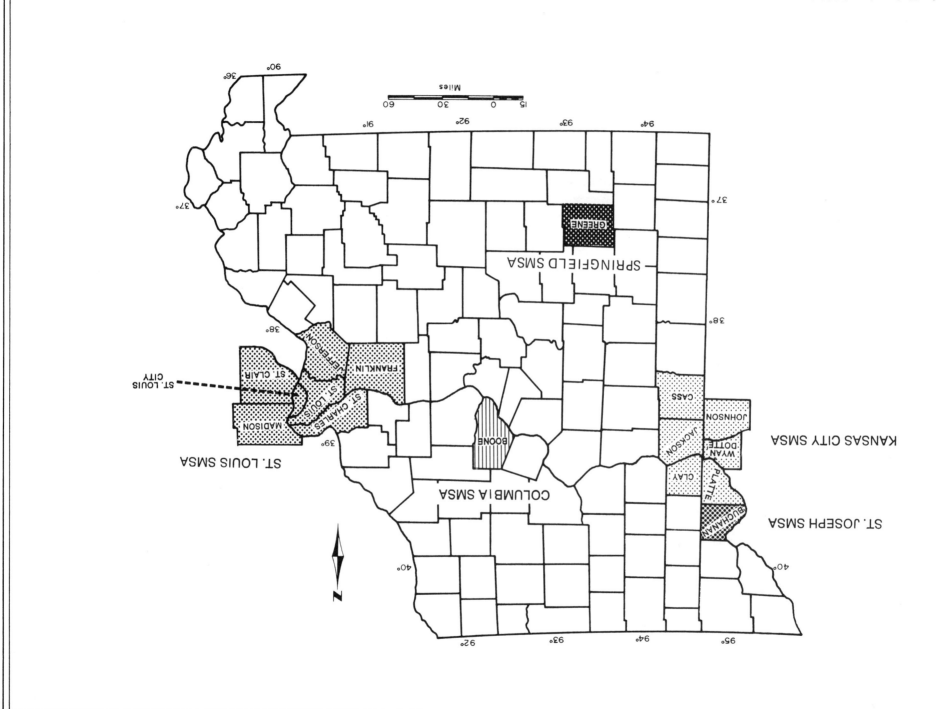

Miles

15 0 30 60

SPRINGFIELD SMSA

GREENE

ST. LOUIS SMSA

ST. CLAIR
ST. LOUIS CITY
ST. LOUIS
JEFFERSON
FRANKLIN
ST. CHARLES
MADISON

FRANKLIN

COLUMBIA SMSA

BOONE

KANSAS CITY SMSA

CASS
JOHNSON
JACKSON
WYAN DOTTE
CLAY
PLATTE

ST. JOSEPH SMSA

BUCHANAN

N

90°
36°
37°
91°
92°
93°
94°
37°
38°
38°
39°
40°
92°
93°
94°
95°
40°

111. STANDARD METROPOLITAN STATISTICAL AREAS (SMSA's)

A standard metropolitan statistical area always includes a city, or cities, of specified population which constitutes the central city and the county, or counties, in which it is located. Such an area also includes contiguous counties when the economic and social relationships between the central and contiguous counties meet specified criteria of metropolitan character and integration. A standard metropolitan statistical area may cross state lines. In New England, standard metropolitan statistical areas are composed of cities and towns instead of counties.

A standard metropolitan statistical area is generally designated on the basis of population statistics reported in a census conducted by the Bureau of the Census. They are sometimes designated on the basis of population estimates published by the Bureau of the Census which have been accepted for use in the distribution of federal benefits. An area designated on the basis of such estimates shall lose its designation if it does not qualify for designation on the basis of population statistics reported in the next succeeding census conducted by the Bureau of the Census.

BASIC CRITERIA

1. Each standard metropolitan statistical area must include at least
   (a) One city with fifty thousand or more inhabitants, or
   (b) A city with at least twenty-five thousand inhabitants, which, together with those contiguous places (incorporated or unincorporated) having population densities of at least one thousand persons per square mile, has a combined population of fifty thousand and constitutes for general economic and social purposes a single community, provided that the county, or counties, in which the city and contiguous places are located has a total population of at least seventy-five thousand.

2. A contiguous county will be included in a standard metropolitan statistical area if
   (a) At least 75 per cent of the resident labor force in the county is in the nonagricultural labor force, and
   (b) At least 30 per cent of the employed workers living in the county work in the central county or counties of the area.

3. A contiguous county which does not meet the requirements of criterion 2 will be included in a standard metropolitan statistical area if at least 75 per cent of the resident labor force is in the nonagricultural labor force and it meets two of the following additional criteria of metropolitan character and one of the following criteria of integration:
   (a) Criteria of metropolitan character:
      (1) At least 25 per cent of the population is urban.
      (2) The county had an increase of at least 15 per cent in total population during the period covered by the two most recent censuses of population.
      (3) The county has a population density of at least fifty persons per square mile.
   (b) Criteria of integration:
      (1) At least 15 per cent of the employed workers living in the county work in the central county or counties of the area,
      (2) The number of people working in the county who live in the central county or counties of the area is equal to at least 15 per cent of the employed workers living in the county, or
      (3) The sum of the number of workers commuting to and from the central county or counties is equal to 20 per cent of the employed workers living in the county.

There are five SMSA's in Missouri: Columbia, Kansas City, St. Joseph, St. Louis, and Springfield. The combined population of Missouri portions of these standard metropolitan statistical areas is 3,041,707, or approximately 65 per cent of Missouri's population.

GRANITE CITY

E. SAINT LOUIS

CAHOKIA

ALORTEN

CENTREVILLE

VENICE

BROOKLYN

NATIONAL CITY

MADISON

SAINT LOUIS

BELLEFONTAINE NEIGHBORS

MOLINE ACRES

BLACK JACK

Dellwood

JENNINGS

FLORDELL HILLS

COUNTRY CLUB HILLS

BERKELEY HILLS

Pine Lawn

Northwoods

Pasadena Hills

Beverly Hills

VILLAGE

HILLSDALE

Wellston

FERGUSON

Normandy

Norwood Court

Glen Echo

Bel-Nor

Pagedale

Greendale

UPLANDS PARK

COOL VALLEY

BELLERIVE

Kinloch

Bel-Ridge

CHARLACK

VINITA PARK

HANLEY HILLS

VINITA TERRACE

SYCAMORE HILLS

St. John

CARSON VILLE

FLORISSANT

HAZELWOOD

St. Ann

Woodson Terrace

EDMUNDSON

SCHUERMANN HEIGHTS

Breckenridge Hills

MARY RIDGE

OVERLAND

Olivette

UNIVERSITY CITY

CLAYTON

RICHMOND HEIGHTS

BRENTWOOD

MAPLEWOOD

Shrewsbury

WEBSTER GROVES

LADUE

Rock Hill

Glendale

OAKLAND

Warson Woods

HUNTLEIGH

CRESTWOOD

KIRKWOOD

SUNSET HILLS

Creve Coeur

WESTWOOD

CRYSTAL LAKE PARK

Des Peres

TOWN AND COUNTRY

COUNTRY LIFE ACRES

BRIDGETON

BRIDGETON TERRACE

MARLBOROUGH

GRANTWOOD VILLAGE

LAKESHIRE

ST. GEORGE

WILBUR PARK

BELLA VILLA

Calverton Park

CALVERTON PARK

Wilbur Park

MACKENZIE

FAIRGROUNDS PARK

Forest Park

Tower Grove Park

FOREST PARK

DELMAR

BROADWAY

GRAND BLVD

KINGSHIGHWAY BLVD

ARSENAL ST.

ILLINOIS

MISSISSIPPI RIVER

MISSOURI RIVER

MISSISSIPPI RIVER

ST. CHARLES CO.
ST. LOUIS CO.

MISSOURI

ST. LOUIS CO.
JEFFERSON CO.

COLUMBIA

DUPO

Scale in Miles

Most of Missouri's large cities are in the St. Louis and Kansas City urban areas. There are six cities with populations over twenty thousand in the Kansas City area and fourteen in the St. Louis area. There are sixty-eight towns and cities over one thousand population in the St. Louis area. Nearly one of every four towns over one thousand population is in the St. Louis metropolitan area.

Because St. Louis attained independent status in 1875, at a relatively early time in its history of growth, a "shatterbelt" of incorporated towns developed around the central city. This was accomplished beginning about 1880 by subdivision development in conjunction with construction of interurban rail-roads connecting with St. Louis. As each subdivision development grew and as surrounding small towns were linked by rails with St. Louis and began to grow, additional services such as fire and police protection and utilities and street maintenance were required. To meet the needs, communities were incorporated in order to borrow money and collect taxes to provide the services.

As the St. Louis metropolitan area continued to grow, the inner belt of suburbs became congested, and a new ring of suburbs grew up. The growth of the automobile suburbs or "outer ring" gained impetus following World War II and has continued to the present.

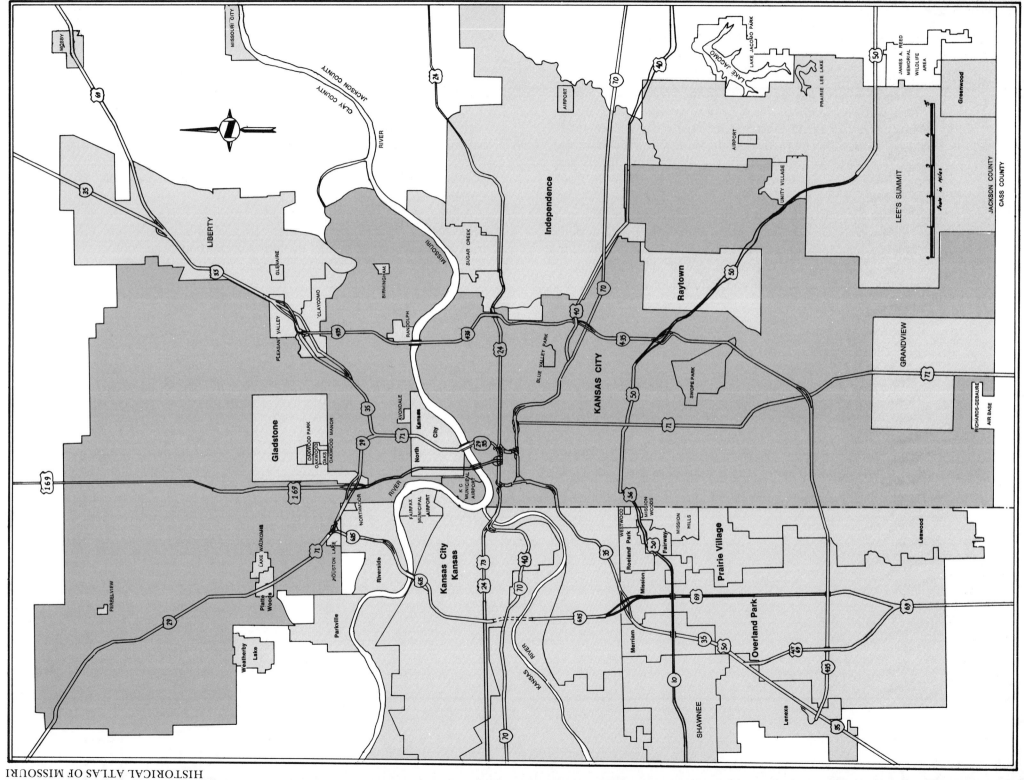

MOSBY

MISSOURI CITY

CLAY COUNTY
JACKSON COUNTY

RIVER

69

35

LIBERTY

24

AIRPORT

70

40

LAKE JACOMO

Lake Jacomo Park

PRAIRIE LEE LAKE

JAMES A. REED
MEMORIAL
WILDLIFE
AREA

50

Greenwood

Scale in Miles

GLENAIRE

Independence

SUGAR CREEK

AIRPORT

LEE'S SUMMIT

CLAYCOMO

BIRMINGHAM

MISSOURI

435

Raytown

JACKSON COUNTY
CASS COUNTY

PLEASANT VALLEY

RANDOLPH

24

435

70

Gladstone

35

OAKWOOD PARK
OAKWOOD
OAKS
OAKWOOD MANOR

AVONDALE

North
Kansas
City

71

29

BLUE VALLEY PARK

KANSAS CITY

435

SWOPE PARK

50

GRANDVIEW

71

77

169

169

NORTHMOOR

RIVER

FAIRFAX
MUNICIPAL
AIRPORT

KC
MUNICIPAL
AIRPORT

29

35

UNITY VILLAGE

50

RICHARDS-GEBAUR
AIR BASE

635

Houston Lake

Riverside

Kansas City
Kansas

73

35

WESTWOOD

Roeland Park

MISSION
WOODS

Fairway

MISSION
HILLS

Prairie Village

Leewood

56

35

FERRELVIEW

LAKE WAUKOMIS

635

24

70

Merriam

Mission

50

69

Overland Park

69

Platte Woods

29

Parkville

70

KANSAS RIVER

SHAWNEE

10

35

50

69/169

635

35

Lenexa

Weatherby
Lake

Kansas City has taken advantage of Missouri's liberal annexation laws to maintain its growth through geographic expansion. Nevertheless, the metropolitan area includes six cities over twenty thousand and twenty-one cities over one thousand population. Unhindered by independent status like that of St. Louis, Kansas City has annexed large areas to the north, south, and east. Several small communities, such as Gladstone, Raytown, and Grandview, have become enclaves surrounded or nearly surrounded by Kansas City.

The growth of towns in the Kansas City area has occurred especially since 1940. In 1890 there were five cities over one thousand in the metropolitan area, and by 1940 only two more attained that population. In the decade of the 1940s four more towns reached one thousand population, and by 1970 ten more towns had reached that level.

Large annexations have helped to hold down the number of suburbs. Between 1958 and 1962 Kansas City annexed 200.8 square miles, and Independence grew to 36.25 square miles. During the 1960s and 1970s outlying areas engaged in defensive annexation, which further restricted the possibility of continued political fragmentation. In 1976, Kansas City, Missouri, was the thirteenth largest city in land area in the United States, with a total area of 316.3 square miles, which makes it larger in area than New York City or Chicago. In comparison, St. Louis' area of 61.2 miles is smaller than that of Independence (77.5 square miles), Lee's Summit (63.7 square miles), or Springfield (62.7 square miles).

REFERENCES

Map 2. The Historic Boundaries of Missouri

Conrad, Howard L., *Encyclopedia of the History of Missouri* (New York, The Southern History Company, 1901), I, 338–43.

Ehrlich, Daniel H., "Problems Arising from Shifts of the Missouri River on the Eastern Border of Nebraska," *Nebraska History*, Vol. LIV, No. 3 (Fall, 1973), 341–63.

Haskell, Henry C., and Richard B. Fowler, "The Attempted Annexation of Kansas City to the State of Kansas," *Missouri Historical Review*, Vol. XLIV (April, 1950), 221–24.

Houck, Louis, *A History of Missouri* (Chicago, R. R. Donnelly & Sons, 1908), I, 2–16.

McClure, Clarence H., and Marguerite Potter, *Missouri: Its Geography, History, and Government* (New York, Laidlow Brothers, 1940), 54–58, 93–94.

McKee, Howard L., "The Platte Purchase," *Missouri Historical Review*, Vol. XXXII, 129–47.

Meyer, Duane G., *The Heritage of Missouri: A History* (St. Louis, The State Publishing Company, 1963), 5, 180–85.

Robins, Ruby Matson, "Americans in the Valley, Part III," *Missouri Historical Review*, Vol. XLV, 275-9.

Shoemaker, Floyd Calvin, *Missouri and Missourians* (Chicago, The Lewis Publishing Company, 1943), I, 5, 59–64, 172–76, 442, 445.

———, *Missouri's Struggle for Statehood* (Jefferson City, Mo., Hugh Stephens Printing Co., 1916), 39–44, 49.

Stevens, Walter B., *Missouri, the Center State* (Chicago, The S. J. Clarke Publishing Co., 1915), II, 763–66.

Thomas, John L., "Missouri-Iowa Boundary Dispute," *Missouri Historical Review*, Vol. 8 (July, 1908), 259–74.

Trexler, Harrison A., "Missouri in the Old Geographies," *Missouri Historical Review*, Vol. XXXII, 148–55.

Van Zant, Franklin K., *Boundaries of the United States and the Several States*, Geological Survey Bulletin 1212 (Washington, D.C., 1966).

Violette, Eugene Marion, *A History of Missouri* (Cape Girardeau, Mo., Ramfre Press, 1951), 105–11.

Map 3. The United States Land Office Survey

Sherman C. E., *Original Ohio Land Subdivisions: Final Report*, III, Ohio Cooperative Topographic Survey (Columbus, Press of Ohio State Reformatory, 1925).

Strahler, Arthur N., *Introduction to Physical Geography* (New York, John Wiley and Sons, 1965), 433–35.

Map 4. Longitude and Latitude of Missouri

Bartholomew, John, *The Times Gazetteer of the World* (London, The Times, 1922).

U.S. Geological Survey, selected topographic maps, 1:250,000 series, covering Missouri and adjacent areas.

Map 5. Northeastern Missouri

Missouri Directory of Manufacturing and Mining, 1976 (St. Louis, Information Data Company, 1976).

Rafferty, Milton D., *Missouri: A Geography of Its Resources and People* (Springfield, Department of Geography and Geology, Southwest Missouri State University, 1976), 168–206.

Writers' Program, Work Projects Administration, *Missouri: A Guide to the "Show Me" State*, American Guide Series (New York, Duell, Sloan and Pearce, 1941).

Map 6. Northwestern Missouri

Missouri Directory of Manufacturing and Mining, 1976.
Rafferty, *Missouri: A Geography,* 168–206.
Writers' Program, W.P.A., *Missouri: A Guide.*

Map 7. Southeastern Missouri

Missouri Directory of Manufacturing and Mining, 1976.
Rafferty, *Missouri: A Geography,* 168–206.
Writers' Program, W.P.A., *Missouri: A Guide.*

Map 8. Southwestern Missouri

Missouri Directory of Manufacturing and Mining, 1976.
Rafferty, *Missouri: A Geography,* 168–206.
Writers' Program, W.P.A., *Missouri: A Guide.*

Map 9. Relief of Missouri

Fenneman, Nevin M., *Physiography of Eastern United States* (New York, McGraw-Hill Book Company, 1938).
Rafferty, *Missouri: A Geography,* 6–11.
U.S. Geological Survey, selected topographic maps.

Map 10. Physiographic Regions of Missouri

Branson, E. B., and W. D. Keller, "Geology," chapter 2 in *Missouri: Its Resources, People, and Institutions,* ed. Noel P. Gist (Columbia, Curators of the University of Missouri, 1950).
Bretz, J. Harlan, *Geomorphic History of the Ozarks of Missouri* (Rolla, Missouri Geological Survey and Water Resources, 1965), Second Series, XLI.
Fenneman, *Physiography of Eastern United States.*
Marbut, Curtis F., "The Physical Features of Missouri," in *Missouri Geological Survey* (Jefferson City, Mo., 1896), X.

Thornbury, William D., *Regional Geomorphology of the United States* (New York, John Wiley and Sons, 1965).
Williams, Walter, *The State of Missouri: An Autobiography* (Columbia, Mo., Press of E. W. Stevens, 1904), 62–70.

Map 11. Geographic Regions of Missouri

Collier, James F., "Geographic Regions of Missouri," *Annals of the Association of American Geographers,* Vol. XLV (1955), 368–92.
Marbut, "Physical Features of Missouri."
Missouri Farm Facts, 1970 (Jefferson City, Missouri Department of Agriculture, Crop and Livestock Reporting Service, 1970).
Rafferty, *Missouri: A Geography,* 98–131.
Sauer, Carl O., *Geography of the Ozark Highland of Missouri,* The Geographic Society of Chicago Bulletin No. 7 (Chicago, University of Chicago Press, 1920).
U.S. Bureau of the Census, *Census of Population, 1970: Missouri* (Washington, D.C., Government Printing Office, 1973), I, Part 27.

Map 12. Precipitation by Season

Bratton, S. T., "Climate," chapter 1 in Gist, *Missouri: Its Resources, People, and Institutions,* 11–16.
Lott, George A., "The World Record 42-Minute Holt, Missouri, Rainstorm," *Monthly Weather Review,* Vo. LXXXII, No. 2 (February, 1954), 50–59.
Martin, Howard H., "Hourly Distribution and Intensity of Precipitation of Kansas City," *Monthly Weather Review,* Vol. LXX, No. 7 (September, 1942), 153–59.

Rafferty, Milton D., Russel L. Gerlach, and Dennis Hrebec, *Atlas of Missouri* (Springfield, Mo., Aux-Arc Research Associates, 1950), 24–25.

Map 14. Soil Textures

Miller, M. F., and H. H. Krusekopf, *The Soils of Missouri,* Bulletin No. 153 (Columbia, University of Missouri Agricultural Experiment Station, 1918).

Scrivner, C. L., and James L. Baker, *Evaluating Missouri Soils,* Circular No. 95 (Columbia, University of Missouri, 1970).

————, et al., *Soils of Missouri: A Guide to Their Identification and Interpretation* (Columbia, Extension Division, University Missouri, no date).

Map 15. Vegetation

Blyth, James E., and Robert Massengale, *Missouri's Primary Forest Products Output and Industries, 1969,* U.S. Forest Service Bulletin NC-16 (St. Paul, Minn., North Central Forest Experiment Station, 1972).

Essex, Burton L., *Forest Area in Missouri Counties, 1972,* U.S. Forest Service Research Note NC-182 (St. Paul, Minn., North Central Forest Experiment Station, 1974).

Ganser, David A., *Missouri's Forests,* U.S. Forest Service Resource Bulletin CS-2 (Columbus, Ohio, Central States Forest Experiment Station, 1965).

Steyermark, Julian A., *Vegetational History of the Ozark Forest,* University of Missouri Studies, No. 31 (Columbia, University of Missouri, 1959).

Map 16. Percentage of Land in Forests

Capps, Osal B., *Forestry in Missouri* (Jefferson City, Missouri Department of Conservation, 1976).

Sharpe, Grant W., Clare W. Herdee, and Shirley W. Allen, *Introduction to Forestry* (New York, McGraw-Hill Book Company, 1976).

Spencer, John S., Jr., and Burton L. Essex, *Timber in Missouri, 1972,* U.S. Forest Service Resource Bulletin NC-30 (St. Paul, Minn., North Central Forest Experiment Station, 1972).

Map 17. Percentage of Change in Forested Land, 1947-72

Rafferty, Gerlach, and Hrebec, *Atlas of Missouri.*

Spencer and Essex, *Timber in Missouri, 1972.*

Map 18. Geology

Branson and Keller, "Geology."

Fenneman, *Physiography of Eastern United States.*

Thornbury, *Regional Geomorphology of the United States.*

Williams, *State of Missouri,* 62–70.

Map 19. Springs

Beckman, H. C., and N. S. Hinchey, *The Large Springs of Missouri* (Rolla, Missouri Geological Survey and Water Resources, 1944), Second Series, XXIX.

Bolon, Harry C., "A Study of Missouri Springs," (master's thesis, University of Missouri School of Mines and Metallurgy, Rolla, 1935).

U.S. Geological Survey and Missouri Division of Geological Survey and Water Resources, *Mineral and Water Resources of Missouri* (Washington, D.C., Government Printing Office, 1967), 313–25.

Vineyard, Jerry D., and Gerald L. Feder, *Springs of Missouri,* Water Resources Report No. 29 (Rolla, Missouri Geological Survey and Water Resources, 1974).

Map 20. Commercial Caves

Bretz, J. Harlan, *Caves of Missouri* (Rolla, Missouri Geological Survey and Water Resources, 1956), Second Series, XXXIX.

Sloane, Howard N., and Russell H. Gurnee, *Visiting American Caves* (New York, Bonanza Books, 1966), 134–57.

Map 21. Groundwater Resources

Davis, Peter N., "Wells and Streams: Relationship at Law," *Missouri Law Review,* Vol. XXVII, 189–245.
Fishel, V. C., James K. Searcy, and F. H. Rainwater, *Water Resources of the Kansas City Area, Missouri, and Kansas,* U.S. Geological Survey Circular 273 (Washington, D.C., Government Printing Office, 1953).
Gist, *Missouri: Its Resources, People, and Institutions,* 67–77.
McCoy, Alexander W., *Artesian Water in Missouri,* Engineering Experiment Station Bulletin No. 12 (Columbia, University of Missouri, 1913).
Miller, Don E., et al., *Water Resources of the St. Louis Area, Missouri,* Water Resources Report No. 30 (Rolla, Missouri Geological Survey and Water Resources, 1974).

Map 22. Rivers and Lakes

Hall, Leonard, *Stars Upstream* (Columbia, University of Missouri Press, 1958).
Hawksley, Oscar, *Missouri Ozark Waterways* (Jefferson City, Missouri Department of Conservation, 1965).
Sauer, *Geography of the Ozark Highland of Missouri.*
Wood, Horace W., and John A. Short, "Water Resources," chapter 4 in Gist, *Missouri: Its Resources, People, and Institutions.*

Map 23. Discharge of Principal Rivers

U.S. Geological Survey and Missouri Geological Survey and Water Resources, *Mineral and Water Resources of Missouri,* 253–81.
Wood and Short, "Water Resources," 58–78.

Map 24. The New Madrid Earthquake, 1811-12

Fuller, Myron L., *The New Madrid Earthquake,* U.S. Geological Survey Bulletin 494 (reprint, Cape Girardeau, Mo., Ramfre Press, 1966).
Gist, *Missouri: Its Resources, People, and Intitutions.*
Penick, James, Jr., *The New Madrid Earthquake of 1811-1812* (Columbia, University of Missouri Press, 1976).

Map 25. Indians of Missouri

Chapman, Carl H., *The Archaeology of Missouri* (Columbia, University of Missouri Press, 1975), I.
——— , and Eleanor F. Chapman, *Indians and Archaeology of Missouri,* Missouri Handbook No. 6 (Columbia, University of Missouri Press, 1964).
Houck, *History of Missouri,* I, 220–36.
Ingenthron, Elmo, *Indians of the Ozark Plateau* (Point Lookout, Mo., The School of the Ozarks Press, 1970).

Map 26. French Claims in North America

Brown, Ralph H., *Historical Geography of the United States* (New York, Harcourt, Brace, and World, 1948).
Davidson, Marshall B., *Life in America* (Boston, Houghton Mifflin, 1954), I, 24–34.
French, Benjamin F. (ed.), *Historical Collections of Louisiana* (New York, Wiley and Putnam, 1846–53), I, 25ff.
Houck, *History of Missouri,* I.
Meyer, *Heritage of Missouri.*
Morison, Samuel Eliot, *The Oxford History of the American People* (New York, Oxford University Press, 1972), I, 75–78.
Shoemaker, Floyd C., *A History of Missouri and Missourians* (Columbia, Mo., Lucas Brothers, 1927), 33–44.

Map 27. Spanish Claims in North America

Adams, James Truslow (ed.), *Atlas of American History* (New York, Charles Scribner's Sons, 1943), 4–7.

Bolton, H. E., and T. M. Marshall, *The Colonization of North America, 1492-1783* (New York, Macmillan, 1922), 32–34.

Houck, *History of Missouri*, I.

Kagan, Hilde Heun (ed.), *The American Heritage Pictorial Atlas of United States History* (New York, American Heritage, 1966), 28–35.

Paullin, Charles O., *Atlas of the Historical Geography of the United States* (Washington, D.C., The Carnegie Institution of Washington, 1932).

Map 28. Spanish and British Claims after 1763

Adams, *Atlas of American History*, 49.

Kagan, *American Heritage Pictorial Atlas*, 52–53, 62.

Meyer, *Heritage of Missouri*, 27–35, 107–14.

Mussey, David S., *The United States of America* (Boston, Ginn, 1933–37), I, 113, 114 map.

Map 29. Louisiana Purchase and Adams-Onís Treaty

Adams, *Atlas of American History*, 94–95.

Kagan, *American Heritage Pictorial Atlas*, 128–29.

MacDonald, William (ed.), *Selected Documents Illustrative of the History of the United States, 1776-1861* (New York, Macmillan, 1901), 160–65.

Meyer, *Heritage of Missouri*, 107–14.

Paullin, *Atlas of the Historical Geography of the United States*, plate 46.

Map 30. Spanish and French Explorations

Houck, *History of Missouri*, I.

Meyer, *Heritage of Missouri*.

Paullin, *Atlas of the Historical Geography of the United States*.

Map 31. American Exploration

Houck, *History of Missouri*, I, II.

Meyer, *Heritage of Missouri*.

Paullin, *Atlas of the Historical Geography of the United States*.

Schoolcraft, Henry Rowe, *Schoolcraft in the Ozarks*, ed. Hugh Parks (reprint of *Journal of a Tour into Missouri and Arkansas;* Van Buren, Ark., Press-Argus Printers, 1955).

Map 32. Spanish Land Grants

Fuller, *New Madrid Earthquake*.

Houck, *History of Missouri*, I, 34–54.

Meyer, *Heritage of Missouri*.

Salberg, Gloria, "The New Madrid Land Claims in Howard County, Missouri," *Missouri Mineral Industry News*, Vol. VII (May, 1967), 69–79.

Map 33. Historic Regions of Missouri

Campbell, Robert A., *Campbell's Gazetteer of Missouri* (St. Louis, R. A. Campbell, Publisher, 1875).

Fuller, *New Madrid Earthquake*.

Gerlach, Russel L., *Immigrants in the Ozarks: A Study in Ethnic Geography* (Columbia, University of Missouri Press, 1977).

Gist, *Missouri: Its Resources, People, and Institutions*.

Haswell, A. W. (ed.), *The Ozark Region: Its History and Its People* (Springfield, Mo., Interstate Historical Society, 1917), I.

Houck, *History of Missouri*, I.

Meyer, *Heritage of Missouri*.

Miller, E. Joan Wilson, "The Ozark Culture Region as Revealed by Traditional Materials," *Annals of the Association of American Geographers*, Vol. 58 (March, 1968), 51–77.

Paullin, *Atlas of the Historical Geography of the United States.*
Rafferty, Milton D., *The Ozarks: Land and Life* (Norman, University of Oklahoma Press, 1980).
Sauer, *Geography of the Ozark Highland of Missouri.*
Schoolcraft, *Schoolcraft in the Ozarks.*
Shoemaker, Floyd C., *Missouri Day by Day* (Jefferson City, State Historical Society of Missouri, 1942), I, II.
Trombly, Albert Edmond, *Little Dixie* (Columbia, University of Missouri Studies, 1955), Vols. 28, 29.
Violette, *History of Missouri.*
Williams, *State of Missouri.*

Map 34. Population Growth, 1810-60

Meyer, *Heritage of Missouri.*
Paullin, *Atlas of the Historical Geography of the United States*, plates 75–77.
Rafferty, *Missouri: A Geography.*

Map 35. Population Growth, 1870-1930

Meyer, *Heritage of Missouri.*
Paullin, *Atlas of the Historical Geography of the United States*, plates 75–77.
Rafferty, *Missouri: A Geography.*

Map 36. Origin of Missouri's Population to 1860

Gerlach, *Immigrants in the Ozarks.*
Gist, *Missouri: Its Resources, People, and Institutions.*
Meyer, *Heritage of Missouri*, 101–106, 136–38, 235, 243, 440, 484.
Rafferty, Gerlach, and Hrebec, *Atlas of Missouri.*
Sauer, *Geography of the Ozark Highland of Missouri.*

Map 38. Origin of Missouri's Population, 1860-90

Meyer, *Heritage of Missouri.*
Paullin, *Atlas of the Historical Geography of the United States*, plates 75–77.
Rafferty, *Missouri: A Geography.*

Map 38. German Foreign-born

Gerlach, *Immigrants in the Ozarks.*
Meyer, *Heritage of Missouri.*
Sauer, *Geography of the Ozark Highland of Missouri.*

Map 39. Irish Foreign-born

Gist, *Missouri: Its Resources, People, and Institutions.*
Meyer, *Heritage of Missouri.*
Rafferty, Milton D. *The Ozarks: Land and Life* (Norman, University of Oklahoma Press, 1980).

Map 40. Population of Missouri, 1890-1970

Campbell, Rex R., and John Hartman, *Missouri Population Characteristics and Changes,* University of Missouri Agricultural Experiment Station Bulletin 765 (Columbia, University of Missouri Agricultural Experiment Station, 1964).
Population Change in Missouri, 1890-1970. Map (Columbia, Department of Rural Sociology, University of Missouri, 1970).
Population Change in Missouri, 1970 to 1974. Map (Columbia, Department of Rural Sociology, University of Missouri, 1970).
Rafferty, *Missouri: A Geography.*

Map 41. Population Density by County, 1974

Gist, *Missouri: Its Resources, People, and Institutions.*
Rafferty, *Missouri: A Geography.*
U.S. Bureau of the Census, *Estimates of Population, Missouri* (Washington, D.C., Government Printing Office, 1975).

Map 42. Slave Population, 1860

Clemens, Samuel L. [Mark Twain], *The Adventures of Huckleberry Finn* (Cleveland, New York, World Publishing Company, 1947).

Meyer, *Heritage of Missouri*, 33–34, 318–22.

Nelson, Earl J., "Missouri Slavery 1861–1865," *Missouri Historical Review,* Vol. 28 (July, 1934), 260–74.

Paullin, *Atlas of the Historical Geography of the United States,* 46, plates 67–68.

Trexler, Harrison A., *Slavery in Missouri, 1840–1865* (Baltimore, Johns Hopkins Press, 1914).

Violette, *History of Missouri.*

Map 43. Blacks in Missouri, 1970

Gist, *Missouri: Its Resources, People, and Institutions.*

Paullin, *Atlas of the Historical Geography of the United States,* 46, plates 67–70.

Rafferty, *Missouri: A Geography,* 72.

U.S. Bureau of the Census, *Census of the Population,* 1970 and earlier years.

Map 44. Population Pyramids for Selected Counties

Campbell, Rex R., *Population Pyramids for Selected Missouri Counties* (Jefferson City, University of Missouri and State of Missouri, Office of Administration, 1973).

Map 45. Origin of County Names

Eaton, David W., "How Missouri Counties, Towns, and Streams Were Named," *Missouri Historical Review,* Vol. 10 (1916), 197–213, 263–87; Vol. II (1917), 164–200, 330–47; Vol. 13 (1918), 57–74.

Rafferty, Gerlach, and Hrebec, *Atlas of Missouri.*

Ramsay, Robert L., "Our Storehouse of Missouri Place Names," *University of Missouri Bulletin,* Vol. 53, No. 34 (1952).

Map 46. County Seats

Johnson, Kenneth M. (ed.), *Official Manual: State of Missouri, 1977-1978* (Jefferson City, Von Hoffman Press, Inc., 1978).

Rafferty, Gerlach, and Hrebec, *Atlas of Missouri.*

Map 47. Public Lands

U.S. Department of the Interior, *The National Atlas of the United States of America* (Washington, D.C., Government Printing Office, 1970).

Map 49. State Senatorial Districts

Johnson, *Official Manual,* 107–85.

Map 50. State Representative Districts

Johnson, *Official Manual,* 107–85.

Map 51. Judicial Regions

Johnson, *Official Manual,* 214.

Map 52. Missouri Planning Districts

Missouri Revised Statutes, 1969 (Jefferson City, Missouri, 1969), Vol. II, chap. 251.

Wharton, Heyward M., et al., *Missouri Minerals: Resources, Production, and Forecasts,* Special Publication No. 1 (Rolla, Missouri Geological Survey and Water Resources, 1969), includes numerous maps of the substate planning districts.

Map 53. Voting Patterns

Friedman, Gordon D., "Voting Trends in Missouri Primary Elections 1908–1972" (paper presented at the 1973 annual meeting, Missouri Political Science Association, Lodge of the Four Seasons, Lake of the Ozarks, November 16, 1973).

Gerlach, Russel L., "Geography and Politics in Missouri: A Study of Electoral Patterns," *Missouri Geographer,* Fall, 1971, 27–36.

Rafferty, Gerlach, and Hrebec, *Atlas of Missouri.*

Map 54. 1976 Presidential Election

Johnson, *Official Manual,* 1283.

Map 55. 1976 U.S. Senatorial Election

Johnson, *Official Manual,* 1283.

Map 56. 1976 Gubernatorial Election

Johnson, *Official Manual,* 1285.

Map 57. The Civil War in Missouri

Brownlee, Richard S., *Grey Ghosts of the Confederacy: Guerilla Warfare in the West, 1861–1865* (Baton Rouge: Louisiana State University Press, 1958).

Grover, George S., "Civil War in Missouri," *Missouri Historical Review,* Vol. 8 (October, 1913), 1–28.

Meyer, *Heritage of Missouri,* 348–404.

Paullin, *Atlas of the Historical Geography of the United States,* plate 162.

Violette, *History of Missouri.*

Map 58. Price's Raid

Grover, "Civil War in Missouri."

———, "The Price Campaign of 1864," *Missouri Historical Review,* Vol. 6 (July, 1912), 167–81.

Meyer, *Heritage of Missouri,* 396–98.

Rea, Ralph R., *Sterling Price: The Lee of the West* (Little Rock, Arkansas Book House, 1959).

Map 59. Leading Religious Denominations, 1950

Gaustad, Edwin S., *Historical Atlas of Religion in America* (New York, Harper and Row, 1962).

National Council of Churches, *Churches and Church Membership in the United States, Series A-E* (New York, National Council of Churches, 1956–1958).

Rafferty, Gerlach, and Hrebec, *Atlas of Missouri,* 16.

U.S. Department of the Interior, *National Atlas of the United States of America,* 264.

Zelinsky, Wilbur, "An Approach to the Religious Geography of the United States: Patterns of Church Membership in 1952," *Annals of the Association of American Geographers,* Vol. 51 (1961), 139–93.

Map 60. Percentage of Families with Incomes under Three Thousand Dollars

Rafferty, Milton D., William Cheek, and David A. Castillon, *Economic and Social Atlas of Missouri* (Springfield, Department of Geography and Geology, Southwest Missouri State University, 1975).

U.S. Bureau of the Census, *Census of the Population, 1970, General Social and Economic Characteristics, Missouri* (Washington, D.C., Government Printing Office, 1972).

———, *County and City Data Book, 1972: A Statistical Abstract Supplement* (Washington, D.C., Government Printing Office, 1972).

Zoubek, Linda, *Missouri County Data Book* (Jefferson City, Missouri Division of Commerce and Industrial Development, 1973).

Map 61. Percentage of Families with Incomes over Ten Thousand Dollars

Rafferty, Cheek, and Castillon, *Economic and Social Atlas of Missouri.*
U.S. Bureau of the Census, *Census of the Population, 1970, General Social and Economic Characteristics, Missouri.*
———, *County and City Data Book, 1972.*
Zoubek, *Missouri County Data Book.*

Map 62. Evolution of Missouri's Railroad Network

Bain, William E., *Frisco Folks* (Denver, Sage Books, 1961).
Cramer, Rose Fulton, *Wayne County, Missouri* (Cape Girardeau, Ramfre Press, 1972).
Douglass, Robert S., *History of Southeast Missouri* (Chicago, Lewis Publishing Company, 1912).
Masterson, Vincent V., *The Katy Railroad and the Last Frontier* (Norman, University of Oklahoma Press, 1952).
Meyer, *Heritage of Missouri*, 256–57, 264, 428, 627.
Millon, John W., *State Aid to Railroads in Missouri* (Chicago, University of Chicago Press, 1896).
Miner, H. Craig, *The St. Louis–San Francisco Transcontinental Railroad* (Lawrence, University Press of Kansas, 1972).
Missouri Pacific Line, *The Empire That Missouri Pacific Served* (St. Louis, Von Hoffman Press, 1957).

Map 63. Abandoned Railroads, 1910–70

Cook, Delbert, "Abandoned Railroads of Missouri (unpublished research paper in geography, Department of Geography and Geology, Southwest Missouri State University, 1977).
Miner, *The St. Louis–San Francisco Transcontinental Railroad.*
Moser, David, et al., *Missouri's Transportation System: Condition, Capacity, and Impediments to Efficiency* (Jefferson City, Missouri Office of Administration, Division of Budget and Planning, 1976).
Writers' Program, W.P.A., *Missouri: A Guide.*

Map 64. Railroads, 1976

Moser, *Missouri's Transportation System*, 148–61.
Rafferty, Gerlach, and Hrebec, *Atlas of Missouri*, 50.
Railroad Mileage by States, December 31, 1974 (Washington, D.C., Association of American Railroads, 1975), 28–29.

Map 65. Interurban Railroads in the Tri-State Area

Chandler, Allison, *Trolley Through the Countryside* (Denver, Sage Books, 1963), 71–100, 229–48, 334–58.
Gibson, Arrell M., *Wilderness Bonanza: The Tri-State District of Missouri, Kansas, and Oklahoma* (Norman, University of Oklahoma Press, 1972).
Megee, Mary C., "The Geography of the Mining of Lead and Zinc in the Tri-State Mining District" (master's thesis, University of Arkansas, Fayetteville, 1953).
Thomas, Richard S., *The Changing Occupance Pattern of the Tri-State Area, Missouri, Kansas and Oklahoma,* University of Chicago Department of Geography Research Paper 21 (Chicago, University of Chicago Press, 1953).

Map 66. Passenger Rail Transportation (AMTRAK)

Amtrak All-American Schedules (Washington, D.C., National Railroad Passenger Corporation, 1975).
Association of American Railroads, *Railroad Mileage by States,* 28–29.
Moser, *Missouri's Transportation System,* 162–65.

Map 67. Water Transportation

Blanchard, R., "Railroads vs. Riverman," *St. Louis Globe-Democrat,* September 30, 1975.
Moser, *Missouri's Transportation System,* 177–219.
U.S. Department of the Army, Corps of Engineers, *Transportation Lines on the Mississippi River System and the Gulf Intercoastal Waterway, 1974,* Transportation Series 4 (New Orleans, Waterborne Commerce Statistic Center, 1974).

Map 68. Missouri Highway Districts

Moser, *Missouri's Transportation System,* 24–26.

Map 69. Interstate Highways

Moser, *Missouri's Transportation System,* 22–27.
Rafferty, *Missouri: A Geography.*

Map 70. Bus Transportation

Moser, *Missouri's Transportation System,* 124–35.
Traylor, Orba F., "Transportation," in Gist, *Missouri: Its Resources, People, and Institutions,* 332–52.

Map 71. Electric Power Lines

Electric Utility Statistics for Missouri (Jefferson City, Missouri Public Service Commission, 1953).
Expressways for Electricity in Missouri (Savannah, Northwest Missouri Electric Cooperative, n.d.).
Rafferty, Gerlach, and Hrebec, *Atlas of Missouri,* 55.

Map 72. Crude Oil Pipelines

Moser, *Missouri's Transportation System,* 260–65.
Shifts in Petroleum Transportation (Washington, D.C., Association of Oil Pipe Lines, 1976).
U.S. Department of Transportation, *Energy Statistics: A Supplement to the Summary of National Transportation Statistics, 1974* (Washington, D.C., Government Printing Office, 1975).

Map 73. Natural Gas Pipelines

Moser, *Missouri's Transportation System,* 260–65.
U.S. Department of Transportation, *Energy Statistics,* 25.

Map 74. Products Pipelines

Moser, *Missouri's Transportation System,* 263–65.
U.S. Department of Transportation, *Energy Statistics,* 25.

Map 75. Airlines Serving Missouri

Meyer, *Heritage of Missouri,* 478, 606, 756.
Moser, *Missouri's Transportation System,* 221–58.
Official Air Line Guide, North American ed. (Oak Brook, Ill., R. H. Donnelly Publishing Co., 1976).

Map 76. Traffic Flow Communities

Angel, S., and G. M. Hyman, *Urban Fields: A Geometry of Movement for Regional Science* (London, Pion Limited, 1976).
Boehm, Richard G., and William B. Wagner, *Principal Interaction Fields of Missouri Regional Centers* (Columbia, Extension

Division, University of Missouri, 1976), 1–37.

Campbell, Rex R., *Highways and Growth Centers in Missouri: Industrial Development* (Columbia, Office of Industrial Development, Studies, University of Missouri, 1967).

Rafferty, *Missouri: A Geography*, 158–206.

Yeates, Maurice H., and Barry J. Garner, *The North American City* (New York, Harper and Row, 1971), 159–212.

Map 77. Circulation of Daily Newspapers

Audit Reports (Chicago, Audit Bureau of Circulations, 1968).

Rafferty, Gerlach, and Hrebec, *Atlas of Missouri*, 58.

Map 78. Historical Geography of the Mineral Area

Gist, *Missouri: Its Resources, People, and Institutions.*

Johnson, Hugh Nelson, "Sequent Occupance of the St. Francois Mining Region" (Ph.D. diss., Washington University, St. Louis, 1950).

Rafferty, *The Ozarks.*

Roome, Charles C., "Selected Aspects of the Southeast Mining Region" (master's thesis, University of Missouri, Columbia, 1962).

Map 79. Mining Camps in Southwestern Missouri

Gibson, Arrell M., "Lead Mining in Southwest Missouri to 1865," Missouri Historical Review, Vol. 53 (1959), 197–205.

———, "Lead Mining in Southwest Missouri after 1865," Missouri Historical Review, Vol. 53 (1959), 315–28.

———, *Wilderness Bonanza.*

Megee, "Geography of the Mining of Lead and Zinc."

Thomas, *Changing Occupance Pattern of the Tri-State Area.*

Map 80. Historical Geography of the Central Mineral District

Bretz, J. Harlan, "Origin of the Filled-Sink Structures and Circle Deposits of Missouri," *Geological Society of America Bulletin,* Vol. 61 (August, 1950), 789–834.

Leach, David L., and Heyward M. Wharton, *Barite Deposits of the Central Mineral District,* Boulder, Colorado, Geological Society of America Field Trip Guidebook, 7th Annual Meeting, 1973, p. 10.

Mather, W. B., *Barite Deposits of Central Missouri,* Technical Publication No. 2246 (New York, American Institute of Mining Engineers, 1947).

———, *The Mineral Deposits of Morgan County, Missouri,* Report of Investigation No. 2 (Rolla, Missouri Geological Survey, 1946).

"Mining History of the Central Mineral District of Missouri," *Missouri Mineral News,* Vol. 13, No. 5 (May, 1973), 84–89.

Map 81. Barite Deposits and Mining

Carriere, Joseph M., *Tales from the French Folklore of Missouri,* Northwestern University Studies (Evanston, Ill., Northwestern University Press, 1937).

Houck, *History of Missouri,* I.

Johnson, "Sequent Occupance of the St. Francois Mining Region."

McMahon, David F., "Tradition and Change in an Ozark Mining Community" (master's thesis, St. Louis University, St. Louis, 1958).

Roome, "Selected Aspects of the Southeast Mining Region."

Schoolcraft, Henry R., *A View of the Lead Mines of Missouri, 1819* (New York, C. Wiley and Co., 1819).

Wharton, Heyward M., *Barite Ore Potential of Four Tailings Ponds in the Washington County Barite District,* Report of Investigations No. 53 (Rolla, Missouri Geological Survey and Water Resources, 1972).

———, et al., *Missouri Minerals.*

Map 82. Coal Deposits and Mining

Bedwell, Shirley, "Missouri Coal Mines" (undergraduate research paper, Department of Geography and Geology, Southwest Missouri State University, Springfield, Missouri, 1970).
Wharton, et al., *Missouri Minerals.*

Map 83. Oil and Gas Fields

Wharton, et al., *Missouri Minerals.*

Map 84. Iron Ore Deposits

Cozzens, Arthur B., "The Iron Industry in Missouri," *Missouri Historical Review,* Vol. 35 (July, 1940), 509–38; Vol. 36 (October, 1941), 48–60.
Meyer, *Heritage of Missouri,* 242–43, 448–49.
Wharton, et al., *Missouri Minerals,* 51–57.

Map 85. Clay and Shale

Hanson, A. William, "The Fireclay Industry of East Central Missouri: The Value of a Resource to a Region" (master's thesis, Southern Illinois University, Carbondale, 1966).
Rafferty, Gerlach, and Hrebec, *Atlas of Missouri,* 45.
Roberts, Clarence N., "Developments in the Missouri Pottery Industry, 1800–1950," *Missouri Historical Review,* Vol. 58 (1964), 464–73.
———, *A History of the Firebrick and Refractories Industry in Missouri,* Technical Series Bulletin No. 75 (Rolla, University of Missouri School of Mines and Metallurgy, 1950).
———, "History of the Paving Brick Industry in Missouri," *Missouri Historical Review,* Vol. 46 (1952), 357–62.
———, "History of the Structural Brick Industry in Missouri,"

Missouri Historical Review, Vol. 47 (1953), 318–28.
Wharton, et al., *Missouri Minerals,* 23–31.

Map 86. Silica Sand

Dake, C. L., "The Sand and Gravel Resources of Missouri," *Missouri Geological Survey,* Vol. 15 (1918).
Rafferty, Gerlach, and Hrebec, *Atlas of Missouri,* 46.
Wharton, et al., *Missouri Minerals,* 96–101.

Map 87. Limestone and Dolomite

Hinchey, Norman S., *Missouri Marble,* Report of Investigations No. 3 (Rolla, Missouri Geological Survey and Water Resources, 1946).
U.S. Geological Survey and Missouri Division of Geological Survey and Water Resources, *Mineral and Water Resources of Missouri,* 126–50.
Wharton, et al., *Missouri Minerals.*

Map 88. Improved Land, 1850-90

Paullin, *Atlas of the Historical Geography of the United States,* 136, plates 145–46.

Map 89. Improved Land, 1890-1920

Paullin, *Atlas of the Historical Geography of the United States,* 136, plate 146.

Map 90. Land Reclamation in the Southeast Lowlands

Bratton, Samuel T., *The Geography of the St. Francis Basin.* University of Missouri Studies (Columbia, University of Missouri, 1926), I (No. 3), 4–8.
Hudson, Charles E., "A Geographic Study, Examining the

Major Elements Involved in the Rise of Cotton Production in Southeast Missouri, 1822–1825" (master's thesis, Western Michigan University, Kalamazoo, 1967), 47 map.

Nolen, John H., *Missouri's Swamp and Overflow Lands*, Report, Forty-Seventh Missouri General Assembly (Jefferson City, 1913).

Map 91. Agricultural Regions

Missouri Farm Facts, 1977 (Jefferson City, Missouri Department of Agriculture, Crop and Livestock Reporting Service, 1977).

Voss, Leonard A., *Productive Missouri Agriculture* (Jefferson City, Missouri Division of Commerce and Industrial Development, 1966).

Map 92. Wheat

Missouri Farm Facts, 1977, 1–54.

Rafferty, *Missouri: A Geography*, 98–112.

——, Gerlach, and Hrebec, *Atlas of Missouri*, 36.

Map 93. Soybeans

Missouri Farm Facts, 1977.

Stamp, Dudley (ed.), *Chisholm's Handbook of Commercial Geography* (London, Longman Group Ltd., 1975), 146–47, 225–26.

Map 94. Corn

Missouri Farm Facts, 1977.

Rafferty, *Missouri: A Geography*, 113–31.

Stamp, *Chisholm's Handbook of Commercial Geography*, 141–42.

Map 95. Grain Sorghum

Garland, John H. (ed.), *The North American Midwest: A Regional Geography* (New York, John Wiley and Sons, 1955).

Missouri Farm Facts, 1977.

Rafferty, *Missouri: A Geography*, 113–31.

World Book Encyclopedia (Chicago, Field Enterprises, 1977).

Map 96. Cotton

Missouri Farm Facts, 1970.

Missouri Farm Facts, 1977.

Map 97. Tobacco

Missouri Farm Facts, 1970.

Missouri Farm Facts, 1977.

Writers' Program, W.P.A., *Missouri: A Guide*, 495–96.

Map 98. Dairy Cattle

Meyer, *Heritage of Missouri.*

Missouri Farm Facts, 1977, 1–54.

Rafferty, Milton D., "Agricultural Change in the Western Ozarks," *Missouri Historical Review*, Vol. 69 (April, 1975), 299–322.

——, Gerlach, Hrebec, *Atlas of Missouri.*

Map 99. Beef Cattle

Meyer, *Heritage of Missouri.*

Missouri Farm Facts, 1977, 1–54.

Rafferty, "Agricultural Change in the Western Ozarks," 299–322.

——, Gerlach, and Hrebec, *Atlas of Missouri.*

Map 100. All Cattle

Kersten, Earl W., Jr., "Changing Economy and Landscape in

a Missouri Ozarks Area," *Annals of the Association of American Geographers*, Vol. 43 (1958), 298–418, reprinted in *Missouri Farm Facts, 1970*.

Missouri Farm Facts, 1977, 1–54.

Rafferty, "Agricultural Change in the Western Ozarks," 299–322.

————, *Missouri: A Geography*, 98–109.

Map 101. Hogs and Pigs

Alexander, John W., *Economic Geography* (Englewood Cliffs, N.J., Prentice-Hall, 1963), 142–43.

Cook, Earl, *Energy: The Ultimate Resource*, Resource Papers for College Geography, No. 77-4 (Washington, D.C., Association of American Geographers, 1977), 3–4.

Missouri Farm Facts, 1977.

Rafferty, *Missouri: A Geography*, 113–31.

Map 102. Charcoal Iron Furnaces

Cozzens, "Iron Industry of Missouri."

Norris, James D., *The Story of the Meramec Ironworks* (Madison, State Historical Society of Wisconsin, 1964).

Map 103. Percentage of Labor Force Employed in Manufacturing

Rafferty, Cheek, and Castillon, *Economic and Social Atlas of Missouri*.

U.S. Bureau of the Census, *Census of Manufactures, 1972*, Vol. III, Part I (Washington, D.C., Government Printing Office, 1972).

Zoubek, *Missouri County Data Book*.

Map 104. Tourism and Recreation Regions

Hall, Leonard, *Stars Upstream* (Columbia, University of Missouri Press, 1958).

Hawksley, Oscar, *Missouri Ozark Waterways* (Jefferson City, Missouri Department of Conservation, 1965).

Sauer, *Geography of the Ozark Highland of Missouri*.

Seven Ways to Get Away in Missouri (Jefferson City, Missouri Division of Tourism, 1977).

Writers' Program, W.P.A., *Missouri: A Guide*.

Map 105. State Parks

Gist, *Missouri: Its Resources, People, and Institutions*.

Meyer, *Heritage of Missouri*.

Map 106. Missouri City

Missouri City: Map and Prospectus (reproduction; Ithaca, New York, Historic Urban Plans, 1967).

Rafferty, *Missouri: A Geography*.

Thompson, Henry C., "Missouri City," *Farmington News*, December 16, 1938.

Map 107. Utopian Communities

Grant, Roger H., "Missouri's Utopian Communities," *Missouri Historical Review*, Vol. 66 (October, 1971), 20–48.

Meyer, *Heritage of Missouri*.

Map 108. The Town of Kansas, 1846

Meyer, *Heritage of Missouri*.

Writers' Project, W.P.A., *Missouri: A Guide*.

Map 109. St. Louis in 1780

Campbell, *Campbell's Gazetteer of Missouri*.

Houck, *History of Missouri*, II, 1–78.

Map 110. Plan of the Fort of New Madrid

Houck, *History of Missouri*, II.
Writers' Project, W.P.A., *Missouri: A Guide.*

Map 111. Standard Metropolitan Statistical Areas (SMSA's)

U.S. Office of the President, Office of Management and Budget, Statistical Policy Division, *Standard Metropolitan Statistical Areas, 1975* (Washington, D.C., Government Printing Office, 1975).

Map 112. St. Louis Metropolitan Area

Missouri: Official Highway Map (Jefferson City, State of Missouri, 1977).
Rafferty, *Missouri: A Geography.*

Map 113. Kansas City Metropolitan Area

Missouri: Official Highway Map.
Rafferty, *Missouri: A Geography.*
U.S. Bureau of the Census, *Boundary and Annexation Survey 1970-1975*, Report GE30-2 (Washington, D.C., Government Printing Office, 1978).